the **INSIDER'S GUIDE**
to getting your book published

AGENTS, editors, AND YOU

edited by **MICHELLE HOWRY**

WRITER'S DIGEST BOOKS
CINCINNATI, OHIO

www.writersdigestbooks.com

Agents, Editors and You: The Insider's Guide to Getting Your Book Published.
Copyright © 2002 by Writer's Digest Books. Manufactured in the United States of America. All rights reserved. No part of this book may be reproduced in any form or by any electronic or mechanical means including information storage and retrieval systems without permission in writing from the publisher, except by a reviewer, who may quote brief passages in a review. Published by Writer's Digest Books, an imprint of F&W Publications, Inc., 4700 East Galbraith Road, Cincinnati, Ohio 45236. (800) 289-0963. First edition.

Visit our Web site at www.writersdigest.com for information on more resources for writers.

To receive a free weekly e-mail newsletter delivering tips and updates about writing and about Writer's Digest products, register directly at our Web site at http://newsletter s.fwpublications.com.

06   05   04   03   02   5   4   3   2   1

Library of Congress Cataloging-in-Publication Data

Agents, editors, and you: the insider's guide to getting your book published / edited by Michelle Howry.
        p.   cm.
    Includes index.
    ISBN 1-58297-152-8 (pbk.: alk. paper)   ISBN 1-58297-141-2 (hc.: alk. paper)
    1. Authorship—Marketing. 2. Authors and publishers. 3. Editing. 4. Literary agents.
    I. Howry, Michelle.
PN161.A34   2002
070.5'2—dc21   2002016811
                                                                            CIP

Edited by Meg Leder
Designed by Sandy Conopeotis Kent
Cover designed by Brian Roeth
Cover photography by Koji Kitagawa/Superstock
Production coordinated by John Peavler

Permissions

Acknowledgments

As an editor myself, I'm in the enviable position of getting to see behind the scenes and understand just how many people it takes to make a book happen. This book would not have been possible without the help of many, many individuals:

First and foremost, the top-notch editors at Writer's Digest Books: Jack Heffron, Meg Leder, Donya Dickerson, and Brad Crawford. Thanks, posse.

The rest of F&W Publications' team and beyond, all of who supported this book throughout the writing: the editors of *Writer's Digest, Fiction Writer, Publishing Success, Writer's Market, Guide to Literary Agents, Novel & Short Story Writer's Market,* and mediabistro.com, and the rest of the editors, past and present, who helped to develop and collect the very best writing about the business of writing.

The F&W sales and marketing team, the designers, the typesetters, the production department, and all the other behind-the-scenes folks who make books happen.

The first-rate writers who contributed their words to the project: Anne Bowling, Robert Lee Brewer, Katie Struckel Brogan, Greg Daugherty, Paula Deimling, Donya Dickerson, Patricia L. Fry, Jerry Gross, Kelly Milner Halls, Robin Hemley, Kirsten Holm, Tara Horton, Jean V. Naggar, Karen Osterman, Timothy Perrin, Don Prues, Tom and Marilyn Ross, John Scognamiglio, Terri See, Laurel Touby, Deborah Way, and John Morgan Wilson.

The agents and editors who offered me their time and their insights: Faye Bender, Fauzia Burke, Richard Curtis, Kristin Earhart, Scott Gold, Betsy Lerner, David Levithan, Donald Maass, Steven Malk, Linda Mead, Duncan Murrell, Joy Peskin, and Jennifer Repo.

To my friends and family, for their unflagging help and support. Your esteem is the truest measure of any accomplishment.

One final note: Book publishing is one industry that's inextricably linked to New York City, and though publishing is thriving in cities and towns all over the United States (and the world), so many people in the book trade are still located in, or have ties to, New York. This book was in the midst of being written on September 11, 2001, and I'd like to thank all the publishing professionals who made the time to contribute to this project in the middle of such a tumultuous period. It's a testament to the dedication and passion of everyone involved in making books. I hope you can take that same passion into your own writing.

About the Editor

Michelle Howry is an associate editor at McGraw-Hill. She has held a variety of editorial positions at other publishing houses, including Newmarket Press, Writer's Digest Books, and the Ohio University Press. Her writing has appeared in publications such as *Writer's Digest*, *Personal Journaling*, and *ID*, as well as several Web sites and online publications. She lives in Brooklyn, New York.

Table of Contents

PART I
Preparing and Submitting Your Manuscript

Chapter 1
Do I Need an Agent?...5

Writer's Digest editors explain the duties of agents, and we give you tips on finding the agent who's right for you.
- Do I Need an Agent?, by Donya Dickerson, Kirsten Holm, and Don Prues.
- Why Publishers Value Literary Agents: One Editor's Perspective, by Don Prues.

Chapter 2
How Do I Find the Right Agent for My Work?...13

Tips for matching your book (and your personality) with the perfect agent.
- Agent Targeting: Finding the Agent Who Fits, by John Morgan Wilson.
- Targeting Agents: Make the Best Fit With an Agent Who Knows Your Market, by Donya Dickerson.

Chapter 3
How Do I Approach an Agent?...28

The art and craft of crafting a compelling query letter—including sample queries that got results—and an interview with the first person your query has to impress: the literary agent's reader.
- Queries That Made It Happen, by Terri See and Tara Horton.
- An Interview With Scott Gold, Assistant at the Zachary Shuster Harmsworth Literary Agency.

Chapter 4
What Does an Agent Actually Do?...48

How agents work, and how they work for you.
- The Agent-Author Relationship: What a Writer Should Expect, by Kelly Milner Halls.

Introduction

What's a mentor? It's a word handed down to us, like so many, from Greek mythology. Mentor was a friend of Homer's Odysseus (hero of *The Odyssey*); while Odysseus was off wandering the Peloponnesian world, he entrusted the teaching and guidance of his son, Telemachus, to his loyal friend Mentor. Today, the idea of relying on the advice of an expert still resonates—*Webster's* defines the word *mentor* as "a trusted counselor or guide, a tutor, a coach."

As a writer, you have probably had one (or many) writing mentors—teachers, friends, or members of your writing group—who read your work, advise you about its merits, and challenge you to constantly improve. A mentor can even be someone you've never met—another writer whom you admire and seek to emulate. Many writers have multiple mentors, people whose insights they seek and whose opinions about their work they trust.

But just as you need support during the *writing* of your book, most writers wish they had someone to help guide them through the *publishing* phase, too—a kind of "publishing mentor" who's available to answer their questions and point them in the right direction. That's where this book comes in.

Agents, Editors, and You is a compilation of some of the best information and advice about writing and publishing, offered by some of the top agents and editors in the business. These are people who have worked in the publishing world for years: the agents who choose to represent your work and the editors who elect to publish it. Some of them are even writers themselves. These are people who know publishing, inside and out. They're the perfect source of advice about how to break into publishing—and how to build a lasting, successful career writing books.

This book is designed to walk you through each step of the publishing process, from deciding whether you need an agent through promoting and publicizing your book—and beyond, to look at the trends that shape the publishing industry and how they affect you as a writer. Here's a brief overview of what you can expect to find inside:

Part I: Preparing and Submitting Your Manuscript tackles some of the basic issues that all writers struggle with when they're preparing to send their work out into the world. Here you'll find the answers to many of your most often asked questions, including

- Do I need an agent?
- What does an agent actually do?
- How do I approach an agent?
- How do I write a query letter?
- How do I meet editors and agents at conferences?

Part II: Selling Your Manuscript includes in-depth Q&A sessions with editors and agents working in publishing today: What do they look for in a manuscript? In an author? What issues are most important to them? And what do you need to know before you even send your material to them? You'll hear a variety of perspectives, from agents and editors working in fiction, nonfiction, and children's books.

Part III: Publishing 101—What You Need to Know *After* Your Book Is Sold addresses the mysterious world behind the scenes at the publishing house.

- What happens to my book once it reaches the editor's desk?
- What do I need to know before I sign a contract?
- How do I work with my editor throughout the publishing process?
- What happens *after* my book is published?

Part IV: Trends in Publishing Today discusses some of the most talked-about recent developments in publishing.

- What do I need to know about e-publishing?
- Do the megamergers in the publishing world mean there are fewer places for me to sell my novel?
- Area all the good agents and publishers located in New York?
- Should I consider self-publishing my book?

Getting a book published is an arduous task. It often seems as if the publishing industry itself was structured to make it as difficult as possible for a first-time author to figure it all out. It's challenging, but there is hope. As you'll see throughout this book, agents and editors really are still searching for talented new writers. Use this book like a road map; inside you'll find the information you need to navigate the unfamiliar publishing landscape and find publishing success. Rely on the advice of these "publishing mentors"—along with your amazingly well-written book—to target an agent, woo an editor, and earn a book contract.

PART I:

Preparing and Submitting Your Manuscript

CHAPTER 1

Do I Need an Agent?

Go to a writers conference, a critique group, or an online chat about writing, and it's probably the most common question: Do I need an agent?

Depending on whom you talk to, you'll get different answers and different reasons why (or why not) to engage the services of a literary agent. It's a question that comes up often within the pages of this book, too, and you'll have to decide for yourself whether hiring an agent is the right choice for you. There's one irrefutable fact, though: Without an agent, it's much harder for you to get your work in front of the editors who might buy it.

In this chapter, three Writer's Digest Books editors explain exactly what it is that agents do to earn their cut. You'll find out what the advantages are to having an agent, and you'll get the information you need to decide whether or not getting an agent is the right move for you. You'll also hear editor Tracy Bernstein's perspective on the matter, and you might be surprised to find out why editors, as well as writers, value what literary agents can do for them.

 Do I Need an Agent?
BY DONYA DICKERSON, KIRSTEN HOLM, AND DON PRUES

If you have a book ready to be published, you may be wondering if you need a literary agent. Perhaps you're not even sure if you want to work with a literary agent. Making this decision can be tough; this article will give you the information you need to make an educated choice about using an agent.

What Can an Agent Do for You?

An agent will believe in your writing and know an audience interested in what you write exists somewhere. As the representative for your work, your agent will tell editors your manuscript is the best thing to land on her desk this year. But beyond being enthusiastic about your book, there are a lot of benefits to using an agent.

For starters, today's competitive marketplace can be difficult to break into, especially for previously unpublished writers. Many larger publishing houses will look only at manuscripts from agents. In fact, approximately 80 percent of books published by the major houses are sold to them by agents.

But an agent's job isn't just getting your book through a publisher's door. In reality, that's only a small part of what an agent can do for you. The following describes the various jobs agents do for their clients, many of which would be difficult for a writer to do without outside help.

Agents Know Editors' Tastes and Needs

An agent possesses information on a complex web of publishing houses and a multitude of editors to make sure her clients' manuscripts are placed in the hands of the right editors. This knowledge is gathered through relationships she cultivates with acquisition editors—the people who decide which books to present to their publisher for possible publication. Through her industry connections, an agent becomes aware of the specializations of publishing houses and their imprints, knowing that one publisher wants only contemporary romances while another is interested solely in nonfiction books about the military. By networking with editors over lunch, an agent also learns more specialized information—which editor is looking for a crafty Agatha Christie–style mystery for the fall catalog, for example.

Agents Track Changes in Publishing

Being attentive to constant market changes and vacillating trends is also a major requirement of an agent's job. He understands what it may mean for clients when publisher A merges with publisher B and when an editor from house C moves to house D. Or what it means when readers—and therefore editors—are no longer interested in Westerns but instead can't get their hands on enough Stephen King–style suspense novels.

Agents Get Your Manuscript Read Faster

Although it may seem like an extra step to send your manuscript to an agent instead of directly to a publishing house, the truth is an agent can prevent writers from wasting months sending manuscripts to the wrong places or being buried in someone's slush pile. Editors rely on agents to save them time as well. With little time to sift through the hundreds of unsolicited submissions arriving weekly in the mail, an editor is naturally going to prefer a work that has already been approved by a qualified reader. For this reason, many of the larger publishers accept agented submissions only.

Agents Understand Contracts

When publishers write contracts, they are primarily interested in their own bottom lines rather than the best interests of the authors. Writers unfamiliar with contractual language may find themselves trapped in situations binding them to publishers with whom they no longer want to work or preventing them from getting royalties on their first books until they have written several books. An agent uses her experience to negotiate a contract that benefits the writer while still respecting some of the publisher's needs. And agents often organize auctions for a book, which ultimately make more money for the writer than she would have made without representation.

Agents Negotiate—and Exploit—Subsidiary Rights

Beyond publication, a savvy agent keeps in mind other opportunities for your manuscript. If your agent believes your book will also be successful as an audio book, a Book-of-the-Month club selection, or even a blockbuster movie, he will take these options into consideration when shopping your manuscript. These additional mediums for your writing are called "subsidiary rights"; part of an agent's job is to keep track of the strengths and weaknesses of different publishers' subsidiary rights offices. After the contract is negotiated, the agent will seek additional moneymaking opportunities for the rights he kept for his client.

Agents Get Escalators

An escalator is a bonus that an agent can negotiate as part of the book contract. An escalator is commonly given when a book appears on a best-seller list or if a client appears on a popular television show. For example, a publisher might give a writer a $50,000 bonus if she is picked for Oprah's Book Club. Both the agent and the editor know such media attention will sell more books, and the agent negotiates an escalator to ensure the writer benefits from this increase in sales.

Agents Track Payments

Because an agent receives payment only when the publisher pays the writer, it is in the agent's best interests to make sure the writer is paid on schedule. Some publishing houses are notorious for late payments. Having an agent distances you from any conflict over payment and allows you to spend your time writing instead of on the phone.

Agents Are Strong Advocates

Besides standing up for your right to be paid on time, agents can ensure your book gets more attention from the publisher's marketing department, a better cover design, or other benefits you may not know to ask for during the publishing process. An agent can also provide advice during each step of this process as well as guidance about your long-term writing career.

When Might You Not Need an Agent?

Although there are many reasons to work with an agent, an author can benefit from submitting his own work. For example, if your writing focuses on a very specific area, you may want to work with a small or specialized publisher. These houses are usually open to receiving material directly from writers. Smaller houses can often give more attention to a writer than a large house, providing editorial help, marketing expertise, and other advice directly to the writer.

Some writers use lawyers instead of agents. If a lawyer specializes in intellectual property, he can help a writer with contract negotiations. Instead of giving the lawyer a commission, the lawyer is paid for his time only. If you know your book will appeal only to a small group of readers, working with a lawyer is an option to consider.

And, of course, some people prefer working independently instead of relying on others to do their work. If you are one of these people, it is probably better to shop your own work instead of constantly butting heads with an agent. And despite the benefits of working with an agent, it is possible to sell your work directly to a publisher—people do it all the time!

Donya Dickerson is an editor at Writer's Digest Books. Kirsten Holm is the former editor of *Writer's Market*. Don Prues is the coauthor of *Formatting & Submitting Your Manuscript* and the upcoming *Writer's Guide to Places* (both Writer's Digest Books).

 ## Why Publishers Value Literary Agents: One Editor's Perspective
BY DON PRUES

Literary agents are not merely a link in the publishing chain but the instruments through which commercially published books must pass. Just ask any editor at a major publishing house.

Tracy Bernstein, who's worked at Kensington Books, Warner Books, and Henry Holt, knows the value of a literary agent. "An agent is the first and most important aid in doing my job," she says. "When an agent sends me a proposal or manuscript, I know it's coming with the assurance that someone—someone highly qualified in most cases—has already read it and likes it. The agent acts as a first filter, prescreening what I'm seeing as opposed to the stuff that just comes in directly from writers."

If the literary agent is a publisher's prized filter, do editors automatically assume an agented submission is better—cleaner, more palatable—than an unagented manuscript that arrives over the transom? "Certainly," says Bernstein. "When we receive submissions from literary agents, we eagerly open the envelopes with high expectations that what's inside is going to be good, especially if it's from an agent we've worked with before. And the more an editor gets to know a particular literary agent (and vice versa), the more likely there is to be something of interest in that envelope."

Despite publisher complaints that agents have been demanding inflated advances during the past few years, editors can't deny how much easier it is to negotiate with an agent than to negotiate directly with a writer. "That's true," says Bernstein, "and true for many reasons: One is that agents have reasonable expectations because of their experience in the business—they're not going to pursue something that's totally ridiculous (an outrageous advance) or have their feelings hurt if you deny their offer. They know the industry standards, and most of the time they know what's reasonable. Dealing with an agent is a more detached kind of negotiation, because the agent looks at negotiation as a businessperson, whereas a writer can't help but look at it from an emotional perspective."

Bernstein is not calling writers unreasonable, emotional weaklings inept at the bargaining table. She simply knows from experience that editors *and* writers win when an agent steers negotiations. "Having the agent be the locus of business affairs allows the editor-author relationship to remain 'pure' as it were, removed from the mundane, nitty-gritty concerns like money. The author can let someone else be the 'bad guy' to the editor: the person who calls to say, 'Where's the check?' The person who tries to retain the best rights. The person who argues about the clauses in a contract."

In addition to the practical benefits of having an agent, there are psychological benefits—less tangible but just as vital—for the author as well. Most obvious is that when an author has someone else bother with the business aspects of publishing, the author can spend his time writing, not negotiating. Also, as Bernstein observes, "Many authors need a tremendous amount of attention editors can't provide. Agents have traditionally been called upon to hand-hold authors—listening to their everyday concerns, helping them with proposals, managing their incomes—and most authors love that."

Clearly, editors and writers are helped by agents, which is why agents are instrumental in publishing. "When a writer and an editor are having problems, it's great for an agent to be involved. I really think the agent needs to step in and mediate the problem. That's a very important role the agent can play. The problem could be over the manuscript itself, or it could be about something that has come up after the manuscript is finished and we're on to publication. Say the author is being difficult (from my point of view, of course) over publicity issues, or something related to promotion. Or say I want to change parts of a manuscript before it goes to publication and the writer objects."

Bernstein also notes that writers who think having a big-time New York agent is a prerequisite and guarantor to getting published are misinformed. "Any agent who really makes an effort to get to know the editor's needs can be very successful. It doesn't matter to me whether someone is available to have lunch so much as it is important the agent keep in mind what I'm looking for and what I publish. I see no reason why someone in St. Louis can't do that as well as someone in New York."

No wonder Bernstein will work with and trust any agent until proven otherwise. "I always assume agents—no matter who they are or where they're from—are being honest with me," she says, "within the parameters of being an agent."

Just what those parameters are can be a matter of interpretation. For Bernstein, however, the parameters are clear: An unmistakable line exists between an agent hyping a book and hoodwinking a publisher. "I consider it acceptable hyperbole for an agent to tell me, 'You know, a lot of people are interested in this. You might want to hurry up and give me an offer.' Things like that to goose my interest are okay. Hyperbole is fine; lying is not. I would be shocked to find an agent had lied about an offer from another house. We know it's happened, but it's rare. Agents I deal with are honest, upfront businesspeople who know the rules of negotiation. Of course, I know their intention is to get the largest advance possible, and good agents do that by offering quality material I know I can sell to the public."

While a reputable, big-name agent can get an editor to read your manuscript, keep in mind that there's still no guarantee of publication. "Certainly there are agents whose taste I admire and whose judgment about a manuscript I respect enormously. I know they're not going to bring me something unless they really believe in it themselves. I'm always happy to read what they send me, but when it comes to publishing a book, the credentials of the author are far more important than the name of the agent who sends me the manuscript."

Author credentials also play an important role when publishers come up with a book idea and need someone to write the book. In search of a talented, specialized writer, publishers will approach agents—because it's much easier for an editor to call an agent and say, "Do you have a writer who can do this?" than for the editor to start looking for a writer directly. "I do this quite regularly," says Bernstein. "I'll go to an agent and say, 'We need to do this book; got any clients who are likely candidates to write for us?' "

From the practical to the psychological, the advantages of having a literary agent are numerous. And while Bernstein acknowledges such benefits to writers, she ultimately values agents for what they offer her. "Quite simply," she says, "I value agents because the submissions we get from them are stronger—more professional, more complete, more intriguing, and more salable—than those we receive from unagented writers."

There you have it, straight from the editor's mouth.

CHAPTER 2

How Do I Find the Right Agent for My Work?

Would you send a snowsuit to your cousin in Florida for Christmas? Of course not. He'd have no use for it. The same principle applies when you're seeking an agent to represent your writing. Your children's picture book could be a Caldecott-worthy classic, but if you send it to an agent who represents only science fiction, everyone's time is wasted.

The best way to ensure positive results when querying agents is by targeting your work to a specific list of agents who represent your kind of writing. In this chapter, you'll find advice about researching agents for *your* book, and tips to help you target the agent who's the perfect match with your work. Then, you'll hear from several top agents working in a few specific areas—science fiction, romance, mystery, self-help, and spirituality books—who discuss what they're looking for and how to impress them.

 ## Agent Targeting: Finding the Agent Who Fits
BY JOHN MORGAN WILSON

Do you absolutely need an agent to get your novel published? No—not if you can self-publish or submit your work to the small presses. But if your goal is to sell your book to a major publisher, you'll want an agent on your side. Increasingly, the big publishing houses look only at submissions received through established agents, letting the agents screen out the material that's unsuitable for them.

But before you go hunting for an agent, you must do some screening yourself. The challenge is this: how to find and land the agent that's right.

The secret is to aim carefully. Create a narrow list of prospective agents—those most likely to respond to your particular work and who have demonstrated the ability to sell similar or related material. Then contact the agents, pitching your manuscript in a manner that further enhances your chances of success.

Here's how this "agent targeting" works.

Step 1: Do the Work.

If you're an aspiring novelist, write your novel. This sounds obvious, but you'd be surprised how many would-be authors try to sell novels they have yet to write. Do not bother to pitch a novel to an agent that is not yet written; it is a waste of his time and yours. Contracts for "ideas" and "concepts" only happen after you've established yourself as a fiction writer. With your novel completed, you move on to:

Step 2: Define Yourself.

Identify as clearly as possible the type of genre of the book you have written or envision writing. Does it fit into the romance category? Horror, fantasy, science fiction, historical, thriller, mystery? Then if possible, define it even further. If it's a mystery, for example, does it fit into a subgenre, such as cozy, hard-boiled, gay male, female protagonist, etc.? Does it qualify as "erotic," an expanding subgenre itself? Or is it less easily definable, falling into the more mainstream, midlist, or literary areas of publishing?

Know what it is you are writing and hope to sell, and where it might fit into an agent's area of interest, a publisher's crowded list, a bookstore's precious shelf space, and the overall trends of the book publishing marketplace. However, do not become a slave to genre; many genres have blurred in recent years, with writers in so-called genre fiction working with greater freedom and latitude than ever before. Remember: Your best understanding of the marketplace always comes from *reading, reading, reading*. The answers you need are all in what is being published.

Step 3: Zero In on Potential Agents.

Now compile a list of those literary agents who are most likely to respond to your particular fiction, whether it's genre or mainstream, while eliminating or temporarily setting aside less appropriate choices. Where do you find such agents, and how do you learn what they might be looking for or are already selling successfully?

Check out books similar to your own. You're probably already reading books similar to your own in style and genre that you particularly value or admire, and are regularly browsing bookstores for more. Check the acknowledgments sections in those books to see if the authors mention their agents by name. The rights departments of many publishing houses will provide agent information of specific authors if you call and request it; or simply search telephone listings and other resources to find them.

Study trade journals. Publications such as *Publishers Weekly* often cover agents and the type of books they sell; reading between the lines of the trade news can give you good leads. Although my agent sells many nonfiction books, I was made aware of her success with novels when her name turned up repeatedly in *PW*'s Rights column in connection with fiction sales; it was through her that I moved from fiction to nonfiction writing. The regular special issues of *PW*—such as those focusing on mysteries, romances, religious books, gay and lesbian titles, and children's literature—are especially valuable for identifying agents who are active in certain areas.

Study the writing guides. Study the *Guide to Literary Agents, Writer's Market* (both published by Writer's Digest Books), *Literary Market Place* (R.R. Bowker), and other resources for information on individual agents. These books are available in many public libraries and bookstores.

Attend workshops and conferences. Meet agents in writing classes and conferences, or make contacts through established writers you meet. A personal reference from a successful writer is probably the single best way to gain access to an agent and to get a faster, more attentive reading of your manuscript. If you decide to "buttonhole" an agent at such an event—something many professional writers and agents advise against—be prepared to discuss your book project clearly, thoroughly but *very succinctly*. Nothing turns an agent off faster than an aspiring writer who hems and haws about a vague, poorly conceived "idea." Agents represent *writers*—not would-be writers.

Join local or national writers organizations. Many of these are open to unpublished writers and often sponsor events attended by agents. The organizations also offer opportunities to network with other writers.

Comb interviews with writers. Newspaper and magazine pieces about successful writers often cite or quote their agents. If an agent sounds right for you and your book, add his name to your growing list.

Caution! Don't search for agents so narrowly or literally that you over-look good possibilities. An agent who has never sold a novel, for instance, but represents several sports journalists might take a look at fiction with a strong sports theme. Use both your common sense *and* your imagination, looking for opportunities to break in that might not appear at first glance.

Step 4: Make the Approach.

Once you've created your "hit list," it is best to approach agents with a query first. Some guidelines:

- Limit your pitch to one page.
- Capture the agent's attention quickly, from the first line.
- Identify your book by genre.
- Describe your main characters, setting, and plot.

Supply background about you, the writer, including your credits, if you have any. Let him or her know briefly why you are the one to write this particular book—what you bring to it that will make it special.

Include important details, such as the fact that your protagonist is intended as a series character, but refrain from overselling yourself or the project. Be sincere, even enthusiastic, but avoid hyperbole.

Never apologize for yourself or your work in any way, or send up red flags signaling your lack of experience. Present yourself confidently and professionally. Above all, be sure your query letter is well crafted and carefully proofread—it is your calling card, the only way the agent will be able to judge you as a writer, a person, and a potential client.

Make it easy for the agent to contact you. With your query, include a self-addressed, stamped envelope (SASE), as well as your e-mail, fax, and phone numbers. Multiple queries to agents are generally considered acceptable and probably best done by mail or e-mail, not fax. If an agent is interested in you as a client, he or she will probably call or write, asking to see a completed or partial manuscript or outline and sample chapters, and perhaps a resume. (If you don't have voice mail, you should; agents who have to repeatedly call potential clients trying to catch them in soon realize these are not professional writers who take care of business.)

Be patient. An agent may take weeks or even months to get back to you, and a few never bother to reply at all. If too many weeks go by and you are keen on a particular agent, you may want to query again with a reminder note, or to call the agent's assistant to see if he or she might check on your query. In the publishing world, a lot of paper gets lost in the shuffle.

Hedge your bets and contact more than one agent, to be sure you're choosing the agent that is right for you and your work—not just the first one who says yes.

Caution! Beware of agents who charge reading or consultation fees, or who steer you toward a particular book doctor to help you with your manuscript. If an agent does suggest you get editing help, he or she should suggest several possible editors with whom the agent has no financial ties and let you pick the one you wish to work with. (This also goes for agents who try to steer you toward a vanity publisher that charges you money to print your book.) If you have doubts about the legitimacy or track record of an agent, diplomatically ask to see a select client list with published titles, then make further inquiries to verify that the agent was actually involved in the sales.

A Guide Through the Publishing World

Some authors grouse and grumble at having to depend on agents for access to the major publishing houses (and a rare few manage successful careers without them). Yet a good agent does much more than just play messenger for your manuscript. He or she has a keen sense of publishing trends and knows which publishers are in need of your kind of book (or already overstocked with them). A worthy agent will know which individual editors are most likely to respond positively to your material and support it down the line—which is crucial for the success of any book. He or she will negotiate a better contract for you, maneuvering past legal and financial pitfalls, and coordinate the sale of ancillary rights in other markets. In the best of situations, an agent will also be your editor, advisor, and friend.

Whichever way you choose to go—with an agent or submitting on your own—never just "shotgun" your manuscript out into the mail. Narrow and prioritize your list of targets and take careful aim. You'll increase your chances of hitting the publishing bull's-eye.

John Morgan Wilson's books include *Simple Justice* (which won an Edgar Award from the Mystery Writers of America as a best first novel), *Revision of Justice, Justice at Risk*, and *The Limits of Justice*—all published by Doubleday— and *The Complete Guide to Magazine Article Writing* and *Inside Hollywood: A Writer's Guide to Researching the World of Movies and TV* (both Writer's Digest Books).

Targeting Agents: Make the Best Fit With an Agent Who Knows Your Market
BY DONYA DICKERSON

As a writer, you are probably familiar with the idea of targeting publishers—identifying a press's interests and successful areas and sending your work to the appropriate place. You may not realize, however, that you should target agents in the same way. You would never send a science fiction manuscript to a religious publisher, so why send a romance novel to an agent who only represents self-help nonfiction?

There are many benefits to targeting agents. First, you'll save valuable time and effort when sending out query letters. Second, you'll connect with someone who has established relationships with the editors interested in your particular field; who knows the current state of your genre; and who is sensitive to other nuances of your kind of writing.

How do you find an agent appropriate for your manuscript? For starters, refer to one of the many agent directories, such as *Guide to Literary Agents* (Writer's Digest Books) or *Literary Market Place* (R.R. Bowker). These books give in-depth listings of literary agencies and organize them according to the subjects they are interested in receiving. Often, an agent directory will even list specific agents at a particular agency and give advice on the types of submissions the agent is interested in receiving.

Another method of finding an agent is to target the agents of your favorite writers. If there is a writer whose work is similar to yours, you can find her agent (if she used an agent) by calling her publisher's Contracts Department. Or check the Acknowledgments page of books similar in topic or tone to your manuscript—many writers include their agents' names in their public thank-yous.

You'll see that the five following agents are specialists. The Virginia Kidd Agency, where James Allen is president, is known for its science fiction and fantasy authors. Pam Hopkins of Hopkins Literary Associates handles only writers of romance and women's fiction. Though his agency is not limited to the suspense/mystery genre, Philip G. Spitzer still considers it one of his main areas. Denise Marcil's agency has a strong emphasis on self-help and self-improvement titles. And Claudia Cross, a member of the larger, more generalized William Morris Agency, represents many of its Christian authors.

For agents, limiting the areas they'll represent has practical consequences. "I handle topics that interest me, and I know the field," explains Marcil. "I have a sense of the competitive books out there in my different areas. I don't think it's essential to specialize, but it makes the job easier. From attracting authors who do those specific topics to focusing on the editors in the houses who buy that type of book—it's a more efficient way to do business."

While some agencies consider any subject, most agents represent a narrow list of specialties. Larger agencies often represent a broad spectrum of material, dividing areas according to each member agent's interests. If you are interested in exploring multiple genres, having a separate agent for each area is not necessary. According to Allen, "Most agents expect and require exclusivity with their clients. There are exceptions—like the nuclear physicist who writes within his career field and also writes men's action adventure. Such a person could make use of two agents and plan to market that different genre work under a pseudonym."

In the following roundtable, the agents interviewed not only discuss the importance of targeting agents but also share their knowledge of the current state of their areas of specialization. While reading, keep in mind that if you choose your agent carefully, you'll have someone who tracks the ups and downs of your genre, follows your competition, and, most importantly, knows the editors who will buy your manuscript. By selecting wisely, you could form a relationship with an agent that lasts your entire career.

Listen to the Pros

Hear what the men and women who will be selling your work have to say about what's selling, what's not, and what you need to do to get your manuscript published.

Science Fiction and Fantasy Markets
James Allen, literary agent

Q Do science fiction and fantasy writers have a better chance of getting published if they use an agent?

A Getting read without an agent is hard. It may sound like I'm puffing agents, but I'm not. It's the publishers making the decisions. It is difficult to find a publishing house that—as policy—will look at unrepresented work. I can remember being shocked better than a decade ago when Bantam Books announced that it—a paperback house—

would look only at agented material for its science fiction line. And now, as paperback houses are getting attached to hardcover houses and conglomerates, it is the almost solid rule rather than exception that publishers require agents to be involved.

Q How have the science fiction and fantasy markets changed in recent years?

A As with the rest of publishing, the conglomeration of genre publishing through mergers has gone far toward killing the concept of midlist. With more of the established houses being taken over by faceless corporations, the look to the bottom line has been stronger than ever. However, I see this being balanced out by the slow but steady emergence of small, specialty presses. Also, with the increase in technologies, there is a real burgeoning and growth of alternative "publication." It's a case of publishing still being healthy but changing direction.

Q Does that mean it is currently easier for a new or an established writer to sell work?

A Authors who are known to be big sellers continue to sell well. There is also room to let in new people . . . on the grounds that you have to pay them less up front. The midlist authors are finding it harder to sell new work. I'm seeing trends where houses will give a first-timer two shots, maybe three. If there is not a breakout within those three books, they won't pick up number four. In days gone by they would have said, "We will keep on publishing him because if we don't pay him too much he'll do okay."

Q How do you see the current marketplace for science fiction and fantasy?

A Still strong. There is something of a return to "the sense of wonder" type of stories—not tedious old space opera, but the sense of wonder that was central to stories when science fiction was truly new at the beginning of the century. There is not a current special focus that would compare to the effect Stephen King had on the horror genre. Thanks to him everybody had a horror line for a while, and then they died. And everybody was doing cyberpunk thanks to William Gibson, and that got passé. A narrowly focused concept becomes old fast. There is just so much you can do in a ten-by-ten-foot room, no matter how cool that room is. You can do so much more on a football field. At present there is no ten-by-ten-foot room. We're back to our football field, and everything is wide open.

Romance Market
Pam Hopkins, Hopkins Literary Associates

Q Does a romance writer need an agent?

A There's a difference of opinion. Many people believe you can do it yourself if you write for one of the category houses like Harlequin or Silhouette. In terms of having access to and an understanding of the market, an agent is always going to be able to provide that and career guidance as well.

Q Do new or established writers have a better chance in this genre?

A I'm not sure today's market favors one over the other. A few years ago, I would have told you an established writer definitely had the edge, but these days, publishing houses are also anxious to start establishing newer voices.

Q Do romance writers have a better chance of starting a career writing single titles or series?

A You can build a career in women's fiction either way. There are many authors who started in category, built a readership, and then moved to single titles. They took their readers with them. In other cases, writers had their first sales in single titles and built equally successful careers.

Q What advice do you have for someone trying to break into the romance market?

A There are a lot of people writing romance and women's fiction, so the competition is for a limited number of slots available at each publisher. It is important to target your market, especially if you are writing category romance. You must understand what each line is looking for and write appropriately for that line. The same can be true for single titles; reading extensively from a publisher's list will help you understand what it might be most interested in. You'll get an editor's attention much faster if you send a submission that fits what her house publishes.

Q How is the current marketplace for romance?

A Romance continues to be a strong market in both the contemporary and historical genres. Unlike some other genres, it has not been as affected by the swings of publishing but has remained steady over the last few years. This steadiness is evidenced by statistics provided by the Romance Writers of America indicating that romance novels constitute 40 percent of all popular fiction purchased in the United States.

Suspense and Mystery Markets

Philip G. Spitzer, Philip G. Spitzer Literary Agency

Q Do you think it's necessary for a writer in the mystery/suspense genre to have an agent?

A It's a question of getting the book to the best editor for that particular book. It's difficult for writers to keep track of mergers like Dell and Bantam combining—that's going to change a lot.

Q What qualities do you look for in mystery/suspense submissions?

A If a book is well written and character driven, I will tend to want to represent it—even knowing it will take me two or three times as long to sell it as it would a plot-driven suspense novel. The market is more plot driven now. Publishers publish down to the reading public, as if they would be less inclined to buy a well-written novel over one that is simplistic. I think that's totally false.

Q Are there any other trends in the suspense/mystery genre?

A Everything is so confused right now. I don't think there are any trends, and that's part of what is confusing. Publishers want best-sellers, but nobody knows what they want from a critical point of view. I've never believed in trends. As soon as you have a book that fits a particular trend, the trend is gone. I discourage any writer from writing to a trend.

Q Is it easier for a new writer or an established writer to sell work now?

A It's easier to sell a first novel than to sell a book by somebody with a poor track record. I have a very good writer whose novel I'm trying to sell now. Two editors said they wanted to buy it, but then they checked on the sales of his last book. The sales were not great in spite of the good reviews. The editors didn't make an offer.

Q How is the current market for mystery/suspense?

A It's very good. Everybody is looking for something new and different, although they often end up publishing the same things.

Q How do you advise writers who are trying to break into the suspense market?

A Don't write to the market, but write the best possible book you can. I've had many experiences seeing writers write to a market or trying to conform to other books that have been successful. The books aren't as good because their hearts weren't in it. I say write the way you want to write.

Self-Help and Self-Improvement Markets
Denise Marcil, The Denise Marcil Literary Agency, Inc.

Q Is it necessary for a writer wanting to publish in the self-help/ self-improvement market to have an agent?

A It's always easier if you have an agent. The idea is that an agent knows which editors buy what type of book. There are a number of houses that won't accept unagented submissions. But some houses do buy books directly from the author.

Q **What are currently the hottest subjects?**

A Health, alternative health—particularly with baby boomers aging—parenting, spiritual self-help. Books for people who are seeking inner peace have surged.

Q **What do you look for in self-help/self-improvement books?**

A A fresh topic that hasn't been written on extensively or new information on a topic, and an author who has an extensive national outreach. Writers can't be just experts in the area. They have to be on a seminar circuit, have workshops or regular media exposure, or be able to sell their books long after publication. That's what publishers want these days.

Q **Is it easier for a new or an established writer to sell a book in your field?**

A A new writer without a track record, and with a good idea and national exposure, is easier to sell than someone with a bad track record. We're in a business controlled by computers. Publishers call the bookstore buyers and ask how so-and-so is selling or how a similar book did. It's all numbers.

Q **Is nonfiction easier to sell than fiction?**

A Absolutely. Publishers think nonfiction is more straightforward. It's easier to quantify who the audience is for nonfiction. It's easier for publishers to do a search on Amazon.com and Books in Print for similar books published. You can't do that with fiction. There's an apprehension on the part of publishers about fiction—what's going to sell?

Q **Are self-help and self-improvement books and health titles growing in popularity?**

A I've been selling these types of books for twenty years, and I've never seen their popularity wane. I've seen certain areas suddenly become more popular, then overpublished, then no longer popular. But, for me, it's always been a strong area.

Christian and Spirituality Markets
Claudia Cross, Sterling Lord Literistic, Inc.

Q Is it becoming more necessary for a writer to have an agent in the Christian market?

A Yes. In the past not every author writing for the Christian market had an agent. Now, however, there are more agents who represent these authors. In general, publishers are relying more on agents to determine the potential quality of a manuscript of a book project.

Q Has the religious market changed in recent years? Are there current trends?

A It's becoming more sophisticated. Publishers in the Christian market are looking for bigger books, better writing, more high-concept thrillers. The religious reader is also becoming more savvy and is looking for certain kinds of books. For example, I represent an author named Penelope Stokes who exemplifies where the market is going. In the past, she had written a historical fiction series, aimed at women. Her recent book *The Blue Bottle Club* (Word Publishing) is the story of four women. When they're about to graduate from high school, they write down their desires—where they think they'll be, what they think they'll do—and put them in a blue bottle. They forget about it and go about their own lives. A number of years later a journalist comes upon this blue bottle. She tracks down the women, who are in their late sixties, and discovers what they've done with their lives. It's a great concept for a book.

Q You represent both fiction and nonfiction. Which is currently easier to sell?

A Celebrity nonfiction sells well if the celebrity is well known and has an inspiring story to share. Fiction in the Christian market continues to sell well, especially for authors with proven track records. I do think, however, that selling fiction by a first-time writer is getting increasingly difficult.

Q **Is it easier for new or established writers to sell their books?**
A It is easier to sell work by an established writer. Publishers are more cautious these days when making acquisition decisions.

Q **When you look at a manuscript that comes in, do you consider the secular market?**
A Definitely. I read a manuscript with an open mind and let the writing, the author's approach, and the content determine the appropriate market and publisher. There's a fine line between the two markets, but, in general, writers for the Christian market write about faith as an integral part of the plot to encourage readers in their own Christian belief, as opposed to spiritual seeking, which would fit into the general market.

Q **Should a writer consider the broad audience when writing?**
A I think writers should just write. And depending on where their passion leads them, we'll figure out where their work fits.

CHAPTER 3

How Do I Approach an Agent?

The query letter is probably the single most essential piece of writing you'll craft as a writer—at least as important, some would say, as your book itself. In one short (oh so short!) page, you're expected to hook an agent's interest, inform him about your project, tell him why you're the perfect person to write it, and leave him hungry to see more from you. A tall order, indeed.

In this chapter, you'll find six query letters that did just that—each letter caught an agent's interest and led to a book deal for its writer. In addition to the letters themselves, you'll find information about the basics of good query letters, interviews with the authors who wrote them, and comments from their agents explaining what each letter did well and why it caused him or her to accept the writer's book. We'll also talk with Scott Gold, an assistant at the Zachary Shuster Harmsworth literary agency and the first person at the agency to read an author's query letter. He discusses common mistakes he sees in queries, and what makes the difference between a query that gets passed on to the boss and one that he'll return immediately.

 Queries That Made It Happen
BY TERRI SEE AND TARA HORTON

Imagine you are on the subway—you and hundreds of others, jostling past each other in your usual routines. You pass through a sea of faces, varied but unremarkable. Then, a certain someone brushes by with just the right "excuse me" or "hello," and, inexplicably, your heart leaps. You're embarrassed to find yourself staring, craning your neck in order not to lose sight of this person. Something caught your attention, snapped you out of your lull, and you're not quite sure what happened. But it's of no matter right now. You're hooked, and you want to know more about that person.

If only your query letter could make such a stunning first impression! But catching an agent's attention is a matter of planning and calculation, rather than chemistry. And your letter has only one to two minutes to hook the agent's attention. Of the countless letters that cross an agent's desk, yours needs to enticingly say "Pick Me!" and not because of an interesting stamp on the envelope. In order to stand out above the competition, you need to know what agents want, what they crave. And you need to give it to them clearly and cleanly.

What agents want is actually quite simple: a succinct letter that tells who you are, what your book is about, and, briefly, why you are qualified to write it. Be specific, concise, and avoid being arrogant *or* self-effacing. Why you do or do not deserve to be published or how your book will make millions has no place in a query. An interesting letter will go far to showcase your writing talent.

Style is important, but in this short space clarity is key. Make your synopsis intriguing but rounded. You don't want to leave the agent thinking, *"What?"* Also, mention whether or not you have been published before. Contrary to common perception, publishing credits can work to your advantage either way. Some agents do prefer to work with previously published writers, but many others look specifically for first-time authors.

Overall, bear in mind that your query letter is a representation of you and, therefore, it needs to appear as professional as possible. Don't handwrite your letter or use distracting, flashy stationery. Be certain you have the agent's name spelled properly (Terri or Terry? Mr. or Ms.?), and take extra care to ensure your punctuation and grammar are correct. These details matter as much as your letter's content and will illustrate how thorough and polished you are—or are not.

Following are the actual queries of four writers who found representation and whose agents have sold their books. The authors discuss how
they selected their agents as well as the snags and surprises in their
query processes, and they share some dos and don'ts they learned on
the path to publication. Their agents, in turn, tell us what made the
letters stand out and what they found appealing about these particular
authors. Let the details of these writers' experiences inspire you to write
your own tempting query letter, and soon you, too, may have an agent
asking for more.

Rainelle Burton

Rainelle Burton took a somewhat winding path to get her book, *The
Root Worker*, published. To begin with, her initial query was not to an
agent, but instead she directly contacted an editor she met at an Oak-
land University writers conference. She pitched her book to Bantam,
and it resulted in a round of letters with a very encouraging editor. The
editor made remarks, asked for changes, and Burton made the changes.
They went back and forth for some time. But, at a point, life got in
the way. In the middle of correspondence with Bantam, Burton suffered
from a serious depression that lasted two years. During that time, she
dropped all work on the book.

Burton eventually left her home and all its belongings to save her
son from street gangs in Detroit. Finding a new home in a small town
and a place to come back to work, she eventually reacquainted herself
with the desire to find a publisher for her book. "When I was trying
to put my life back together, the editor was the first person I called. But
she was gone," says Burton. "She had left Bantam, and they couldn't tell
me where she went. I was back at square one."

Determined to move forward, she looked up a friend who had contacts at Houghton Mifflin. He asked Burton what her agent had to say
about her situation. "I said, 'I don't have an agent,' and he looked at
me like I was crazy. He told me that having a publisher interested in
taking on my book should get me my pick of an agent. 'Okay,' I
thought, 'I didn't know that. I'll get an agent.' " Then, another turn

Rainelle Burton
1702 Query Lane
Writers Town, MI 48111
(626) 555-1234

August 30, 1998

Amanda Materne
James Levine Communications
307 Seventh Avenue, Suite 1906
New York, NY 10001

> This letter didn't have ridiculous mistakes, such as spelling or grammatical errors, or being addressed to the wrong person.

Dear Amanda Materne:

Thank you in advance for taking the time to consider representing *The Root Worker*, my recently completed first novel.

> This letter does not come off as pompous. Instead, the letter makes you want to read the actual novel.

The Root Worker, set in the 1960s, is based on the real life lower east side Detroit community that I grew up in, where root working—an urban African-American derivative of West African voodoo—is not only practiced, but controls the lives and relationships of its people. The story chronicles the tension and despair of a family and community that is bred, perpetuated, and exploited by one woman, the Root Worker. It explores the conflicts and similarities between the precepts of Catholicism and paganism, and their existence in a larger community that embraces traditional African-American religion.

The Root Worker also gives a view of the phenomena and effect of the urban flight of the 1960s, and the mass exodus of Catholic institutions in Detroit from the perspectives of those who remained behind.

Thank you again for your consideration. I look forward to hearing from you.

Sincerely,

> Writers need to have their query letters pretty spotless if they want an agent or publisher to consider their work. If you're careless with the query letter, it isn't the best "preview" of your writing ability. You want to have as much as you possibly can going your way when your piece is pulled from the stacks.

Rainelle Burton

Comments provided by Amanda Materne

in the road: "I picked up the book, after all this time had gone by, and said 'Whoa, this needs some work.' In some ways, my depression was clarifying."

Burton worked on revisions to the book for some time, then put it down for several months and picked it up again to see how it would read. Finally, when she felt the time was right, she looked for an agent. "I did a lot of reading in *Guide to Literary Agents, Writer's Market,* and *Writer's Digest* magazine, listened to agents at conferences—their dos and don'ts—and got all the information I could. I looked at listings of agents and made lists of the agents who took fiction, then I looked at the interests of those agents. I queried about thirty agents." (See query letter on page 31.)

Burton received several letters requesting to see her manuscript. Amanda Materne with James Levine Communications, however, *called* her, and that more personal effort made a difference. Burton held off on responding to the other requests for her manuscript because it seemed the right thing to do. Even though James Levine Communications handles only 2 percent fiction, Burton says, "When I read the company's short biography and learned its interests, I thought my book was a possible fit." Upon request she sent Materne the other chapters. Burton was excited to hear from her again. "She said, 'Can you send the whole manuscript?' Then she asked if I would be interested in her representing me, and I said, 'Hell, yes!' " As a happy result, *The Root Worker* was published in the spring of 2001 with The Overlook Press.

While Burton does not consider herself a highly organized person, she does believe strong organizational skills have played a helpful role in her career, first as a technical writer and freelance editor, and now as a published novelist. In the search for an agent, good record keeping is vital. "List the agents you sent manuscripts to," advises Burton. "List when you sent them, including the dates and their responses. You need to log these things so that you do not appear confused when you're dealing with an agent."

Although Burton did not get her query format from a book, she knew through her research what the letter should include. "It has to be polite and to the point," she explains. "It should draw the agent's attention and express appreciation for the agent's consideration. Say what you need to say up front and never mind all that other stuff. Make your book sell without being overly pushy or tooting your own horn. Don't tell an agent, 'You'll regret it if you don't get this book!' And skip the fancy paper with all the squiggles. They'll be suspicious of your writing. A good synopsis will help, too."

When asked if she encountered any surprises in the process, Burton says, "The biggest surprise I had was finding that both the agent and the editor were approachable. From my reading, I thought they would be these people who sit up in the sky and pass judgment on you. And that you should not call an agent or an editor, and you must ask permission to speak. Not so! They are warm, genuine, and very human. I was able to ask questions."

Burton's advice in dealing with agents is to "be patient because the process takes time, and once your manuscript is out there, it's out there. You can't pull it back."

Marcus Wynne

Marcus Wynne has been a paratrooper, diplomatic bodyguard, close combat and counterterrorism instructor, and emergency medical technician. He has traveled to more than fifty countries, many of them listed in *The World's Most Dangerous Places* (Harper Resource), coordinated embassy evacuations in Haiti during the 1991 coup, led a counterterrorist Federal Air Marshall unit during the Gulf War, and was invited to South Africa to train Nelson Mandela's bodyguards. And if all that were not dangerous enough, Wynne decided to dive into writing a novel.

Wynne has made a living as a freelance magazine journalist since 1983, writing articles on everything from psychology to military affairs, as well as crossing over to plays and industrial films. He credits this experience as a great leg up in getting his book out. "I was used to writing as a business, and I didn't bog myself down with the preciousness and naïveté of the 'artistic' writer. I was used to writing for money and working as a writer in the business sense, and I'm one of the few freelancers who makes a decent living freelancing in journalism. I think anyone who expects to succeed at writing books has to separate the creative function from the business function, which includes marketing, public relations, and promotion. You need to learn to be your own best advocate because until you sell as many books as Tom Clancy, most publishers won't be." With this attitude in mind, Wynne was able to see the process of querying an agent purely as a business matter.

As was necessary in many of his other adventures, Wynne approached getting *No Other Option* published with careful, methodical preparation. Part of his caution was a result of a prior experience with an agent. As it happens, *No Other Option* is his second novel, and Ethan Ellenberg of the Ethan Ellenberg Literary Agency is his second agent. Wynne wrote a first novel, *Air Marshalls*, based on his experience in the Gulf War. His first agent had the book for a year and a half, and in that time only sent the book to three editors. Of those three editors, one wanted to publish it but held it for six months and eventually decided to pass on it. The second publisher did not want *Air Marshalls* but offered Wynne a nonfiction book contract, and the third publisher simply passed on it. "Knowing what I know now about the publishing industry, those are good signs," Wynne says. "But the agent told me that I should shelf it after just three rejections. I later discovered he sent out my manuscript without a cover letter. After that I decided it was best for us to part ways, and by then I was kind of discouraged with the book, so I shelved it. Then I immediately went to work on my second book, *No Other Option*."

Later, this seeming failure actually helped Wynne make a valuable connection. Before the offer of representation by his first agent, Wynne had done a mass query mailing. "Out of that huge mailing, I got a few responses, a whole lot of rejections, and a couple of nice letters," he says. One of the positive letters he received was from Ethan Ellenberg. Ellenberg, he says, looked at the book and said it needed more work than he was willing to put into it. But he also indicated that when Wynne had another manuscript, Ellenberg would be interested in look-

Marcus Wynne
48 Published Way
Authorville, FL 54210
(989) 555-4953

April 8, 1999

Mr. Ethan Ellenberg
549 Broadway
Suite 5E
New York, NY 10012

Dear Mr. Ellenberg:

> Marcus's letter is very focused—it has a lot of passion and self-awareness.

My name is Marcus Wynne. I'm a novelist seeking representation for the enclosed psychological thriller. Last year you looked at my previous novel manuscript, *Air Marshalls*. While the book wasn't for you, you offered me some useful feedback and extended an invitation to send any new work to you. I've enclosed the first 100 pages of my new novel, *No Other Option*.

This book: The technical accuracy and thinly fictionalized real-world accounts of Richard Marcinko or Tom Clancy; the psychological insights of Thomas Harris; the narrative drive of John Sandford or Stephen Hunter. There's darkness, sex, and

> He knew what he had written and felt strongly that it was a good book. That confidence appealed to me.

violence in it, interesting characters, and some great dialogue. There's also a lot of hidden truth in it—enough to worry some highly placed people in the special operations world.

Me: Writer/consultant with a gun-toting past. Been publishing nonfiction nationally since 1983. This is my second novel. The first one (unpublished) is on the shelf where I won't trip over the training wheels.

I've enclosed an SASE for your reply. Return of the material is not necessary. Thanks for taking a look. I look forward to hearing from you soon.

Cheers,

> I liked everything about the book. It is very well written and has a page-turning quality that will always be the hallmark of the thriller. It's fresh, it's different. There are appealing elements to the villain, similar to what the great Thomas Harris does with Hannibal Lecter. Discovering a great read and a great writer remains job number one for any agent serious about fiction, as I am.

Marcus Wynne

Comments provided by Ethan Ellenberg

ing at it. This brief note would make a difference later when Ellenberg's name again popped up in Wynne's agent search.

For *No Other Option*, Wynne began his precision campaign for an agent by closely reading *Guide to Literary Agents* and other sources. Next, he scanned bookstore shelves for books in genres similar to his and made note of the agents and editors mentioned in the authors' acknowledgments. Then he condensed this information into a short list and used Agent Research & Evaluation (www.agentresearch.com) to obtain a detailed breakdown of these agents and the names of their clients.

"Then I crafted individualized letters," Wynne explains. "I geared them toward each agent's particular area of interest. Out of my ten initial queries, I received seven requests to see the manuscript. Of those, I got solid offers for representation from three, including Ethan Ellenberg." (See query letter on page 35.) Wynne called and interviewed all three agents, after first deciding what qualities he wanted in an agent. He recommends to writers, "Ask yourself if you are willing to trust your career to this person. If so, why? First impressions are important, but they're not always the answer. Ask hard questions, and be specific about what you expect. And listen carefully to how the agent treats you. If he is condescending or brusque, ask yourself if you are willing to put up with that behavior. Or ask if he treats you like a professional. Because that's what we all want to be, right?"

After interviewing the offers for representation, Wynne decided to go with Ellenberg because he owns a smaller but highly regarded agency, offering personal attention. "He took the time to explain how things worked and what to expect," Wynne says, "so I was quite comfortable and felt I could trust him." Wynne was surprised to find an agent willing to do business on a handshake. "He basically recognized my hesitation borne of inexperience in the publishing world and said we could enter a written agreement or go on a verbal agreement and see how it went. While I might not recommend that approach for everyone, I was comfortable with it. Also, he let me be an active participant when I needed to be." Wynne further compliments Ellenberg's professionalism, saying he tirelessly pushes a book until there is a buyer. "That's what an agent needs to do—find the one editor who believes in your book." And Ellenberg found that editor at Tor/Forge.

Looking back on his query letter, Wynne feels, "It was written to get Ellenberg's attention. It was a subject matter he knew, and it was short, sweet, sexy, and to the point." He feels his self-promotion in the letter was not only appropriate but, in this case, very helpful. "Having a marketable and promotable background that lends real authenticity to the work really helps, and anyone with a sense of publicity and promotion will sit up and notice. And I had to learn to push that aspect to the front, instead of being modest about it."

But, Wynne says, behind a good query letter needs to be a clear understanding of an agent's job. He explains, "Don't mistake the desire for an objective evaluation of your work with needing an agent. An agent's job is to sell your work. He may help you shape your manuscript and so on but only after he recognizes he can sell it. You need to have your craft down, and you need to be writing up to your own personal best. Learning how to edit my own writing and really working at my fiction gave me confidence—as did a carefully chosen cadre of readers."

Do Your Groundwork: How Research Led One Writer to an Agent and a Contract

Even with sales to magazines like *Aboriginal SF*, Jan Lars Jensen felt it might be difficult to find an agent for his science fiction novel, *Shiva 3000*. "I realized the initial payoff for an agent would be small. A good strategy, I thought, might be to first interest an editor with a query and then use his or her response to land an agent. I quickly realized how few publishers consider unsolicited work."

The next step was finding an agent. Using the Internet and *Science Fiction Writer's Marketplace and Sourcebook* (Writer's Digest Books), Jensen compiled a list of potential agents. He ordered the agents according to his criteria: (1) a proven track record getting science fiction/ fantasy writers published; (2) associated with authors he is familiar with; and (3) based in New York. A resident of British Columbia, Jensen sought an agent in New York, where the major publishers of science fiction and fantasy are based. His ideal agent would specialize in this genre and have what Jensen did not: "a lot of experience and a lifetime of publishing contacts."

By taking advantage of other available resources, Jensen pared down the list. A member of the Science Fiction and Fantasy Writers of America (SFWA), he perused this organization's directory to learn who agented some of his peers. "Richard Curtis caught my attention because he represented several authors I admired," says Jensen. "From another source, I learned that Richard had actually been the SFWA's agent for a period, which suggested to me that he was respected within the field. I discovered that Richard had himself written some novels, and I liked that; he was a writer too, and if he did represent me, he might better understand writers' issues." Curtis went to the top of Jensen's list.

While putting together the query letter, Jensen tried to imagine the situation of the person who would read it. "I kept the letter short, assuming (1) agencies receive many queries and (2) the more succinct, the more attention the contents of mine would receive. I also thought it important to establish my 'qualifications' quickly so the reader would know I took my writing seriously. That's why I mentioned my degree and short story sales in the second line."

Describing the novel took more thought. Working against Jensen was a recent shrinking in the science fiction market. In addition, there were no comparable novels to his on the shelves. "I wasn't going to tell a potential agent I thought my novel would be a tough sell—so even though I thought originality was one of the novel's strengths, I didn't emphasize this. I would let Richard draw his own conclusions from the description, and when I compared my work to that of other writers, I chose authors whose success lay in offering something fresh and new." (See query letter on page 39.)

Jensen sent off his carefully crafted query to Curtis, and soon after, a positive reply came from his number one pick. Curtis had several publishers in mind for the book and received from Harcourt Brace a response that Curtis says, "agents only dream of." Harcourt Brace's

6534 Science Fiction Rd.
Chilliwack, British Columbia
Canada A1B 2C3

March 1, 1998

Richard Curtis
Richard Curtis Associates, Inc.
171 E. 74th St.
New York, NY 10021, USA

> *Validates himself as one worthy of serious consideration.*

Dear Mr. Curtis:

I have recently completed a science fiction/fantasy novel entitled *Shiva 3000* and I hope you might consider taking me on as a client, with the goal of selling it to a major American publisher.

Since obtaining my BA in Writing from the University of Victoria, I have sold fiction to several professional magazines (such as *Fantasy and Science Fiction, Interzone, Aboriginal SF*) and anthologies (*Tesseracts 5* and *6, Synergy 5*). My novel blends literary aesthetics with the razzle-dazzle of contemporary science fiction, and I believe it would appeal to the same audience that has made bestsellers of works by William Gibson, Neal Stephenson, Jeff Noon, Dan Simmons, and Nicola Griffith.

> *If he did his homework he would have easily learned Simmons is a client. If Jensen's notion was to subtly flatter me—well, he did.*

Nineteenth-century missionaries returning from India reported seeing Hindus throwing themselves under the wheels of a towering temple cart that carried a representation of the Hindu god, "Jagannath"; from these tales, we derived the English word, "juggernaut." *Shiva 3000* is set in a far-flung future India, where the million-plus gods of Hinduism have become real, where the god Jagannath does roll through the cities on an unstoppable chariot, massive, inexorable, crushing.

> *This synopsis is irresistibly exotic. I said to myself, "This story is so bizarre, I have to read it to see if he has pulled it off."*

Another god, Kali, confronts the protagonist, Rakesh, with a task. Kali says a famous celebrity known as the Baboon Warrior must die. He must be killed by Rakesh.

Rakesh accepts. People are appalled to hear his goal, incredulous of his claim that it is his holy duty. Among the doubters he meets is a government Engineer, with his own problems. The Engineer has been expelled from the Palace, the victim of political skullduggery that soon comes to undermine stability of the government and the country. The Engineer vows to expose the young Prince who framed him, and joins Rakesh. Sex, violence, and human computers figure into the unfolding of events. In the end, Rakesh uncovers the true nature of the gods that guide their lives, and seizes control of the Jagannath—piloting it into the capital, to force the truth from the anomaly calling himself the Baboon Warrior.

> *He nailed me with this line. Now I absolutely had to see the manuscript to determine if the author was a master or a madman.*

The mythology and culture of India proved to be an inspiring milieu for a speculative novel. You are the first agent I have queried, and I hope you will take the time to consider *Shiva 3000.*

Yours truly,

> *This flattered me again. I had to send for the manuscript before he decided to query his second and third picks. I contacted him moments after finishing this letter.*

Jan Lars Jensen

> *An interesting, stimulating, inviting query letter.*

commitment to publish the book in hardcover and to give it a high profile was exactly what Jensen had hoped for his novel. As a result, *Shiva 3000* was published in the spring of 1999.

Reflecting on his experience, the only thing Jensen might have done differently was to go directly to the agents. "I would not bother querying editors until you've exhausted possibilities with agents," he says. "In addition, writing short fiction and taking courses in writing have not only improved my skills but also—in situations like querying an agent—given me some valuable credibility. I have also benefited in unexpected ways from my membership in the SFWA, so I suggest writers join organizations appropriate to their goals.

"I didn't become a writer so I could spend my time struggling to put together the right query letter," Jensen says. "But the rewards are worth the effort, because, with luck, it can lead to a situation where the author never needs to write another."

A Dose of Luck: The Elements of a Successful E-Query to an Agent

The last thing Rubén Mendoza expected when he made his collection of stories into Christmas presents was to end up with a publishing deal. "At the time, I was not at all interested in being published or attracting sales," says Mendoza. "I figured I had another five, ten years at least before anyone cared enough for me to start seeking publication."

The ball began rolling for Mendoza after "much pushing and prodding" from his girlfriend. "I asked a local author friend of mine what she thought I should do with the book. I was really just seeking editing advice and trying to get a feel for how this kind of thing worked, expecting tips on how to improve my writing. She recommended I send a copy to her publisher, and I did; about a month later, the publisher sent me a contract offer."

Acting on advice from *Writer's Digest* magazine not to sign a contract on his own, Mendoza decided to get an agent. "I didn't know anything about getting an agent or why one would need an agent or how any of this worked at all. I conduct most of my business online, so my first

Sample E-Query to an Agent

Dear Ms. Gusay:

I was recently offered a deal to publish a book of short stories. This is my first offer and I am unfamiliar with the publishing industry; I am therefore seeking agency representation to deal with contract negotiation issues.

The book is finished and is provisionally titled *Lotería*. The stories range in length from about 700 to about 8,000 words, and would probably be best classified as serious literary experimental fiction.

I am 25 and have been writing fiction as long as I can remember. In 1994, I earned a degree in American Literature from the University of Southern California. Born and raised in East San Jose, California, I now live in the Los Angeles area.

If you are interested, I would very much appreciate the opportunity to send my work and/or meet with you to further discuss the possibility of establishing a professional relationship. Thank you for your time. I look forward to hearing from you soon.

Best regards,

Rubén Mendoza

---

step was to look up a few agents on the Internet. I was looking first for someone who was not afraid of communicating this way. I told them my situation through e-mail—that I had an offer in hand and needed help on it, as well as what I was working on at the time. Obviously it helped that I had an offer—I'm not sure how much response I would have received without it." (See query above.)

Charlotte Gusay of The Charlotte Gusay Literary Agency was one of the first to respond to the e-mail query. "She was local, and that was a plus for me," says Mendoza. "While I like doing business online, I also need eventually to be able to meet with people face-to-face. Later, I got hold of a copy of the most recent *Guide to Literary Agents* and

Sample E-Query Follow-up Letter to an Agent

123 Short Stories Blvd.
Alhambra, CA 98765
emailaddress@email.com
(818) 555-2468

21 February 1997

Ms. Charlotte Gusay
The Charlotte Gusay Literary Agency
10532 Blythe Avenue
Los Angeles, CA 90064

> *It's not unusual to be approached by a writer with a deal already in hand. This tells me, "Maybe I should have a look at this."*

Dear Ms. Gusay:

Thank you for your response to my e-mail. As I indicated, I was offered a deal to publish a book of short stories. This is my first offer, and I am unfamiliar with the industry. I am therefore seeking agency representation and/or advisory service to deal with contract negotiation issues for this deal. I am also seeking agent representation in general for future work.

I located your agency first with Yahoo!, and then in the *Guide to Literary Agents*, which indicates that you might be interested in representing work similar to mine. I am seeking an agent in California. Your response was one of the warmer and more personal responses I received, so I am sending you

> *Very helpful. He knows his market, and knows where he fits in and where he departs.*

a completed copy of my self-published short story collection. Also included are copies of the contract I was offered and a counteroffer I drew up. I realize the counteroffer is probably inappropriate in both content and format, but it gives you an idea of the things I wish to negotiate.

As a Chicano writer and reader, I think this book would appeal to Chicano and other Latino readers like myself. My work is a very conscious effort to straddle the two cultures—Latin American and U.S.—that have formed my life and literary sensibilities; I am just as indebted to Latin American authors like García Márquez, Vargas Llosa, and Borges, as I am to U.S. authors like Vonnegut, Hemingway, and Barth. In addition to this completed collection of stories, I am also currently at work on an experimental crime detective novel with film potential. I have included a one-page synopsis and a page of sample text from the novel.

I am 25 and have been writing fiction seriously for two years. In 1994, I earned a degree in American Literature from U.S.C. I was born and raised in San Jose, California, and now live in the Los Angeles area (Alhambra).

I would appreciate the opportunity to meet with you to further discuss the possibility of establishing a professional relationship. I can be reached at (818) 555-2468. Thank you for your time. I look forward to hearing from you soon.

Best regards,

Rubén Mendoza

Enclosures

> *Overall, this query has a very positive and professional tone. It stands out because I represent his type of writing—it's a good match. Happily, his book was published within a year of this query and sold out its first printing.*

Comments provided by Charlotte Gusay of The Charlotte Gusay Literary Agency in Los Angeles looked her up there. I liked what her listing said about her, even though she was emphatic about not representing short stories (I was naively optimistic enough to figure I could change her mind—I think I was partly right). I received responses to my other e-mail queries as well, but Charlotte's was the warmest."

It is typically Gusay's rule to request further information upon receiving an e-mail query. In response to this request, Mendoza sent a second query letter (see this query on page 42), a copy of the book, and the contract he was offered.

Mendoza kept the queries basic, honest, and to the point. "I tried to maintain a very professional tone and imagined I was sending a formal resume cover letter to apply for a job." The letters took about fifteen to twenty minutes each to compose. "They were not difficult to put together quickly, because I was very clear from the beginning on what I needed—and perhaps because I had no preconceived notions or fears of how one should approach an agent." His professionalism and confidence were apparent—Mendoza received several positive replies.

During his communication with these interested agents, Mendoza got the feeling he was the one who should be happy about getting an agent's attention and not the other way around. The exception was Gusay. "I found we were able to establish an equal footing and respect for one another in terms of the value of what each of us contribute to this partnership and how we treat one another," says Mendoza. "I don't know that I would work with an agent otherwise—even if it meant not getting published.

"Gusay's response was immediate and very positive," says Mendoza. "She was aggressive and showed an understanding not only of the work's commercial potential but of its value as literature as well. That was most important to me considering how I'd stumbled into this whole situation from an almost purely noncommercial perspective. She also seemed to know the business, and that was the perfect combination of what I was looking for: good business sense coupled with good literary sense."

Gusay assured Mendoza the offer he received was quite acceptable, but she wanted to shop *Lotería* around to other publishers just to test the waters. Not long after, St. Martin's Press made an offer for publication under its Buzz Books imprint. Mendoza says, "I liked the idea that Buzz Books, which claimed to be promoting Los Angeles writing, was actually interested in publishing such an explicitly Latino work." This focus, along with Buzz's satisfaction with the book's title and concept (the other publisher wanted changes), convinced Mendoza he had found a home for his stories.

Mendoza advises aspiring authors to adopt his attitude of not being afraid of the rules. "As long as the writing is good, as long as you continue to focus on writing for the sake of the writing . . . the rest will tend to 'fall into place,' as they say."

Terri See is a freelance writer and a former editor for WritersMarket.com. Tara Horton is a freelance editor and a former editor of *Songwriter's Market* (Writer's Digest Books) and *Decorative Artist's Workbook*.

 ## An Interview With Scott Gold, Assistant at the Zachary Shuster Harmsworth Literary Agency

Scott Gold is an assistant at Zachary Shuster Harmsworth, a literary agency that represents both fiction and nonfiction, including authors Ha Jin (*Waiting*, winner of the National Book Award, Pantheon) and Dr. William Pollack (*Real Boys*, Random House). Gold is the "first line of defense" for the agency—it's his job to review the slush pile of query letters and manuscripts and decide which ones are worthy of further consideration. He explains what it takes to make him give your query a second look and what easy-to-avoid mistakes will brand you as an amateur.

Q How many queries would you say you look at in a year?

A We get upward of about two thousand queries a year. And the fact is that we'll probably end up representing only a few of all those people.

Agents have a vested interest in the authors we pick to represent—when we do take on a project, we end up investing a lot of time and effort into it, hoping it will sell. Agents are looking for something that's polished and professional, something that will be as easy to sell as possible.

Q **And you're the one reading this slush pile—the first reader that writers have to impress, the one in charge of forwarding materials that look promising to the individual agents at your company?**

A That's right. And they all have their own submissions piles, too—queries and proposals that they've solicited—in addition to what I give them.

Q **So what materials does your agency require for making a decision about whether to represent a writer?**

A We want to see a one-page query letter, a synopsis of the work, a sample of the material, and a self-addressed stamped envelope (SASE). That SASE is hugely important—if they don't have that, we're not even going to respond to them. We just can't.

Q **Does your agency accept electronic submissions?**

A We're starting to, but it's rare. We're kind of old-fashioned, I guess; we like to have the materials in hand. But some places are starting to accept and even prefer electronic submissions; it's important to find out what each particular agency wants. It's a personal thing for each agent. The technological revolution is still becoming part of the publishing industry. I know of one top editor who still has her assistant print out all of her e-mails for her to read every morning!

Q **What are some things that writers commonly do in queries that are "red flags" for you—things that make it easier for you to reject a writer's work?**

A Flags that pop up are typos, spelling errors, grammatical errors, syntax errors—anything that shows a lack of professionalism. If someone has a spelling error or a dangling participle in a one-page query letter, how does that speak for the person's writing? The writer has this opportunity—twenty or thirty seconds—to make an impression on an agent.

I also don't like "gimmicky" stuff—when writers try to shock me or get my attention with something clever. Or writers who start off writing about the weather. ("It was a dark and stormy night.") Or queries that come without an SASE. Or an unsolicited 500-page manuscript—chances are I'll just throw that out.

You know a huge red flag? Spelling the name of the agent or agency wrong. We get a lot of those. And try to find something out about the agent or agency you're submitting to. For example, Todd Shuster, one of the agents I work with, does a lot of serious nonfiction: science, psychology, memoir. So if you've written a science fiction novel, why submit it to him? It's worth a quick call to the agency to find out something like that.

Q **But you do want to see some writing samples, right?**

A Yes—a couple of chapters. Something to get me into your story, something to let me see your writing talent. This is true for fiction and nonfiction. Because that's what will really sell a manuscript—the quality of the writing.

Q **So what are the things that really attract you about certain query letters?**

A When a writer has some experience—has published, has won an award, even has gone to a writers conference. Something that tells me that he takes himself seriously as a writer, and that he's not just doing this in a weekend and sending his query off to an agency on a lark. A person who has an M.F.A. in creative writing will probably get more consideration. As will someone who's been to one of the big writing workshops, like Iowa. Anything that tells us that you're serious and that you're marketable. A writer who has some publishing credentials is simply easier for us to sell to an editor.

Q Do you and the agents at your company ever go out and solicit writers yourselves?

A We go out and we find writers. I cold-call award winners: people who have won scholarships, grants, prizes for their writing. We find these listings in trade journals. I read a lot of literary journals and online writing to keep up on up-and-coming writers. We also represent a lot of journalists—we read a lot of newspapers and magazines to find these people. We want to find writers who are talented, writers we can promote and sell. We always recommend that aspiring writers try and get some magazine writing done.

Q Do the agents at your agency attend writing conferences?

A Yes, we do a lot of writing conferences. It's another good way for writers to make a connection with an agent—if you've met an agent at a writing conference and you mention that in your query letter, your letter will get a closer look. There are so many ways for a writer to bypass the general "slush pile" and make it onto an agent's desk, and that's one of them.

Q Is there anything else you want to convey to writers who are sending query letters to agents?

A Just to say again that there are so many ways to make a "connection" with an agent. Conferences. Writing credentials and experience. And plain-old good writing. Take the time on your query letter—it's so important, and yet some writers don't take much time with it at all.

CHAPTER 4

What Does an Agent Actually Do?

It's standard practice in the publishing industry today for agents to get 10 to 15 percent of the writer's cut on a book project. Fifteen percent! That can seem pretty steep, particularly if you don't understand just what it is that an agent does to earn that piece of the pie.

In truth, the role of the agent is a lot more than simply sending the book to an editor and waiting for the cash to come pouring in. Agents today wear a variety of hats: career guide, writing coach, author's advocate, sometimes even friend. In this chapter, you'll hear from three agents about the many roles they play in their clients' careers and the relationships they forge with the writers they represent.

 ## The Agent-Author Relationship: What a Writer Should Expect

BY KELLY MILNER HALLS

As the number of manuscripts annually contracted shrinks, the competition for publication grows proportionally fiercer. As competition swells, so does the budding author's need for reliable professional associations. But what should a new writer expect from the most infamous of symbiotic literary relationships—the union of agent and author?

Three respected professionals—David Hale Smith, founder and head of DHS Literary, Inc., an agency that handles mainstream fiction and nonfiction out of Dallas, Texas; Bert Holtje, whose firm Ghosts & Collaborators International in Tenafly, New Jersey, represents not only traditional professionals but a string of successful ghost and coauthors;

and Margaret Basch, former trial lawyer who founded her own literary agency in Chicago after being encouraged by Simon & Schuster's Michael Korda—eagerly mapped out the nuts and bolts of this sometimes mysterious joining. "If the author knows what the agent expects and the agent knows what the author expects," says David Hale Smith, "it becomes a win-win proposition. Then we can sell some books."

Q Can you briefly describe and define your "job" as an agent?

Smith: I define the work of agents in several different ways. We are managers and we are salespeople for our authors' works. We're our clients' number one fans. And we also have an editorial role. I have never looked at being an agent as taking on just one role, which is probably what makes the job fun.

Holtje: There are a couple of ways to approach that question. First, it's important to note that I handle only nonfiction. So when I take on clients, I look forward to helping build their careers. I also help authors develop appropriate projects. Most agents are looking for "the big book." I tend to represent authors who write backlist books—books with long shelf lives. As a result, most of my clients have been with me a long time.

Basch: I'm not accepting any new clients at this point. I think that's important to say up front. But my job is to stay on top of the various markets so I know not only what is "out there" and what sells but also what publishers are looking to buy in the immediate future. It is *not* my job to get books published. It *is* my job to make money, both for my clients and for myself.

Q How many clients do you represent?

Basch: I have about a hundred clients, but not all of them have manuscripts ready to go at the same time, thank goodness. I usually have a few dozen books for sale at any given time. Any more than that would be hard to manage.

Holtje: I currently have more than fifty clients, but they are not all active at the same time. Only about half of them are active constantly. The others write and submit only occasionally. For example, I represent a number of academics—authors who write general reference and professional trade books—who write only when a specific topic arises.

Smith: I tend to represent about twenty to twenty-five, maximum. But when you have a great staff you can handle more, which occasionally I do.

Q How often should a contracted writer expect a call from his agent?

Holtje: It's generally on an "as needed" basis. Over the long haul, my clients become accustomed to when they can expect a call. But when something significant happens with a project, I call them right away.

Smith: As often as necessary. One thing I tell people is the only way I can work effectively is for them to understand the process. When we're getting ready to send out a manuscript, we may talk quite often. But we don't need to talk every time I pitch the proposal to an editor. After the project is pitched, we wait. There's no need to talk then. But when I get an offer on a manuscript, the first person I call is the client. Just remember, if I'm on the phone *with* you, I'm not on the phone *for* you.

Basch: From what I've heard, I call more than other agents. I call to ask questions, either about the content of a manuscript or about the author's credentials, or sometimes just because I want to chat and get a "feel" for the person I will be working with. I only work with people I like. (Yes, it *is* nice to have that luxury.)

Q How often should a writer call her agent?

Smith: Same answer—only as often as is necessary. But it's important we agree on what "necessary" means. One of the first things I do with a new client is make sure our expectations are in line so we go forward with a common understanding—a common vision of what our goals actually are. I can't handle it when my clients get passive-aggressive on me, when they get frustrated but don't tell me why.

Basch: A writer should call his agent any time he has questions or just wants to talk. A writer has a right to expect his calls to be returned promptly, even if just to say, "Sorry, I don't know anything right now."

Q Should a writer consider an agent a preliminary editor?

Basch: I do not edit, although sometimes it is tempting. I only accept manuscripts that are perfect. If the first page has typos or grammatical or punctuation errors, guess where I'm going to stop reading! If you cannot copyedit your own writing, pay someone else to do it. I do not appreciate having my time wasted. I will make helpful suggestions about the text if I like it but think I could love it if something specific were changed.

Holtje: To a certain extent, yes. But most of my clients are professional writers, so very few need editing in an expansive sense. If you're asking from the perspective of a beginning writer who needs some editing, yes. I'll do that when I see potential. But an agent should edit only in very broad strokes.

Smith: I think that's a matter of an agent's personal style. A writer should look at his agent as an industry professional and a partner in the process. If the agent thinks there is a way to improve the work, whether through his own input or some other legitimate professional, the client should take heed. I consider myself a serviceable editor, but I also appreciate when my clients recognize that it's not necessarily in the job description. I always tell people I do my best work when they give me something that's ready to go. The biggest sales I've made happened quickly because the work was ready to show.

Q What common mistakes do new writers make in establishing relationships with agents?

Holtje: They often try to overwhelm me with all sorts of possibilities. They have ten thousand ideas, and they to present them all right away. That's one of the major problems. I look for good writing skills and the ability to be flexible—to write on a number of subjects, but one at a time to start.

Smith: Too many writers expect agents to spend a great deal of time telling them about their agency and their client lists, before they've even submitted writing samples, before they've been signed. That's why we publish an agency profile in directories like the *Guide to Literary Agents* each year.

Send in your stuff first. Make that leap of faith. We evaluate based on the printed page, not a cold call asking questions about who we represent, our best-sellers, submission fees. Those are all valid questions— but ask them after we say we love your work, after we say we want to work with you.

Basch: I have had unpublished authors act as if I should feel lucky to have them, the world's greatest authors, and demand my credentials, etc. Every author I accept is great, in my opinion. Almost all of them are published. I do not mind working with a new author, and I do not mind answering questions. But if you are new and do not know this business, and I do not have your book sold in a week, don't call me incompetent (or words not as nice).

Q **What kind of advice do most agents offer their authors?**

Smith: Editorial advice is only one kind of advice we offer. Remember, in today's market, your work as an author has only just begun once you sell your book. Don't expect to sit back, now that you have a publishing contract, and let other people make you rich and famous. You should adopt the attitude that an author can and should be an integral part of a book's sales and promotion.

Basch: Advice? I think I learn more from the authors than I could begin to teach them. My clients know their craft. I let them write, for the most part, and I stay on top of the markets and foster my contacts.

Holtje: I like to give authors a clear picture of the economics of writing. A lot of people don't understand. They think the streets are either paved with gold or that they'll struggle all their lives. I try to give them a realistic idea—very sound, practical advice.

Q **How long does it take to place most works of fiction?**

Basch: Well, if you're already known, you can be sold before the book is written. A first novel by an unknown can take a year or longer. Reading your manuscript is just not a priority for most busy editors. They will get to it, but not always in the month it is sent.

Smith: The market is highly competitive when it comes to the best work. I once negotiated a two-book deal and a $150,000 advance in just five days. I got another client, Boston Teran, an advance in the high six figures for his first novel, *God Is a Bullet* (Knopf), in just twenty-one days. Literary fiction takes longer. But a good literary thriller—the perfect hybrid of compelling plot lines and gorgeous writing—can sell in a month or less.

Q Does that differ when placing nonfiction books?

Holtje: That depends on the project. A lot of the books I help negotiate are publisher driven. I represent a number of ghostwriters and professional collaborators. Where the average agent gets maybe half a dozen calls a year from publishers looking for a writer to transform a good idea with an unpublishable manuscript, such calls represent a significant part of my business. Since those are publisher driven, they move forward quickly.

Smith: It depends on whether it's personality-driven nonfiction. Frequently, in nonfiction, who the author is has as much import as the subject matter. Those books sell quickly. Others take longer because publishers tend to take more time thinking about and researching exactly who the book will appeal to. But good narrative nonfiction is very hot and will continue to be hot. If nonfiction grabs you like a novel might, it'll go pretty fast.

Basch: I think it depends on the nonfiction. If the author knows the market pretty well and can tailor the book to what a specific publisher or group of publishers does, like self-help for women, then nonfiction can sell relatively quickly.

Q Should your agent be your friend as well as your colleague?

Smith: If that kind of relationship develops, it's wonderful. But don't expect it. There's a little danger in getting too close because remember, it is a business relationship. But if your agent is not a fan of your work, it's a bad sign. The agent-author-editor triangle is the perfect form of professional symbiosis.

Basch: I was an attorney before I was an agent, and all my clients considered me a friend. They were always inviting me to their kids' christenings and weddings and things. It is hard being friends with clients. It takes a lot of energy, but in my case, I can't not be friends with them.

Holtje: I think so. I don't make clients of friends, but I make friends of my clients.

Q. Should contracted writers actually meet their agents face-to-face?

Basch: I like to know my clients. Certainly if they are in town I will go out of my way to meet them. It isn't always possible, so I make sure I talk to every author on the phone, and if they're online, I'll send my photo so they can see me.

Holtje: It's nice, but not necessary. I have clients scattered all over the world. In this age of electronics and telecommunications, the relationship can move forward without meeting. When I do meet my clients, it's often in an airport, on the run.

Smith: I would advise it, if possible, but I don't think it's necessary. I would venture to say that a high percentage of authors haven't met their agents. In fact, lots of New York agents have writers from all over the country. In today's world of high-tech communications, it's normal not to know them face-to-face. And you don't have to meet for your agent to do a good job for you.

Q. How long do most agent-author associations last?

Holtje: My oldest client goes back about fifteen years. I like to build a good steady relationship with my authors. I like helping them build their careers.

Smith: For some clients, I've sold five books. For others, only one because there was only one book they really wanted to do. An agent's goal should be to represent authors throughout the course of their careers. But it doesn't always work out that way.

Basch: I don't know. I haven't lost one yet.

Q Describe the perfect client, from an agent's perspective.

Smith: The perfect client is talented—an extremely good writer. He is passionate about his craft. He is a professional. He is a progressive thinker and an effective communicator. And the perfect client is financially independent—not depending upon this one book to pay the rent.

Holtje: The perfect client is someone who can write well, someone who is adaptable and flexible, someone not intimidated by new challenges. The perfect client is also someone who sees writing as a career rather than ego enhancement.

Basch: The perfect client understands I care about every client and I do my best for each. He appreciates me and all the hard work I do, both to keep his work "out there" and to keep him informed. If I could get every client a multi-million-dollar contract the same day I receive the manuscript, I would. Trust me!

Kelly Milner Halls has been a full-time professional writer for more than a decade. Her work has been featured in *The Atlanta Journal-Constitution*, the *Chicago Tribune*, the *Denver Post*, the Fort Worth *Star-Telegram*, *FamilyFun*, *Guideposts for Kids*, *Highlights for Children*, *Teen People*, *U.S. Kids*, and *Writer's Digest*. She regularly contributes to electronic publications on America Online and has been a contributing editor at *Dinosaurus* and the *Dino Times*. Her first book, *Dino-Trekking* (Wiley), was a 1996 American Booksellers Association Pick of the Lists science book.

CHAPTER 5

How Do I Evaluate My Agent?

Y ou've heard the horror stories. The agent who won't return an author's phone calls. The agent who charges a steep reading fee— then never seems to sell his authors' work. The agent who just doesn't seem to share the writer's vision for the book. Earlier in this book, you learned what an agent is supposed to do for you, the writer. But once you understand all this, how can you be sure your agent is doing his job right and acting as the best representative for you and your work?

Happily, most author-agent relationships are professional, friendly, and mutually beneficial. In chapter two, we looked at ways to target a literary agent who is a good fit for your work. But once you've found an agent who's interested in representing you, how can you be sure the agent has your best interests at heart? In this chapter, we talk about how to evaluate the working relationship between author and agent and how to be sure it is still working for you. Agent Jean Naggar offers some history about one of the most established organizations of agents, the Association of Authors' Representatives (AAR), and offers her advice about the qualities a writer should insist upon when selecting an agent.

 ## Agents and Ethics: Getting Published Without Losing Your Shirt
BY JEAN V. NAGGAR

Writing is usually a lonely occupation. When at last, after months, even years of wrestling with words and ideas, the writer types in "The End," prints up the result of mighty labors, and feels the thrill of hefting a bulky pile of crisp pages, it would seem that the Herculean task is over. Now, surely, it is merely a matter of locating the right agent, getting the right publisher interested, and the words and ideas, elegantly bound and jacketed, will appear on the shelves of bookstores everywhere.

Easy, right?

Wrong.

These days, the writer must not only create a fine work of the imagination, the aspiring writer must also learn a good deal about how the publishing business works, who the players are, and how to avoid falling into the clutches of a growing number of "agencies" and "editorial services" that survive on fees paid up front and not on commissions from a job well done. Throughout the years, hardworking, reputable literary agents have striven to distinguish their ways of doing business from the ways of the less particular.

A Brief History of the Association of Authors' Representatives

Early in the 1970s, a small group of independent literary agents who had recently moved to agenting from editorial and other positions in publishing houses began getting together informally, to network and to exchange gossip, war stories, and survival tips. The group quickly coalesced into something more formal, and it named itself the Independent Literary Agents Association (ILAA).

This energetic, proactive group of then relatively new agents operated alongside the venerable and respected Society of Authors' Representatives (SAR) for some years, maintaining an independent-minded approach to reading fees as it did to other matters.

The SAR had long held its members to a code of appropriate behavior, and in time, a committee formed in the ILAA to discuss many questions of ethical behavior that came up in conversation and in practice. They discussed appropriate behaviors of member agents with each other, with their authors, and with the publishers and editors with whom they dealt. While not wishing in any way to impinge on the free and independent operation of its members, or to create a policing body, certain red-flag issues came up again and again, and the committee decided to develop a code of appropriate behavior for its members.

In 1990, the two associations joined forces and emerged as the Association of Authors' Representatives (AAR), an energized association of literary agents, committed to following high standards of behavior in their professional dealings, charging no reading fees, and avoiding any situation that might introduce a conflict of interest, although it took some time for some differences in philosophy to be resolved to the satisfaction of all.

The AAR currently numbers some 350 member agents nationwide. Member agents subscribe annually to a code of ethics that is fast becoming a standard in the publishing industry, and concern themselves with following the latest developments in contracts, royalties, and the optimal dispensation of all rights.

Creating an Ethical Standard

The Canon of Ethics that developed from this joining is signed yearly by every member of the AAR when dues are paid. It has produced high standards within an unregulated, unlicensed industry. It is notable that publishers have not developed a similar set of ethical guidelines for their behavior, nor are they likely to do so!

Briefly, the Canon of Ethics ensures the following:

- That members maintain two separate bank accounts so there is no commingling of clients' monies and the agency's operating expenses.
- That prompt disclosure and payment are made to clients regarding monies received for them from both domestic and foreign sales.
- That members are forbidden to charge reading fees to clients or potential clients, directly or indirectly, beyond the customary return postage charges. In an attempt to deflect potential author abuses, the Ethics Committee recently extended this provision. Now, agents who belong to the AAR may not charge fees for reading manuscripts and proposals at writers conferences.
- That members of the AAR may not receive a secret profit or enter

into any arrangement regarding a client's work that might create a conflict of interest.

While providing this very unique standard of ethical behavior authors can depend upon, the AAR still affirms the total independence of its members' individual operations, adoption or rejection of author-agents agreements, commission structures, and negotiations with publishers.

Sometimes, an author attempts to involve the cooperation of the Ethics Committee of the AAR in connection with a particular agent who is not an AAR member or for reasons outside the scope of the Canon of Ethics. Most of these matters, however, are not the purview of the Ethics Committee, which was never intended to be a policing body regarding general "agenting" complaints. Any complaints addressing *a member's* violation of the Canon of Ethics are taken very seriously indeed, and no decision is taken without a thorough exploration of all circumstances surrounding the complaint.

Cooperating to Keep Up With a Changing Industry

The AAR also works to inform and educate its agenting community on developments within the publishing industry. At present, the contractual and conceptual problems arising from new electronic technologies and the shrinking of publishing venues due to recent consolidations are taking much of the organization's attention. AAR members have formed task forces to work with publishers on these issues, and have organized forums for the discussion of cutting-edge technologies and their impact on all of us. The AAR makes sure its members are equipped with the information they need to make the decisions that best benefit their writers.

The association also appoints individual agents to act as liaisons with all the major writers organizations. They keep abreast of issues concerning these writer communities and, in turn, inform them of AAR developments, maintaining a steady flow of information. It is more important than ever before that authors and agents share information and insights and move forward together into the changing world of today's publishing scene.

Making Informed Choices

Obviously, in choosing an agent, whether through the AAR list or otherwise, there are vast differences in temperament, sensibility, day-to-day practice, and personal style to take into account. To gain a sense of the personalities of several agents, read John Baker's *Literary Agents: A Writer's Introduction* (Macmillan). Every writer should choose the agent best suited for her own needs and disposition. By choosing an agent who is an AAR member, a writer can be sure that the agent cares about ethical standards enough to sign on to them on a yearly basis, and because admission to membership requires several recommendations and sale of a specific number of books, it also ensures that the AAR agent you approach is respected by her peers and not a fly-by-night operation.

Your writing career is worth all the advance power you can find to fuel it, and although the temptations out there are many, be advised that reputable agents rarely if ever advertise—most reputable agents obtain new clients through referrals and word of mouth. Agents also cannot make promises about getting your work published. And if your book is going to be published, a reputable publisher will be paying you an advance, not the other way around.

There is no more precious a thing than the painstaking creation of a work of the imagination. Writers are the lifeblood of the publishing industry, the only indispensable element in a continuum that links writer to reader. But the publishing industry is becoming increasingly bound by corporate politics and policies, forcing writers to seek out other kinds of feedback. Publishers are also at the mercy of the media, whose enormous hyping of superlative advances and celebrity has created its own quicksand, into which many writers founder, lured by the pot of gold at the end of the rainbow.

Using Freelance Editors

Just when technology has provided aspiring writers with wonderful tools like "spellcheck" and the ability to restructure a manuscript several times without having to retype the entire work, the publishing industry itself has chosen to batten down the hatches, jettison imprints and editors in droves, and consolidate lists—all of which leave little room for the unpublished writer to slip a toe in the door.

Publishing has undergone seismic change. Mergers and consolidations have led to firings and departures of editors, and have caused a general sense of unease among those who are still employed. Departing editors are often not replaced, placing a greater burden on the shoulders of fewer editors, giving them neither the time nor the energy to take on projects that require a lot of editorial work. Unwilling to take risks that might land them among the unemployed, most people in publishing houses hold back on making decisions and choose the path of least resistance.

Consequently, many reputable and not-so-reputable individuals now offer "book-doctoring" services to evaluate material and pummel it into shape before it even reaches the critical eyes of agents and editors. Offering promises of magical editorial input, some of these self-styled "editorial services" exist solely to tease money from the hopeful and empty the pockets of the uninformed. The pitfalls are many along the road to publication, and shape-shifting monsters lurk in the deep to seize the unwary and relieve them of their savings.

However, the happier side of this picture is that there *do* exist groups of seasoned professionals working as individual freelance editors and exercising editorial skills honed from many years spent making decisions at publishing houses. Finding themselves out of jobs in the new corporate groupings, they offer an important entrepreneurial opportunity within the changing landscape of the publishing industry. Some of them are beginning to coalesce into associations of their own. Others work alone. They usually do not advertise, and their services are expensive. But they are true publishing professionals and take genuine pleasure in using hard-won skills to help writers find their voices or to pull a publishable work out of chaos.

Above all, bear in mind that a reputable publisher *will pay you* for

Finding Reputable Freelance Editors and Literary Agents
How can a writer tell which face of Janus is smiling in her direction? How do you sift the reputable from the disreputable when you live far from the centers of publishing activity and feed on hope to keep your dreams alive? When you have been rejected by an entire flotilla of agents and someone out there offers you (for a "small" fee) the opportunity to have your manuscript read by a self-styled "professional" or, better yet, offers you publication if you will come up with an "advance" toward it, could this be opportunity knocking at the door? Use these guidelines to help you decide:

- Read *Publishers Weekly* for several months before you will need the services of either a book doctor or a literary agent, focusing on new agents who come out of substantial publishing (not necessarily agenting) experience.
- Attend writers conferences, and ask around for names of freelance editors and agents with whom people have had positive experiences.
- From freelance editors, request an advance breakdown of fees before signing any contract, including the cost of a reading and editorial letter and the cost of a subsequent in-depth editorial job. Beware of empty promises. A freelance editor cannot guarantee you publication.
- Ask freelance editors if they will provide samples of previous editing jobs, and discuss the level of editing you will receive for the fees you pay.
- Request a list of published writers who have worked with this editor, and try to check it out by looking at Acknowledgment pages, etc., unless you are fortunate enough to have access to one of these writers.
- Ask your librarian or local bookseller if the name of the editor you are considering is at all familiar. Librarians and booksellers read *Publishers Weekly* and attend book conventions, where they sometimes meet editors. They can also make inquiries for you and steer you toward a reputable editor.
- Familiarize yourself with what services a good agent can and should be able to provide.

the right to publish your book and will not require you to put up your own money.

The Authors Guild and other writers organizations can provide information about editors and agents. The AAR has also moved consistently, over the years, to help prevent author abuses within the ethical framework for its members. It has never been more important to be wary of golden promises. It has never been more important to enlist the help of a reputable professional.

Happily, writers are hard to discourage. I would only urge you to put as much energy and research into the "tools" with which you hope to achieve publication as you put into writing the work you hope to publish. In achieving a realistic understanding of the limitations and benefits of the publishing industry, and in gaining a sense of the names and roles of the players in that industry, you can avoid costly mistakes and make choices that lead to publication, rather than insolvency.

Jean V. Naggar is the president of the Jean V. Naggar Literary Agency in New York, begun in 1978. She is a past president of AAR and has worked in publishing for thirty years.

CHAPTER 6

How Do I Approach Agents and Editors at Conferences?

For many writers, making the commitment to attend a writing conference is a big step. In a very real way, it's an investment in your writing—a statement to yourself and to the world that you're serious about improving your work, meeting other writers, and just maybe finding an agent or an editor who is as enthusiastic about your writing as you are.

Writing conferences are a great way to put a "face" on the sometimes daunting world of publishing. Most conferences invite agents, editors, and successful writers to attend and give seminars. Sometimes you'll have the opportunity to meet with them for a one-on-one session about your work; sometimes you even have the chance to "pitch" your book to an editor or agent. It's important to learn as much about what's offered at your conference as possible before you get there: Who is attending? (Any agents who represent works like yours?) What classes or sessions are available? (Large workshops or personalized critiques?)

But most importantly, you must set some clear goals for yourself about what you want to get out of your time. In this chapter, you'll learn nine guidelines to help you make the most of your experience at a writing conference. You'll also hear from agent Meredith Bernstein about conference etiquette, impressing agents, and how to follow up with that great agent who seemed so interested in your work.

Maximize Your Writers Conference Experience
BY KAREN OSTERMANN

Firsts can be frazzling or dazzling. Take for instance one's first date, first job—or first writers conference. Seizing the opportunities that a conference presents sounds easy, but insecurity, indecision, and inertia may impede the moment. Sometimes the excitement and anticipation of the event obscures practical preparation.

Use these nine tips to help storm these roadblocks.

1. Don't Hug the Wall

Network, network, network! Get started during registration and coffee hour. Introduce yourself to the person standing next to you. Everyone wears name badges to break the ice—including authors, guest speakers, and volunteers—and they all have something to offer.

2. Don't Arrive Without a Plan

Don't forget to research the speakers via the Internet, libraries, or bookstores. The itinerary is set in advance, identifying the speakers and their topics. Search for information regarding their published works, literary connections, and credentials. Then prepare an outline listing the workshops you wish to attend, including the presenters' names and their scheduled rooms and times. Try to arrive early, and scout out where the rooms are to save time later.

3. Don't Forget Your Pen

Don't hesitate to start writing the minute you arrive. Carry a small bag or briefcase for your notebook, pens, and free handouts. Jot down the names of new acquaintances, their projects, and e-mail addresses. Editors always need new material, so if an idea pops into your head that might work for an editor you just met, you want to be able to jot it down and know whom to send it to.

4. Don't Be Shy

Don't pass up opportunities to speak up at the workshops. The audience usually is invited to participate, and questions prepared in advance can give you an edge.

5. Don't Be Nameless

Don't go without business cards. They create a professional impression and are easy to exchange in a pinch of time. Any print shop can make them up. You can order them online—five hundred for less than twenty-five dollars at Web sites like www.bizcardpro.com, for example—or you can make your own on the computer with software such as Print Shop Publishing by Broderbund.

6. Don't Be Bogged Down

Don't carry around too much baggage. You want to have your hands free to write, and you want to be able to move quickly between workshops. Coat and luggage check rooms are worth the few dollars if you are not spending the night on site.

7. Don't Hide

Don't forget to position yourself strategically at workshops. If you are encouraged to ask questions, sitting close to the front is a prime spot to be noticed. A third to midway back on the aisle is a safer bet if you intend to leave a session early. Climbing over chairs and their occupants can be noisy and distracting.

8. Don't Be Afraid to Share

Bring some writing samples. Sharing, during breaks and lunches with new acquaintances, promotes confidence and opportunities. Everyone in attendance is looking to share information or to get feedback no matter how successful they are. If your book piqued the interest of an agent or editor, he or she may be interested in seeing an outline or the first few chapters.

9. Don't Ignore Opportunities

Don't fight fate and opportunity. At an American Society of Journalists and Authors conference, I happened to make eye contact with author Dominick Dunne during his book signing of *The Way We Lived Then* (Crown). Emboldened, I immediately charged over and secured a book, handshake, and signature, completely unaware that I had run to the head of the line. (Oops!) Seize the moment, and follow your instincts.

Insecurity and the writer seem to be familiar bedfellows. Enduring firsts—whatever they may be—is often the toughest part of any journey, whether it be putting pen to paper, sending out a query, or attending your first conference. Minimizing those self-conscious moments with preparation and forethought boosts confidence. Being there, taking action, and heeding advice may hurtle you to places of which you only dared to dream.

Karen Ostermann, a freelance writer and editor based in New York, is working on her first novel.

Meeting Agents at Conferences: How to Get Your Foot in the Door
BY DONYA DICKERSON

"I just sold a book from that conference," says literary agent Meredith Bernstein referring to the annual International Women's Writing Guild's Big Apple: Meet the Agents conference. "It's a first novel by Sharon Wyse called *The Box Children*, and I absolutely flipped for it. I sent it out to a large selection of publishers, and within a month and a half we had a deal with Riverhead Books."

Throughout her twenty years running the Meredith Bernstein Literary Agency, she has found attending writers conferences a valuable way to discover potential clients. Besides the IWWG conference, Bernstein frequents conferences across the country, including the Golden Triangle Writers Guild in Beaumont, Texas, and the Pacific Northwest Writers Association Conference in Seattle, Washington. Not only does she share insights into her job as an agent and the publishing industry, but she often meets one-on-one with new writers. For any budding author, conferences provide a unique opportunity to network with agents like Bernstein.

With a client list that includes mystery series writer and Agatha winner Nancy Pickard; National Organization for Women president Patricia Ireland; and Dennis Conner, author of *The America's Cup* (St. Martin's Press), Bernstein says her start in the agency business was "kind of a fluke. I wanted to be a writer when I was growing up. And I actually wrote a full-length novel when I was twelve—I thought I was Anne Frank reincarnated."

Nevertheless, she avoided finding a job in publishing. "I thought publishing was dark and dreary. I started out being things like a story editor and a freelance reader, then worked as a scout for a network producer. One day I called up a literary agent and said, 'What's new?' She said, 'I'm getting married. Do you want my job?' So I was hired by Henry Morrison. I worked for him for five years then left to open my own agency."

Almost as serendipitous as Bernstein's introduction to the agenting world is the story of how she met her first client—and made her first sale. After being with Morrison only three months, a friend asked Bernstein to accompany her to a conference held by the IWWG. "I was full of vim and vigor, telling everybody at the conference I was an agent," says Bernstein. "I convinced the woman running the conference that I should speak on agenting—all my three months' worth of knowledge. There was a woman there, Christina Baldwin, who described a book she had written, and I thought she was also Anne Frank reincarnated. I asked if I could read her book, and I fell in love with it. I only knew one publisher—a client of Henry's—so I pitched the book to him. He called me the next day saying he wanted to buy it." That book, *One to One: Self-Understanding Through Journal Writing* (M. Evans & Company), is still in print more than twenty years later.

Since her first sale, Bernstein has continued to search conferences for new clients, claiming, "They have paid off for me." Nevertheless, the number of writers she meets forces her to be discerning about whom she chooses to represent. "At this stage in the game, I'm interested in somebody who's committed to her work, has some knowledge about the publishing industry, is focused, has a clear idea of what she wants to do and where she wants to go with her work, and who is passionate about what she is doing."

In order to impress an agent, it's important for a writer to prepare for a conference. "Do your homework," advises Bernstein. "If you know who's going to be there, check out the books and magazines that talk about these people. Decide who is a good person to spend your time talking to." A common mistake, she says, is when writers approach agents who are inappropriate for their manuscripts. "If people line up to talk to me about military history, my eyes are going to glaze over. I'm not the right agent for that subject, and if they don't know that, they should."

Before speaking to Bernstein at a conference, a writer should know that her agency represents an even split of fiction and nonfiction. "The fiction has traditionally been a lot of romance—everything from the real category stuff to the single title romance—and a lot of mysteries," she says. "I'm open to commercial and literary fiction, but it has to have a very strong voice. Commercial fiction should have characters you can't get out of your mind and a story that makes you want to turn the page. I'm also interested in thrillers and suspense, but not horror or science fiction. For nonfiction, I do absolutely everything across the board. I like narrative nonfiction, memoirs, parenting, health, spiritual, pet books, women's issues, humor, sports, business . . . you name it."

Bernstein is extremely honest with the writers she meets to avoid being swamped with submissions after a conference. "I don't want to encourage people to send me things I'm not interested in because I'm too far along in my career. I don't want to waste my time looking at things just to be a nice guy. It's not fruitful for them, and it's not fruitful for me." There are, of course, exceptions. "Sometimes I'll look at something because a person touches me in a particular way."

Bernstein is adamant about maintaining "publishing etiquette," and she expects potential clients to, also. This means that writers should contact her after the conference through a one-page query letter with an enclosed self-addressed, stamped envelope. Because of the number of people she meets at conferences, she emphasizes how important it is that a writer mentions that Bernstein showed interest in a particular manuscript. "If you talk to sixty people for five minutes at a time, it's hard to remember each one." Nevertheless, she admits, "If the person says, 'I'm sitting with a deal from a publisher. Would you handle it?' I might remember that."

For writers who aren't able to attend conferences, Bernstein, like many other agents, is always open to receiving written queries. Still, she believes an important part of her job is meeting with writers and dispelling their fears about agents. "Being a presence at conferences gives writers the opportunity to see who you are. A lot of writers have a picture of agents as these people who live in an ivory tower or who are unapproachable. I like to show up at a conference and make people feel like of course they can write to me, of course they can call me. But the most important thing is for them to realize that we are approachable."

CHAPTER 7

Should I Send an E-Query?

To e-query or not to e-query? It's a question that didn't even exist just a few years ago, but today more and more writers are eschewing the traditional query letter in favor of an electronic version. There are definite advantages to sending your query through cyberspace instead of the U.S. Postal Service, including speed, convenience (both for the writer and the editor or agent), and cost.

But e-queries became even more accepted—and crucial—during the anthrax scares in late 2001. Suddenly, those bundles of unsolicited mail and bulky manuscripts weren't just a necessary burden for editors and agents to sort through. They became a potential danger. Many publishing professionals wouldn't even accept unsolicited queries or manuscripts anymore, throwing away such packages unopened. E-queries became the sole way for writers to establish contact with some editors and agents.

Many publishers and agents officially changed their submissions policies after the anthrax scares, specifying that they will accept only e-queries. Still others are just as adamant about their refusal to look at anything other than hard-copy versions of letters and manuscripts. The most important thing, as always, is to find out what each individual agency or publisher requires—e-query or standard letter, sample chapter or entire manuscript. This information is usually available at the company's Web site, in a listing of editors and agents in a book such as *Writer's Market*, or by simply picking up the phone and asking. In this chapter, you'll learn some basic tips on e-query etiquette. You'll also hear firsthand from several editors and agents how the anthrax scares affected their submission requirements, and whether or not their companies are more open to e-mail submissions.

E-Query Etiquette
BY GREG DAUGHERTY

With e-queries, success is often in the e-tails. Here are ten pointers for writing—and sending—e-queries that work.

1. First, find out if the editor or agent accepts e-queries. This may seem too basic to even mention, but there's no point in sending out e-queries to companies that won't consider them. So check *Writer's Market* (the print edition or online at www.writersmarket.com) or send a quick e-mail and ask. Or use that quaint old tool, the telephone. Many editors and agents spell out whether they take e-mail queries and where to send them in the writer's guidelines posted on their Web sites.

2. Remember that most basic of basics. The job of a query letter is to persuade an editor or agent to ask for more materials from you— a proposal or sample chapters. So whether it's printed on paper or glowing on a cathode-ray tube, any query you send should be built around a solid idea—one that's right for the editor or agent and for which you are, of course, the ideal writer.

3. Be a little formal. E-mail is often more casual than conventional letters. But if you wouldn't call an editor or agent by his or her first name in a letter, don't do it in an e-mail. An editor accustomed to being addressed by strangers as Robert So-and-So may not appreciate an e-mail that begins "Hi, Robert" or "Yo, Bobbo."

4. Watch your spelling. Even in the brave new world of e-mail, editors and agents still expect you to know how to spell. Your e-mail program may have a spell-check feature just as your word processing software does. If it doesn't, one option is to write queries in your word processor, spell-check them there, and then paste them into an e-mail.

5. Make good use of the SUBJECT: line. The last thing you want to do is carefully write and polish a query and then have some harried editor delete it unread because it looks like spam. One simple way to prevent that is to put the word "query" prominently in the subject line of your e-mail, such as "Query about a new way to garden" or "Query about a new horror novel."

6. Provide enough contact information. Put your phone number and snail mail address on your e-mail. If you have a fax number, you might as well toss that in, too. Anything that makes it easier for an editor or agent to reply to your query increases the odds that one may actually do so.

7. Offer to supply samples of your work on request. But don't load up your e-mail with attachments. Some editors and agents won't even open attachments from strangers for fear of viruses. If samples of your work are available at your own Web site or somewhere else online, by all means mention that, but don't count on the agent to spend a leisurely afternoon reading them. Again, check the company's Web site for information about the best way to submit sample chapters or other supplemental material.

8. Save your resume for job applications. Just because you can easily attach your resume to an e-mail doesn't mean you should. As with any writing samples you attach, many editors and agents won't give your resume so much as a click. Far more effective is a paragraph somewhere near the end of your letter in which you sum up any experience and publishing credits you have that would be relevant to the project you're proposing.

9. Go easy on multiple submissions. Pitching the same idea to several different editors and agents at the same time couldn't be easier than with e-mail. But think twice. Even editors and agents who are willing to look at simultaneous submissions may be put off by a TO: line with the e-mail addresses of a dozen other places. When I get those, I often just delete them, figuring that any writer who wrote to that many publications will never notice whether I replied or not. If you want to try that kind of scattershot approach, be sure to mention that it's a simultaneous submission, but send out separate e-mails, with just one addressee each or use the BCC: option.

10. Don't expect an instant answer. E-mail can make it easier to churn out queries, but editors and agents still need time to think about your projects and respond, just as they would with a paper query. An idea is an idea, whether it arrives via modem or mailbag. If you haven't heard anything after several weeks, there's no harm in e-mailing back with a gentle inquiry. But whatever you do, don't get testy about it. Editors felt overwhelmed long before e-mail, and it has only added to their burdens. Remember that the easiest thing any editor or agent can do is hit the delete key.

Greg Daugherty was editor in chief of *Reader's Digest New Choices* magazine and is the author of *You Can Write for Magazines* (Writer's Digest Books).

 ## The Effects of Anthrax on Writers' Submissions
BY ROBERT LEE BREWER

"I think we would all be willing to get our mail a day or two later if we didn't have to worry about infection," remarked one editor in the aftermath of September 11. As a result of all the coverage in the media, it's probably common knowledge now that anthrax is a bacterial disease typical in farm animals, such as cattle and sheep, which can also be spread to humans. Though easy to cure, if it goes long enough without detection, it can be fatal. The spread of this disease through the mail has people in all professions on the alert.

During the anthrax scares, many writers contacted WritersMarket .com to report return-to-sender mail from magazines, book publishers, and agents. These leads often mean a certain company has changed address. Usually, we follow up on such leads and make the appropriate contact changes in our online databases. However, most of these markets have not moved; they just changed their submission policies, at least for a while.

Since September 11, it seems almost every piece of information regarding terrorism has been playing up the negative possibilities, often looking at just how bad things could get at any minute. Some theorize that many media outlets have been promoting terror to increase ratings, often by running stories before all the facts are reported and verified.

For this article, more than 150 editors, book publishers, and literary agents completed a survey to assess the current state of the publishing industry in relation to the anthrax scares. Here are the results.

Book Publishers

Perhaps because they deal with bulkier packages, a high percentage of book publishers changed their submission guidelines in response to the anthrax scares. And many of the publishers that did not change their policies mentioned they're still *considering* a change from the norm a possibility.

Quite a few literary agents, who deal with publishing houses frequently, mentioned they've heard the days of slush piles at major publishers are officially over. Whether this rumor pans out remains to be seen. However, book publishers are still accepting manuscripts, and for the most part, the rules are still the same.

"Nothing yet suggests to me that publishers need to take extraordinary precautions in the post-9/11 world," states Sharon Woodhouse of Lake Claremont Press. "I think overreacting, misplaced fears, and the erosion of common sense in times such as these, though understandable, can interfere with recognizing and responding to real dangers should they occur, while reducing our sanity, security, freedoms, and quality of life along the way."

Whether book publishers have changed policies or not, the decisions seem to be made rationally and not in a frenzy or panic. In some cases, the full conversion to e-mail submissions was only pushed forward by the recent anthrax scares. In fact, many of the book publishers have been accepting e-mail and snail mail submissions simultaneously for years.

"Most of our unsolicited submissions come in regular mail, but an increasing number are coming over e-mail. I personally prefer e-mail," explains Mary Lou Bertucci, senior editor for Swedenborg Foundation Publishers/Chrysalis Books. She adds, "I don't feel any sense of panic, but I do wonder about mailed submissions. However, I still tear them open as I always have—no gloves or face mask or anything like that."

Just like Bertucci, most publishing houses have kept relatively calm and separated the media-portrayed threat from the real threat. Most have acted appropriately by preparing their employees for action without letting it stop their businesses altogether. In fact, many of those surveyed expressed that e-mail-spread computer viruses concerned them more than the threat of anthrax. At the moment, computer viruses certainly do seem more likely to affect a book publisher's bottom line.

As Laurence Jacobs of the Craftsman Book Company says, "You're much more likely to die in a car accident on the way to work than from an anthrax attack. And we all drive to work every day without a trace of fear."

Literary Agents

Literary agents deal with many of the same packages that book publishers do. It then comes as no surprise that agents responded to the survey pretty much in line with the publishing houses. There have been some changes in submission guidelines. There is some fear. But for the most part, agents are trying to get on with their work in a cautious but productive manner.

"No," responds Justin E. Fernandez, literary agent–attorney, in response to whether or not he feels threatened by the recent anthrax scares. "But I would never open a package with no return address, or with wires sticking out, or with oil stains, a funny smell, or an odd shape. There are plenty of nonterrorist lunatics out there. So anything suspicious would be tossed unopened—after a call to the bomb squad or other authorities."

Many of the agents surveyed seemed to have a good handle on what the real threats of anthrax are and the chances of getting infected. In fact, the major scare is not that they'll be targeted but that they may receive a piece of cross-contaminated mail, something many feel is highly unlikely.

"One can't grow so paranoid as to not live one's life, but in light of recent events one needs to be alert and aware," says agent Felicia Eth. "I see this as a trial balloon of some sort. Which is to say, I don't feel any particular immediate threat at the moment. I don't anticipate receiving a letter with anthrax spores, mostly because as a one-person agency who is not 'well known,' I don't see myself as the symbol (of American capitalism) these individuals are looking to attack."

But at the same time, Eth says she feels threatened by the attack (as several agents and book publishers have expressed). "I received two queries last week in small envelopes and addressed by hand, with a writing similar to the envelopes containing anthrax," explains Janet Kobobel Grant from Books & Such literary agency. "I paused, checked the postmarks to see if they were from New Jersey or Florida, and opened them carefully. I'd say I've become a bit more cautious and nervous."

The consensus seems to be that people in publishing do feel threatened. But these same professionals are moving on with business. As literary agent Alison Picard believes, "We should not allow terrorists to create an atmosphere of fear and paranoia. I'm conducting business as usual, and I encourage all writers and publishing professionals to do the same."

The Effect on Writers

At the moment, the publishing industry does not seem to be a direct target of whichever group is sending terror in the mail (with the exception of American Media, which unfortunately has a misleading name). It makes no sense to quit everything you're working on to prepare for a threat that may never present itself. However, because the threat is present, writers can expect magazine editors, book publishers, and literary agents to take certain precautions to avoid being infected. As a result, the need for professionalism from writers is perhaps at its highest level ever.

This professionalism means that writers may need to be more patient with response time. The possibility of a slower postal service is real. Also, many of the people surveyed mentioned that their mailing service departments are moving a little slower to check postmarks against return addresses. Many submission policies have changed rather quickly.

The speed of change should not be interpreted as anything other than what it is though. The publishing industry is not under attack, and writers are still encouraged to submit good books on all subjects and in all genres. The way writers submit work will always be in a state of revolution. Why else would a directory like *Writer's Market* exist if this wasn't the case? So the effect on writers . . .

The effect on writers is that they need to be even more professional with their submissions than usual. Period. And get back to your writing, because the world can't go on without some form of positive creative energy.

Robert Lee Brewer is the assistant editor for *Writer's Market* and co-editor for WritersMarket.com.

CHAPTER 8

What Should I Do Once I've Caught an Agent's or Editor's Interest?

You've made the first cut—the literary agent (or editor) was intrigued by your query and wants to see more information about your book. After you've uncorked the champagne and done a little celebrating, it's time to get to work on the next important piece of writing you'll be sending out: the book proposal. Whether you've written the next great American novel or the next great American diet book, there are certain components you must include in your book proposal. In this chapter, you'll learn what they are and how to craft them.

 ## Commanding Book Proposals: The Rejection Slip's Greatest Enemy
BY DON PRUES

Many writers approaching a publishing house or attempting to find an agent to represent their books perceive themselves to be a diminutive David staring down a monstrous Goliath. Even worse, they think no weapon exists to slay the giant and prove their books are worth publishing. Such folks are wrong. An effective weapon does exist: It's called a book proposal. The hitch, however, is that writers must build this weapon themselves.

And therein lies the problem: Most writers don't know which materials to use or how to put the pieces together to stand a fighting chance. But hang in there—in this chapter, you'll learn what you need to include in your proposal and how to assemble it, ultimately equipping you with the necessary weaponry to conquer even the most colossal rejection pile.

Before we get into the specifics about composing and organizing your proposal, we need to get one fact out of the way: The proposal you create depends upon what the agent or editor wants. And the most nonintrusive way to know what she wants is to consult her listing in a directory like *Writer's Market* or *Guide to Literary Agents*, or to do some background research on a company's Web site, or to write and ask for submission guidelines. And follow the submission specifications to a T—nothing more, nothing less.

The Novel Proposal

The golden rule in publishing fiction is your novel must be completed before you solicit an agent or editor. Will you be permitted to send

The Components of a Novel Proposal:
- Cover letter
- Cover/Title page
- Contents page
- Synopsis
- Chapter-by-chapter outline (rarely requested)
- Author biography
- First three sample chapters (or about fifty pages)
- Endorsements (if possible)

The Components of a Nonfiction Book Proposal:
- Cover letter
- Cover/Title page
- Contents page
- Overview
- Marketing information
- Competitive analysis
- Promotion ideas
- Chapter-by-chapter outline
- Author biography
- Sample chapter(s)
- Endorsements (if possible)
- Attachments (if possible)

your entire novel upon initial contact? Probably not. Unsolicited manuscripts are ignored, returned, and sometimes even thrown away when sent to an agent or editor who does not accept them. That's the catch with fiction: You need to have your novel finished before soliciting an agent or editor, but rarely are you allowed to send the complete manuscript. Don't waste your time, energy, paper, and postage sending material to someone who doesn't care about it.

Many agents and editors prefer first to receive a one-page query letter, and they will ask for the proposal or the manuscript only after having their interests piqued by the query. Check to see what this particular agent or editor accepts—rarely will it be a complete manuscript, but often it will be a novel proposal.

Novel proposals are easy to put together. You can anticipate sending a cover letter, a synopsis, three consecutive sample chapters (almost always your first three chapters) or the first fifty pages, possibly an author biography, and an endorsements page. These are by far the most important—and most requested—parts of your proposal. Some agents and editors require only a cover letter and three sample chapters, because with fiction, the writing itself (your sample chapters) matters most. Again, what you send is determined by what the agent or editor demands.

The Nonfiction Book Proposal

Although you can still showcase your writing style with a nonfiction proposal, the *concept* of your book is much more important than the writing itself. Strong prose can only help your proposal, of course, but the agent's decision to represent you or the editor's decision to buy your book will rest with the project's commercial viability. Unlike fiction, you do not need to have your nonfiction book completed before soliciting an agent or editor. (You will, however, need to send some sample chapters.) But there's still a lot of work to be done when creating a nonfiction proposal.

Compared to novel proposals, nonfiction book proposals are complicated pitches that must contain a variety of elements—an overview, a marketing section, a competition section, a promotions section, a chapter-by-chapter outline, an author biography, and attachments. With your nonfiction proposal, you can expect to send a big package with lots of individual parts that hover around your unique and salable concept.

The Components
Cover Letter (for Novel and Nonfiction Proposals)

The type of cover letter you compose depends on whether you're sending a blind ("unsolicited") proposal or a requested ("solicited") proposal. Some agents and editors accept (or even prefer) to see an entire proposal upon initial contact instead of a query letter, particularly for nonfiction books. In any case, you'll need to tailor a sharp cover letter to hook her and encourage her to dive eagerly into the rest of your proposal. A cover letter accompanying a blind proposal submission is like a tightened version of a query letter (for more on queries, see chapter three). Similar to the query letter, your cover letter tells who you are *and* what you have to offer. You don't need to spend much time arguing that your proposal is worthwhile, because what you have to offer (the proposal) is actually enclosed.

If you've already sent the agent or editor a query letter and she has requested a full proposal, keep the cover letter short—just a paragraph

---

The Basics of a Cover Letter

A good rule of thumb is to keep your cover letter to one page, containing three or four short paragraphs organized in the following order:

1. The introductory paragraph. State the book's title, and then spend two to five sentences hooking the agent with a brief description of your book and why it will sell.

2. The biographical paragraph. In one or two sentences, explain a bit about yourself, including only information that's pertinent to the book, such as previous publishing credits or why you're sending it to this particular agency.

3. The concluding paragraph. Politely close the letter.

or two will do. Simply let her know what material you've enclosed, and mention whether anyone else is considering the same proposal.

Cover/Title Page (for Novel and Nonfiction Proposals)

Although the title is but a small part of a large book, a telling and catchy title can be so important. The difference between an adequate title and a superb title can mean the difference between mediocre book sales and gargantuan ones. Think about some of the successful titles you know—most are under five words (excluding the subtitle) and present a unique feature of the book. Titles are particularly important with nonfiction; make them convey and convince.

For both nonfiction and fiction proposals, the cover page, or "title page," follows your cover letter. When formatting the cover page, be sure to put the book's title in all caps about a third of the way down the page. Include your contact information (name, address, phone number, fax, e-mail) with the date in the bottom right corner. Put the word count in the top right corner.

Table of Contents (for Novel and Nonfiction Proposals)

Your contents page lets the agent or editor know precisely what's in your proposal package and lends order and organization to all the disparate proposal elements. Be sure to list every item you're sending and the corresponding page numbers in the order they appear in your proposal. You obviously need to make your contents page neat and easy on the eyes. It should be double-spaced and organized according to its sections. The contents pages should *not* be numbered.

Synopsis (for Novel Proposals)

A synopsis is a brief, general overview of your novel, sometimes referred to as a "short summary." The goal of your synopsis is to tell what your novel is about without making the agent read the novel in its entirety. You need to supply key information about the primary elements in your novel (plot, theme, characters, setting), then show how all these aspects work together to make your novel worthy of publication. The trick with the synopsis, however, is doing all of the above quickly.

How quickly? Well, that depends on the person you're soliciting. There are no hard-and-fast rules about the synopsis—some agents and editors look at it as a one-page sales pitch, while others expect it to be a comprehensive summary of the entire novel. Not surprisingly, there's conflicting advice about the typical length of a synopsis. Over the years I've contacted numerous publishing people to get their take on just how long it should be, and nearly everyone prefers a short synopsis that runs from one to two single-spaced pages, or three to five double-spaced pages. Because every novel is different—with its own number of important characters, plot twists, subplots, etc.—there is obviously some disagreement on this point. Nevertheless, every agent and editor agrees there's one truism about a synopsis: "The shorter, the better." That's why one to five pages is generally the preferred length for a novel synopsis.

That said, some plot-heavy fiction, such as thrillers and mysteries, might need more space, and can run from ten to twenty-five double-spaced pages, depending on the length of the manuscript and the number of plot shifts. If you do opt to compose a longer synopsis, aim for a length of one synopsis page for every twenty-five manuscript pages (a 250-page manuscript should get a ten-page synopsis), but attempt to keep it as short as possible. And *always* follow the agent's or editor's guidelines if they're available—your twenty-page synopsis may be poetic, gripping, and insightful, but if the agent you send it to is adamant about only reading two-page synopses, there's a good chance your brilliant book will never make it onto her desk.

A few other important aspects of your synopsis:

- Write in third person (even if your novel is written in first person).
- Write in present tense (even if your novel is written in past tense).
- Focus only on the essential parts of your story, and try not to include sections of dialogue unless you think they are absolutely necessary.
- Make your story seem complete. Keep events in the same order as they occur in the novel (but don't break them down into indi-

vidual chapters), and be sure your synopsis has a beginning, a middle, and an ending. And yes, you *must* tell how the novel ends.

Overview (for Nonfiction Proposals)

The overview should be the power punch of your nonfiction proposal. It is the quick pitch that tells an agent or editor whether the rest of the proposal is worth reading. Make sure you immediately state what your book is about, why it should be published, and why you're the perfect person to author it. Start with a perfect lead sentence that both sums up your book and makes the agent or editor eager to read on (ideally, such a sentence will be enticing and encouraging without being gimmicky). Although the overview typically runs only a few pages (even up to ten), it must be persuasive and should highlight the book's key concepts. It should also touch upon marketing, competition, and author information.

Marketing Analysis (for Nonfiction Proposals)

Although the concept of your book is important, the marketing section is arguably the most crucial part of any nonfiction book proposal. The goal of this section is to convince the agent or editor that your book is worth her time and that she'll make money from it. Prove to her why, how, and where your book will sell. Show you know the audience for your book, and give compelling reasons why this audience will buy the book.

Unlike other parts of your proposal, your marketing section has no length limits; it's important to spend as much time as you need to prove your book will sell. Don't ramble, of course, but don't hold back either. Do as much research as possible, and provide as many facts as you can.

Your marketing analysis section should cover two things: your book and its readers. Provide the agent answers to the following questions when writing this section:

- **Who will buy this book?** Can you describe the audience? How big is your readership base, and will it increase? What organizations do potential buyers belong to? Where do they shop? How do they spend their money? Will they spend money on your book?

- **Are there any trends that might help sell your book?** For example, if you're writing a cookbook, can you prove more people are cooking at home these days?

- **In what other venues could your book be sold?** Any specialty outlets? Are there seasons of the year during which the book could sell particularly well?

- **What ideas do you have for the book that will increase its appeal to readers?** Will it have sidebars, callouts, interviews, pictures, charts, or other special features? Keep in mind, though, that publishers have final say over any book's visual elements.

Competitive Analysis (for Nonfiction Proposals)

Your competitive analysis outlines why your book is outstanding in its field and why it should be published. In this section, you should size up the competition and prove your book has what others lack. The best way to do this is to mention books similar to yours, how well they sell, and why your book is superior. While the temptation exists to say your book is the "only one of its kind," a lack of competition can actually hurt your cause. Agents and editors need to be able to show that books similar to yours have sold well.

Begin your analysis with an overview of the genre or category into which your book fits. Show how those titles are doing in general, then specify what books are selling the best. Next pick the top four or five competitors, analyze why those books have done well, and prove why your book is still needed to fill a category void. Are some of the books poorly organized, terribly written, or even outdated? Good. Mention any flaws you can find among your best-selling competitors, and then delineate how your book's sales could capitalize on their shortcomings.

Three ways to find information on your competition:

- Go to a large, well-stocked bookstore, look for competing titles, and discuss with bookstore employees how those books are selling.

- Do some research with the industry standard *Books in Print* (R.R.

Bowker). The electronic version is available through many libraries (www.booksinprint.com/bip). Notice the number of titles in print compared to the number of titles on the bookstore shelves. How can you ensure your book will be one of the ones that gets a prized shelf space?

- Search the large online booksellers (www.amazon.com and www .barnesandnoble.com) to find competing titles and to see how well they are selling. Although you can't get actual sales figures from these sites, you do get to see where the competing titles rank among all other titles. You also get to read comments from readers and see what other books and authors are popular with readers who might buy your book. Reviews of the books might also help you identify shortcomings in your competition.

Promotion Ideas (for Nonfiction Proposals)

The promotions section of your proposal is the place where you tell the agent or editor what you can do to help sell your book. Authors often overlook this part of the proposal, but it's a great place for tossing out ideas about what you have to offer the publisher in addition to what's contained in the pages of your book.

Are you already a promotable author? What makes you so promotable? Do you already have a loyal following? Do you have a Web site? Are you an awesome public speaker? Why will your book benefit from a tour? Do you have any contacts who could prove useful when promoting your book? Do you know of any special events or venues that would benefit from your presence (and help sell hundreds or even thousands of copies of your book)? Do you look good on television? Have you done radio interviews before? Do you have an interesting slide presentation? What other promotion ideas can you come up with?

Any promotion you do for your book is called your "platform." Most publishers only consider books from nonfiction writers who have already established a platform. Make this section brief but to the point.

Don't hold back on your suggestions, and don't hesitate to prove you are willing to be your book's strongest salesperson.

Chapter-by-Chapter Outline (Usually for Nonfiction Proposals; Occasionally for Novel Proposals)

An outline describes each chapter as its own entity; the descriptions range from a few paragraphs to two pages per chapter. In short, you're expanding and specifying what you've generally written in either the synopsis (for fiction) or the overview (nonfiction).

Few agents or editors want chapter-by-chapter outlines with fiction (most just request a cover letter, a short synopsis, and a few sample chapters). Therefore, you should never submit an outline for your novel proposal unless one is specifically asked for. Chapter-by-chapter outlines will be requested occasionally with genre fiction, which often has numerous plot shifts. When possible, limit the novel outline to one paragraph per chapter.

With nonfiction proposals, a chapter-by-chapter outline is essential. Providing a very thorough one lets the agent and editor know precisely what your book covers and in how much detail.

Author Biography (for Novel and Nonfiction Proposals)

If you think aspects of your life are important and relevant to the salability of your book, then include an author biography. The goal of your author bio is to sell yourself in ways that complement the proposal. Don't include information that doesn't directly help the pitch. Do tell about your profession, particularly if it's pertinent to your book, and always highlight noteworthy publishing credits, if you have any. Try to keep the author bio to one page.

Endorsements Page (for Novel and Nonfiction Proposals)

An endorsements page is not essential, but having one can improve the salability of your manuscript. Your endorsements must come from noteworthy people, typically prominent industry insiders (well-known authors, agents, experts on the topic) who've read your manuscript and commented favorably on it. Unless you have contacts, though, it is difficult to obtain a quote from someone noteworthy. But don't fret if your proposal doesn't have an endorsements page—few authors include one.

Attachments (for Nonfiction Proposals)

You might wish to send some attachments with your proposal. These include any radio, television, magazine, newspaper, or electronic mentions on your topic. Your goal with sending attachments is to show tangible proof that people are interested in your book's topic. Even feel free to supply copies of scholarly research articles conducted on your subject. In short, attach anything that helps prove your book matters. Be sensible, though, by making sure your attachments come from reputable sources and by supplying proper documentation for everything you send. Like endorsements, attachments aren't necessary; they simply help your cause—convincing the agent or editor to represent you.

A Reply Postcard (for Novel and Nonfiction Proposals)

If you're a bit paranoid about whether or not your material actually makes it to the agent or publisher, you may send a reply postcard with your proposal package. Having it signed by someone on the staff and sent back to you will alleviate any worries that the package didn't make it to its destination. Two caveats: (1) Not all agents and editors are gracious enough to send your reply postcards back—but most do. (2) Just because you receive a postcard reply, you cannot assume your proposal has been read or will be read in the next few weeks. Your reply postcard's only function is to let you know your package has been received.

Now you have all you need to know to craft a powerful proposal. Just be smart, target the right agent, honestly acknowledge the commercial viability of your proposal, and *send the agent or editor what she wants to receive.* Sound doable? Good. Go do it—Goliath is waiting.

PART II

Selling Your Manuscript

CHAPTER 9

What Are Nonfiction Editors and Agents Looking For?

The umbrella of "nonfiction" covers a lot of territory—everything from memoir to self-help to health to history to business. But according to editor Jennifer Repo, an editor with Perigee Books (an imprint of Penguin Putnam) and Faye Bender, a literary agent with the Doris S. Michaels Literary Agency, Inc., some constants remain, no matter what area of the nonfiction spectrum you're writing in: Writers must establish strong credentials, maintain superior writing standards, and make a first-rate effort to promote their own books.

An Interview With Jennifer Repo, Editor at Perigee Books

Jennifer Repo started her career in children's publishing but admits she "never really had the knack" for kids' books. When the opportunity arose for her to work at Riverhead Books (an innovative imprint of adult fiction and nonfiction by such A-list authors as Junot Díaz, Nick Hornby, and the Dalai Lama), Repo leapt at the opportunity. From there she moved to Perigee Books, where she edits a variety of nonfiction books: health, women's issues, spirituality, and other self-improvement titles.

Q Do you find most of your books from agents, or do you work with unagented authors, too?

A I think that maybe only one time in the past two years I've developed a project I found in the slush pile, but I didn't end up acquiring it. I think that we do treat those submissions very seriously—we've heard it time and time again: Don't overlook the slush pile. But with the amount of stuff that comes in, we just don't have the time to go through unagented manuscripts as thoroughly. Agents can really help shape the proposal into something that an editor wants to see. Agents know publishing.

Q And target it to the individual editor, I'm sure. They know you, know your preferences.

A Exactly.

Q A big catchphrase I've heard a lot in nonfiction lately is "prescriptive nonfiction." How does this differ from "self-help"?

A Yeah, that's the term that I use more than ever. Because I think it sounds perhaps more glamorous than "self-help." And I think perhaps the term "self-help" is really kind of a misnomer anyway. A lot of the books we do don't advocate reliance upon self. The books we publish are prescriptive—there's some type of formula, there's some type of program, whether it's a spiritual book, or a women's how-to book, or a business book, or a teen finance book. There's a program, there are suggestions of how to get from point A to point C. And that to me is the huge value of them. But ultimately, most of our books are shelved in that general self-help category in the bookstore at Barnes & Noble.

Q What kinds of projects are you, as a nonfiction editor, interested in acquiring right now?

A I'm doing a lot of women's issue books. That's a personal interest of mine. It's nice to do books that I love. Also spiritual books, but those are harder to do because Perigee doesn't have a track record with the booksellers for those types of books. It's a harder battle to fight. And also, there are very few prescriptive spiritual books out there. A lot of literary spiritual titles, the Riverhead Books type of title, but not as many prescriptive.

Q. That surprises me. It seems like that would be the next logical step.

A I know, because you think you would go to God or spirituality for answers. And there are books like that out there, but finding the right balance of an author who has a platform to deliver the goods in the spiritual market is a challenge anyway. A lot of them are just really entrenched in doing their own denominational stuff, whether it's Buddhist or Christian or Judaica or whatever. So to find an author with a national platform, and who is not already taken by one of the larger spiritual houses such as Tarcher or Riverhead, is a challenge.

Q. Let's talk a little bit about the idea of an author needing a "platform" to publish. The idea of what an author has to do these days, particularly in the nonfiction arena, to be attractive to publishers is amazing. It's so competitive—authors have to come to the table with a lot more, such as speaking engagements, publications, etc.

A It really, really is necessary. It's something that everyone in publishing is bemoaning, especially authors and agents. It used to be that publishing houses would have the funds, the time, and the manpower to market and publicize an author so that the responsibility didn't rest upon the author as much as it does today. They could help "launch" an author.

Today, with the consolidation of so many of the big publishing companies, one publicity department is publicizing four to six imprints, maybe each imprint with twelve to fifteen titles minimum per season . . . and they've got a staff of maybe seven people. You can see that timewise, it's not possible for them to pay extra attention to each author. Therefore the responsibility shifts to the author.

Also, there's simply more product in the marketplace. We're publishing so many more books today. It just behooves an author to come to the marketplace with something extra.

Q What has been the reaction to this change?

A I think that nobody likes change, but the business itself really has changed. Agents, authors, and people who have been in publishing for eons and are *not* embracing the change and acknowledging what authors have to bring to the table now will have trouble.

It's actually a good thing—whatever helps bring the product out there and increases its visibility is obviously good for the author and the book. Yes it's more work and more responsibility on the author. But if it's going to help the *Today* show book an author, and it's going to set that author apart from all the other people who have written books, it's helping everybody.

Q Do all nonfiction books require that the author have a strong platform?

A Seeing an author in print, on TV, radio . . . those things are all helpful. Of course, as I said, for some authors such widespread publicity might not be as necessary or appropriate. There are some books that don't require it. Literary nonfiction and memoir, for example. Credentials help, too—if you're a doctor, a Ph.D., a therapist, then you don't necessarily have to have a lot of articles written for *Self* magazine to write a book on why relationships fail. It would be nice to see, but it's not always the case.

Q What sort of experience do you look for in a nonfiction author? What sort of background constitutes a strong author platform?

A It really varies from subject to subject. For example, in the spiritual area, the first thing I look for is, are they speaking at all the major conferences? And if you're a finance author, I look to see if you're well regarded by *Money*, *Kiplinger's*, and those types of publications. Have you written any articles for them? Do you have contacts with them?

Do you go to the big financial retreats? These are the key things I look for first.

What's disheartening is when authors say that they "have plans" to speak at these retreat centers, because if they haven't planned it or haven't booked it yet, they probably don't know just how hard it is to get in to speak at these places.

I also look for an author to have a national presence. They may be Tampa, Florida's most liked person, and they might be on the air all the time there. But are they getting any sort of coverage at all on a national level—whether it's writing for a national publication, or appearing on MSNBC, or anything like that? Unfortunately, being a local hero is not enough. But it's a start, and I don't want to denigrate that, because that is important.

Q Is an author's online presence helpful in establishing a platform?

A There are a lot of proposals that really emphasize an author's Web presence, and I think such grassroots efforts are important, too. But even when I see that an author's Web site receives fifty thousand hits a month, that doesn't necessarily mean that we'll sell books. It doesn't mean as much to me as an appearance on the *Today* show does.

Q Tell me a little about the type of editing that you do with a nonfiction author.

A I was really uncomfortable when I started out editing nonfiction. I didn't feel confident putting my opinion down on paper . . . I didn't know anything about these topics my authors were writing about! But then after doing a couple of rough draft edits, I got more comfortable with it.

Nonfiction editing is really quite formulaic—in a good way. It's really got to be clean, organized, have a structure. You have to prove your point. I'm really a very organized person, so when I'm looking at a 300-page manuscript, I can sort of see the layout of the book. I can see that chapter seven needs to be chapter one, or whatever. And I think that's the difference between someone who is a good editor and someone who struggles with it. You need to have those skills—to remember that page 65 is repeated on page 3—if you don't have those skills, you'll have disastrous books. Now the passion I have for nonfiction is amazing. I would never change to fiction.

Q In addition to the structural edits, do you also have a hand in helping your authors to craft their language and clarify their ideas?

A I'm very much a hands-on editor—I tell all my authors that up front. But I'm also very fair. I've recently worked on a few books where all that was required was a light line edit, and I'll never change something just for the sake of editing. But I'll definitely pick my battles. I was working on a book in the months following September 11, and my author wanted to include something about September 11 in there. And I deeply, firmly believed that the author should not put anything about September 11 in the book. The book didn't have anything to do with September 11, it was already in production before September 11, he wasn't an authority on the topic. I stood firm in that instance. But most stuff, if the author is really passionate about something, I let it go.

Sometimes I work on books where the authors are brilliant professionals in their field but they're not the best writers. And I've had to get into their text and work hard. But that's okay. I like hands-on editing. It's like a puzzle.

An Interview With Faye Bender, Agent With the Doris S. Michaels Literary Agency, Inc.

Agent Faye Bender originally thought she wanted to be an archaeologist, but a last-minute decision to attend the Radcliffe Publishing Course after college changed her direction entirely. She took a job working with the Nicholas Ellison Agency, and a few years later joined the Doris S. Michaels Literary Agency. She has extensive experience with nonfiction but is also branching out and representing more fiction authors, too. Bender was the agent for Patricia Henley's book *Hummingbird House* (MacMurray & Beck), which was a finalist for the National Book Award in 1999.

Q. How is selling nonfiction to editors different from selling fiction?

A I think that nonfiction is just much easier to sell—it's easier to know if you have something salable. With fiction, it's just incredibly subjective. I've done some pop culture, some popular science, self-help, and also some more literary fiction.

Q. What are some recent projects you've worked on that you're most proud of?

A Well, there's an anthology of writing by Asian American teenage girls that I sold to HarperCollins, called *Yell-Oh Girls*. It was number three on the *L.A. Times* best-seller list, which was really exciting. When we were sending it to editors around town, we were getting some resistance from publishers, who were saying, "How do we know Asian Americans will buy books?" Particularly teenagers, who are not a "proven" market. But HarperCollins really went out with it in a big way and has been doing a terrific job with it. And the author's been doing a lot of publicity, so that's been really exciting and gratifying. It's one of those projects that just feels like it should be out there. It's probably helping some of these girls feel like they're not alone and that their experiences are pretty common. I feel good about that book.

Q. Let's talk a little about what materials you like to see from authors when they're submitting to you.

A For the initial query, our agency prefers to get the query online. That's been our preference for a while, but particularly with the post–September 11 mail scares, an online query is just easier and faster and easier to respond to. I think a lot of agencies have Web sites now with submissions guidelines on their sites, which will let you know if they prefer getting online submissions. So in the letter itself, things like descriptions of the author's previous publishing credits (magazines or journals), any awards or lectures. A good synopsis of the project, down to 300 words, is so difficult—but important. And for me, one of the most important things in an initial query is the author information. If the project is of interest to me, I'll ask for a proposal or a few sample chapters.

Q What's the most important section of a proposal to you?

A For me, particularly in nonfiction proposals, the most important section is the marketing section. It's become more and more important for authors to really work on the marketing of the books themselves. It's no longer the job as much of a publishing house's editorial department. For an author to have really given thought to how his book can be marketed and how he can help market it is a huge selling point. And it's something that authors can really work on themselves—having access to the Internet opens them up to a whole new world now. They have access to much more information, and they can really compile lists of sites where their material might be featured and do a lot of research beforehand, which is really helpful to the agent and the editor.

Q Editors, too, seem to place great importance on nonfiction authors having a strong "platform"—published magazine or journal articles, radio or TV appearances, speaking engagements. How important is this for you when you're evaluating a project or an author?

A It is important, pretty much across the board. It's not true 100 percent of the time, though. I have an author whose nonfiction book I sold to Crown, and she really doesn't have a platform. She's just an incredible writer. Some of it, too, just comes down to the writing.

But mostly I do believe that an author needs a platform. An author needs to be able to say, "This book need to be on the bookshelf because . . . and here's why I'm the person who needs to write it." Particularly in nonfiction, writers do need to have some kind of visibility from which they can launch publicity and marketing. I think it's kind of an unfortunate circumstance of publishing today that authors need to be "celebrities" in their own right before their books can come out. But it is, to a degree, true. We do get that response all the time when trying to sell proposals to editors.

Q **What experience do you look for that will make an author attractive to editors?**

A I'm not sure an author has to have radio or TV appearances to be salable. Going on the lecture circuit, or having written a column for a magazine, or having years and years of expertise in a certain field are all important. Also, having access to other writers or other experts in your field is helpful—these are people who could endorse your book and provide cover blurbs. That can also make a big difference.

Q **How closely do you work with your authors before even sending their work out to editors?**

A I work a lot editorially with my authors before submitting anything. I think I came into agenting at a late enough point that this was just expected—I didn't go through that transformation. I think perhaps five or ten years ago, agents didn't do that; they'd just get something in and send it right out to editors. But I do so much editorial work with my authors, and I find that really gratifying. It's something I really love about the job.

Also, I think that agents are a real point of stability for authors now. With editors moving from publishing house to publishing house, the agent is often the only stable figure for an author, and the one who can continually fight for the author. I have one author—her book was the first one I sold—whose book is still not published because it went through three editors at the first house. I finally had to break the contract at that company because the editors kept putting off the book's publication. Then I resold it, so it's now with its fourth editor. And throughout this whole process, the author has only had access to me as somebody to rely on.

Q **And had you not been there to act as her advocate, she might have been in an even worse situation!**

A I think the book would have still been at this first publishing house being recycled through more editors and more changes, and the publication date delayed more and more. It's really important for authors to have someone solid to rely on. And that also speaks to building substantial and long-term relationships with authors—I think that's the goal of every agent, and that's one of the gratifying things about this job. We have so much personal contact with authors that we can build these really strong long-term relationships. Editors may not be able to do that as easily, because they move around so much.

Q **Is having an agent more important for nonfiction writers than fiction writers? Less important?**

A This will probably sound completely self-serving, but I think it's really important for both. Someone to play good cop/bad cop, someone there to follow up on things for authors . . . it's just really important for writers to have an advocate. Authors are trying to build comfortable relationships with their editors, so they don't necessarily want to have to call and complain that their second payment is now three months overdue. That's what agents can do with all kinds of writers. Plus, negotiating contracts can be so difficult. I've seen the boilerplate contracts that go out to agents as compared to those that go out to un-agented writers—the differences are amazing.

Q **There are a lot of questions about what will happen with e-books in the coming years—particularly with nonfiction titles, which seem to have a lot of e-book possibilities. How do you try to protect your writers' e-rights for the future, and even make the most of those rights today?**

A We haven't actually done much with e-rights right now. We're trying really hard to retain all of the enhanced rights and the multimedia rights, but there just hasn't been much to do with them once we have them. So we're really just waiting right now to see what might open up and what we can do with them. But at this point, I really haven't found many forums for the e-book rights.

Q Do you frequently attend writing conferences? Tell me about the role they play in your business.

A I attend one or two conferences per year. I haven't yet found an author at a conference, which is unfortunate—I would love that. And meeting with people in the industry is important. It's much more relaxed, and you spend more time together than you would, say, over lunch in New York. Also, to go away and talk about what I do gives me great perspective on what I do—I come away remembering that what we do is really important and special, and that joy and passion of all of these hundreds of writers who have traveled from far away and are staying in hotels and paying for these one-on-ones. That's easy to forget, too, when you're slogging through queries on e-mail. Conferences are great to reinforce my excitement for what I do.

Q Nonfiction has been really popular lately—self-help, self-improvement, memoir. Is this an area that will continue to grow?

A I see great growth potential. Particularly with prescriptive nonfiction—after, say, three years many nonfiction books are dated enough that someone can publish a new book in that area. I also think that narrative nonfiction is really of interest right now, and many of the proposals I'm getting in right now are narrative nonfiction. In some ways, selling narrative nonfiction is much more like selling fiction. It's much more about the writing, about the ability of the author to get the readers to connect with his or her story. But when you hit on something really great, it sells very, very well.

Q Do you have any general words of advice for writers?

A One of the things I think is so important—and I know it's a horribly frustrating process—is getting published in literary journals and magazines before sending out your queries to agents. It really does make a difference; it's such a worthwhile endeavor. A lot of writers say, "I'm not a short story writer. I can't do that." Well, take a chapter from your book, modify it, and try sending that out. It's so worthwhile.

Also, just think creatively about ways to market your work. With the Internet, it's a whole new world with new ways of doing things. If, as an author, you can come to your agent, your editor, or your publicist and say, "I think there's this list of 350 Web sites that would link to my site," it's such a help. Authors need to be involved more than ever. The success of one book will only lead to greater success with the next book. If you really want to become a career writer, then put that work into it. At every stage. At any stage.

CHAPTER 10

What Are Fiction Editors and Agents Looking For?

I n this chapter, we'll hear from three of the best editors and agents working in publishing today. Nan A. Talese is the publishing equivalent of a superstar—she's helped build the careers of such writers as Margaret Atwood, Pat Conroy, and Antonia Fraser, and she runs her own imprint (Nan A. Talese/Doubleday Books). She'll discuss the challenges involved in publishing literary fiction in today's best-seller-oriented publishing climate. Jonathan Galassi is the editor in chief of Farrar, Straus and Giroux, another prestigious literary house that publishes award-winning authors such as Alice McDermott, Jonathan Franzen, and Michael Cunningham. Galassi debunks the "Maxwell Perkins myth" of the omnipotent editor, taking a modest view of his contributions to his writers' work and describing the excitement of working to develop new voices and fresh talent. And agent Donald Maass, president of the Donald Maass Literary Agency and author of *Writing the Breakout Novel,* discusses the agent's role in "growing" an author's career and explains what it is he needs to make a decision about representing a new novelist. All three agreed on one point: The best part of their jobs is discovering a gifted new writer.

 ## A Conversation With Nan A. Talese, Publisher and Editorial Director of Nan A. Talese/Doubleday Books
BY LAUREL TOUBY

Nan A. Talese is head of Nan A. Talese/Doubleday Books, an imprint known for publishing quality fiction and nonfiction. A few of the critically acclaimed and best-selling titles she has published in the last decade include *The Blind Assassin* by Margaret Atwood and *Beach Music* by Pat Conroy, as well as the work of Peter Ackroyd, Kevin Canty, Antonia Fraser, Thomas Keneally, Robert MacNeil, Gita Mehta, George Plimpton, and Mark Richard, among others.

Q **With the consolidation of the publishing industry in general, do you feel pressured to create instant best-sellers?**

A Not instant best-sellers. Take Margaret Atwood, who is now a best-selling author: When I published her twenty-five years ago, she sold about 5,000 copies at best, as did Joan Didion and John Irving. Very few writers suddenly sell 100,000 copies. Careers are built gradually, although I think corporations have less patience than they used to.

One often hears about M.B.A.'s who come newly into the world of publishing, who look at the best-sellers and say, "Why don't you only do best-sellers?" They suggest we mustn't contract for books that we're going to publish fewer than 15,000 copies of. But the fact is, many of those best-sellers come from those low numbers. If anyone could predict what it is that makes a book a best-seller, we'd have fewer publishers. We never can tell what new book is going to suddenly appeal to readers and have marvelous reviews—and even marvelous reviews cannot guarantee sales. It's not predictable.

Reading is the most personal of all the arts. A reader reads alone and has only the voice of the author. So, unlike a film, or where you have a shared experience, books are a one-on-one experience. And it does take longer to build an audience.

Q **Are there enough readers out there to make literary fiction into best-selling fiction?**

A It depends. Literary essentially means a book that is well written, that has an intelligent mind behind it. Now, inevitably, there are fewer intelligent minds than unintelligent minds, so you have a smaller audience to start out with. Also, in this country we're very brand conscious. When writers begin, they are relatively unknown.

Q Can you create a bigger audience for literary fiction?

A I think a good deal of patience is required on the part of both authors and publishers. For example, for one of the books I published recently—*How the Irish Saved Civilization* by Thomas Cahill—it was thought that we shouldn't publish more than 6,000 copies of this book. But by getting some of our sales reps to read it, we built enthusiasm for the book and printed 15,000 copies. The book has now sold over a million copies. I do a lot of guerilla marketing. And as the author pointed out to me, "There are 40 million Irish Americans out there." We haven't gotten to all of them yet.

Q Do you feel that the Internet has had any effect on literary fiction?

A At one time, a book that sold 15,000 copies would be considered a best-seller. Americans weren't reading as much. Today, the bar is much higher. Contrary to what people may think, computers and the Internet have had a lot to do with an increase in interest in literary works. Your generation is more comfortable with writing than the previous generation.

Q You've had a very successful publishing career. How does someone in the publishing business get his or her own imprint?

A The first step is to gain credibility by publishing fine writers whose work finds readers. And that takes reading a lot—not only the books that are submitted to you by agents, but also general reading—and you really have to enjoy it. When you take a writer on, you should understand who the potential readers could be and have strong ideas about how you can reach that readership. That takes experience. In order to have credibility, you have to put in the years. One of the things that trips up every creative industry is hype. A lot of money is spent on hyping films that, in the end, don't speak to the public. The only thing to be secure in is your own belief in an author's talent. What happens once the book is in the bookstores doesn't have much to do with you or the author. It doesn't mean you should lose faith in that author if you really think the author is good.

Q What do you think is the job of an editor today?

A The job of an editor is to help the writer produce the best book he or she possibly can; you are the person that the writer trusts to be a sounding board, knowing that you share the writer's vision. A writer trusts that when a manuscript is submitted, you respond productively, intelligently, and in a spirit of goodwill. But what's important is to point out what does really work. What I find is the most valuable when I'm working with a writer is saying, "I don't understand why this happened this way. You don't explain this enough." An editor is a sounding board for the author.

Q What is your daily job? What does your job really entail? I know you oversee marketing, you oversee editing, you edit.

A Well, today I'm writing notes to booksellers. I have a list of around eleven hundred booksellers who really are interested in hand-selling the books to the public. I am sending them a book and reminding them why I wanted to publish it and why I think it will do well for them.

Q You have forty authors—do you read every single one of their manuscripts?

A Absolutely. But they're not all turning them in at the same time, and I also have a wonderful assistant editor who is a superb reader and has a good sense of both literary quality and the marketplace.

Q Is there anything in particular that you look for in nonfiction?

A For all the books we publish, the three things are a good use of language, passion about the subject, and storytelling—a compelling narrative.

Q You're an artist in a lot of ways. That is what an artist is. You focus on what you love doing and what resonates with you.

A Exactly. Although I cannot say I am an artist, my work is to promote the work of the artist.

Q **And it's not about getting somewhere; it's about loving where you are.**

A You've summed it up exactly. That truly is success.

Laurel Touby is a New York-based freelance writer who has written for *Working Woman, Business Week, Glamour, New York, Travel & Leisure, Self, Redbook, McCall's, Family Circle, Good Housekeeping, Working Mother,* and *The Daily News.* She is the founder of mediabistro.com, an online community of media professionals.

An Interview With Jonathan Galassi, Editor in Chief, Farrar, Straus and Giroux
BY ANNE BOWLING

When the pages of Alice McDermott's first novel landed on Jonathan Galassi's desk, he had no way of knowing that he was picking up a future National Book Award winner. Nor would it have mattered to him, in all likelihood. In his twenty-seven years of publishing—at Houghton Mifflin, Random House, and now as editor in chief of Farrar, Straus and Giroux—Galassi has earned a reputation as an editor of refined instincts and discerning eye, to whom industry accolades and commercial success are not as important as publishing books of substance. In the case of McDermott's first submission to Galassi, which became *A Bigamist's Daughter,* Galassi says, "The voice there was very secure, and that was certainly clear in the pages . . . that's an editor's greatest gift, if he can find something that's truly new. That is very, very exciting."

Not that the authors Galassi has edited have gone begging for attention, from readers or the publishing community. McDermott's *Charming Billy* won the National Book Award in 1998, narrowly passing Tom Wolfe's *A Man in Full,* also edited by Galassi. And the editor does not restrict his talents to fiction. A National Book Award nonfiction winner, Edward Ball's *Slaves in the Family,* was acquired by Galassi, who also counts Nobel Prize winner Seamus Heaney and poet laureate Robert Pinsky among those he has edited. And there's the tale of Scott Turow. Like McDermott, Turow was picked up by Galassi as an untested author, and his best-selling first novel, *Presumed Innocent*, set sales records in publishing, launching a wave of renewed interest in the legal thriller genre.

"Jonathan bought my first novel on the strength of the first one hundred pages," says McDermott. "And on that strength and a conversation we had about my plans for the rest of the novel, he took the risk. So a sense of trust has been there from the beginning. Jonathan has many wonderful qualities, but probably foremost is he trusts me to know what I'm doing. He does not impose himself or his will on my work, and I trust his opinion as an excellent reader. So when I'm ready to have a reader, I know he's a good person to go to."

Galassi is noted for his instincts and diplomacy as well as his restraint, evidenced in the told and retold story of Galassi's work with Tom Wolfe on *A Man in Full*. Wolfe had reached an impasse in the novel, and over lunch, Galassi suggested Wolfe set the book entirely in Atlanta. The suggestion required that Wolfe, eight years and nearly one thousand pages into the book, eliminate New York as a setting and dump hundreds of pages of manuscript. Wolfe agreed.

But despite Galassi's literary instincts and influence, he declines to be tagged as his generation's Maxwell Perkins, legendary editor of F. Scott Fitzgerald, Thomas Wolfe, Ernest Hemingway, Marjorie K. Rawlings, and other top writers of the twentieth century. In an interview in *Harvard Magazine*, Galassi says, "The Maxwell Perkins myth . . . glorifies the editor, but the real creative figure in a book is the author. The better a book is, the less it needs an editor."

Galassi came to editing in 1973, as an editorial intern at Houghton Mifflin. The publishing industry moved more slowly then, he says, with a greater interest in cultivating long-term writer-editor relationships. "There was a sense of loyalty to a house, working for a house for a long time, and building a list of authors." Galassi says. One of the first manuscripts he was given to read was Robert Stone's National Book

Award–winning *Dog Soldiers.* Galassi moved to Random House in 1981, which he left for Farrar, Straus and Giroux in 1986.

Here Galassi takes time out to share his views on strong writer-editor relationships and how industry consolidation is bringing long-term changes to the business of publishing fiction.

Q Can you credit the current publishing climate with creating a renaissance in fiction writing, in that the much-publicized "death of the midlist author" has opened doors previously closed to new writers?

A First of all, I don't think it's true that midlist is dead. You can't just publish best-sellers. You have to publish other books. You do still have to build authors, and even though people try to get around that system, I think that's how it really works. Midlist is still the meat and potatoes of publishing. People seem to think publishers don't want midlist books, but if you look across the board, that's what they are publishing by and large, because that's what they've got. That's what people write and that's what the market really bears.

Q Do you see more room now in publishing for experimentation with both the novel and short story forms?

A I think there's more openness to experimentation across the board. I don't think you're going to see a lot of short shorts on the best-seller list, but people are more willing to try anything. I think there's more openness to foreign books and more tolerance for experimentation. For instance, we published Michael Cunningham's *The Hours*, which is quite an experimental book. We've now sold over 140,000 copies of that experimental novel, which people have responded to very, very strongly. So I think the reading public for literary books is very sophisticated. *The Hours* is not a book that has best-seller written all over it. But it's a very beautiful, original, substantial book that has garnered a huge amount of attention and sold very well.

Q You've been widely compared to legendary editor Maxwell Perkins for your similarities in style and close working relationships

with high-profile authors. Yet you've been quoted as saying the Perkins myth "hangs like a cloud over editing" by elevating the status of the editor to that of the writer. Does that speak to your overall philosophy of the editor's role in the development of a writer?

A In the case of Perkins, there were some writers, especially Thomas Wolfe, who needed a special kind of editing, which amounted to carving books out of manuscripts. This is very seldom what really goes on in editing, and I think it's true that a kind of mythology of the editor grew out of that relationship that is grandiose. I don't think most editors do anything like that, and most books don't call for that kind of thing.

I think a more realistic vision of what an editor does is that an editor is like a shrink—he or she listens to the book, listens to what the author is trying to do, and in the end gets the author to see what needs to happen. A really good shrink doesn't fix you; you fix yourself through the shrink, and I think that's what an editor should be doing.

Q You've edited Alice McDermott's novels from her first, *A Bigamist's Daughter*, through National Book Award–winner *Charming Billy*. From an editor's perspective, what's it like to find a really promising manuscript from an unpublished author? And what does an editor look for?

A There's something about the excitement of starting out together— starting out with an author on her first work—that is among the most exciting things an editor can do. I think what it takes, especially, is open-mindedness, an ability to hear something that hasn't been heard before, to spot something fresh.

With Alice McDermott, I had not a whole manuscript but pages, which is not often how it happens. But the voice there was very secure, and fresh, and assured, and so we decided to publish the novel. Her voice was there, from the beginning. She's often quoted saying that a teacher once told her, "I've got bad news for you—you're a writer." And you could just tell. It was clear from the get-go that she had a voice, and that was certainly clear in the pages—her sardonic humor, and crispness, and tone.

Q What does a writer need to be prepared to bring into a successful writer-editor relationship?

A A writer should be prepared to be open-minded, to listen without any prejudice to what the editor has to say about the work, and be willing to consider the opinions of the editor. That doesn't mean you should blindly follow what the editor suggests, because editors are fallible people. But I think the best relationships between editor and author are where the editor feels free to be as honest as possible, and where the author then knows that he or she has the freedom to respond as openly as possible. In other words, when there is as little diffidence between them as possible.

I think the editor has to be prepared to bring the same things: to be open to what the author is really doing, to try to respond to that as fully as possible, and not to try to twist the author's book to suit some idea that he or she has. They're both ideally working toward the same thing, which is getting this book in the best possible shape it can be for the public.

Q How has the spate of mergers, acquisitions, and consolidations among publishing houses in the last five years affected the writer-editor relationship? Do you believe that has had a negative impact?

A In a way, that would be like complaining about TV. We have to deal with reality. And I think what people really want to hear about is not what's wrong with the situation but what to do about it. When I was trained at Houghton Mifflin in the 1970s, an editor's career was somewhat less entrepreneurial than it is today. There's more a sense of editors as quasi-independent operatives who are trying to strike gold fast, and I think there's more movement among authors and editors. People say that today the real stable element in an author's career is an agent rather than the publisher. I think that's not the ideal situation.

Ideally, an author, agent, and editor should settle down for a long winter's nap together. That's the ideal situation for building a career. Because the trouble with a fast shot is if it doesn't work, you've got a problem. You hear a lot about big deals for first novels, and the problem is what if it doesn't work? Where is the author with the publisher the next time around? They lose that continuity, the history, the building. Let's face it, very few writers can count on a career where that building happens. I think that's what's needed, but I think that's very hard to come by today.

Q **At the Jerusalem International Book Fair a few years ago, where you were a moderator, the keynote speaker addressed this question: How can young people who enter publishing with idealism be progressive forces in a world in which serving the marketplace has become the standard for a new "excellence"? What's your take on that?**

A You have to start out with the right kind of philosophy in the publishing house. A publishing house is only as good as the fostering it does of the relationship with authors. So if a publisher doesn't care what's published, then you're in trouble. And I don't think that's true, by and large. I think most major publishers are interested in quality, because I think quality is the only thing that sells in the long run.

But then, I do think that editors have to be good ambassadors for authors in the publishing house; they have to explain to the rest of the team why those books are important, why they are good. If they're good, they will sell. They may not sell a million, but good books have a market. It's part of their definition. So I think there's plenty of room for idealism in publishing today. There's also plenty of room for people to pursue their interests and their passions within the context of the marketplace, because in a shrinking market quality is more important than ever.

Q **How do you view the long-term effects of mergers, acquisitions, and restructurings on the publishing industry?**

A There has been more change in the time I've been in publishing than there was in the past two hundred years in the way business is done, and the rate of change seems to be exponential. I think that's something that causes a lot of concern, because if you're an agent and you're trying to place a book, the number of options you have is limited by the consolidations. Even if you still have a lot of editors in different units of a big company, still the number of clear shots you have at different houses is smaller. Agents and authors are losing options, freedom, alternatives. The consolidation has gone very, very far.

Q Has it worked to homogenize the industry?

A I would say that the companies that result from the homogenization tend to be more like one another than they would have been had they remained independent. I think that's undeniable. There's a theory on war that you end up becoming like your enemy so you can fight your enemy better, and I think some of that applies in this situation.

Q What are your predictions for changes in publishing in the early part of the twenty-first century?

A I think change is the way we live today—we live in a technological society where change is a constant, so there definitely will be a huge amount of change in publishing in our lifetime. I think many of these changes are positive: Books will be available in many different formats, they will be instantly available, and there will be no out-of-print books. We're living in an information bath now—we drown in information—and books are a part of that. And I think books will continue to have a very important role in our culture, because there is no substitute. Film and visual media cannot convey the complex information that books can. So we're not in danger of losing books.

The way books are sold, and the way they're published, that's bound to change. It's changing as we speak. Publishers will change, because they're really going to be kind of brands for books more than anything else. That's already true today. If you go online, you can see how many people are publishing books, so the publishers are really going to be the guardians of quality. But as far as what that all means for writers—it's hard to know. I guess the real question is how is the world going to know about the individual writers—how are the writers going to stand out in this? That's what publishers are going to be there for, to discriminate.

Anne Bowling is the editor of *Novel & Short Story Writer's Market*, and a columnist on children's and young adult literature for *Pages* and *BookStreet USA*.

An Interview With Donald Maass, President of the Donald Maass Literary Agency and Author of *Writing the Breakout Novel*

Donald Maass is the president of the Donald Maass Literary Agency, which he founded in 1980. Today, Maass represents more than one hundred fiction writers, including Anne Perry, David Feintuch, and David Zindell, and is himself the pseudonymous author of fourteen novels. He's also published two nonfiction books on writing, *The Career Novelist* (Heinemann) and *Writing the Breakout Novel* (Writer's Digest Books), and he serves as the president of the Association of Authors' Representatives (AAR). Maass discusses what it takes to build an author's career in today's bottom-line publishing environment and talks about the four things he wants to know from authors before representing their work.

Q One of the first questions out of any writer's mouth is: Do I need an agent? Why do you feel that having an agent is an asset to writers, particularly fiction writers?

A I think the traditional reasons to have an agent—to gain access to publishers and editors that one might not otherwise have access to, to have an expert negotiator on your side during contract negotiations—these reasons are still very true. What has changed in the past twenty years is that the editorial role of the agent has grown, and I think today this is even acknowledged readily by publishers and editors. Agents are partners in the creative process; they frequently contribute ideas, certainly offer comments and revisions—and some agencies even have staff editors who will groom proposals. I think it's very clear that the first line of editorial help that novelists get from the industry is at their agencies, rather than with their publishers.

Also the continuity over the course of a career comes from the agent, too. Editors change jobs, companies are sold, and conglomerates become ever larger. But the agent is the one consistent advisor for a novelist. This has been part of my practice for more than twenty-one years. Today, I think many, many agents do what I've been doing all along, which is to advise their clients, right down to which book to write next—being part of the very conceptual process. Is this book a good idea, or is that book a better idea? That's advice I offer my clients, advice that they take.

Q How much editorial work do you do with a novelist before sending his or her work out to an editor?

A A great deal. I have gone so far as to give my clients the very basic ideas and premises. There was a book that was recently nominated for the World Fantasy Award, *The Grand Ellipse* by Paula Volsky (Bantam). It's a fantasy take on *Around the World in Eighty Days* by Jules Verne. I suggested the idea to the author. She, of course, turned it into a wonderful novel. To say it was my idea is not to say very much— she fleshed it out in a unique way. She wrote it in her own inimitable style and wound up with this award nomination. But knowing the author, I was able to suggest the idea that really sparked in her and produced an extraordinary work.

That said, I don't just hand my writers ideas and expect them to write only those stories. But I do like to see projects in development at the earliest stages so I can make comments, issue challenges, ask questions, test the ideas in the early stages, and hopefully move the authors toward deepening the inner conflicts in their main characters— layering the plot with extra material and extra narrative lines, raising the stakes (both public and private), and all the other things that really make a good idea a great novel.

Q **So knowing the market and knowing a particular author's strengths gives you a real advantage—it allows you to join together an author and an idea.**

A You know, it's very infrequent that I give advice to authors that comes from what I perceive "the market" to be. I think chasing market trends is a loser's game. You cannot get ahead doing that. What you *can* do is to take any idea that an author has and help them, challenge them to make it better than they ever thought they could.

I think it's dangerous to tamper too greatly with an author's purpose in writing a particular story. I think most stories occur to an author for a reason—there's something they want to say in a story, there's something about it that's itching to be told through their voice. I don't want to squelch that or derail that in any way. If you take away the deep reason somebody's writing a novel, you take the life out of it.

I think it's more important to work with the impulse, the purpose, whatever inner thing is causing the author to write a particular story, and then shape the story itself—work with the characters, deepen the characters, add to the narrative lines. Help them craft it into a bigger, larger feeling story—a higher-stakes story. That's my job. I don't really see my job as saying: "This is what I can sell." I see my job as saying: "This is how I can take what you're doing and help you to make it the best novel it can be."

Q **Do you find too many fiction writers making the mistake of chasing a hot trend?**

A Yes. And you know, if you think about it, the business of fiction is *not* a business of trends; it's a business of brand-name authors. The authors who tell a very distinctive kind of story, and do that consistently over time, find a following. The ones who adapt themselves to the hot genre of the moment may get contracts, but they don't build a following. I've noticed that again and again over the past twenty years. You can maybe sell a book if you imitate John Grisham, Scott Turow, or Stephen King, but you can't become your own novelist with your own very loyal and powerful following.

Q Let's talk about an idea that I know you're really passionate about—the idea of "growing" the writing careers of your clients. How do you do this?

A It requires a couple of things. It requires an author with a very clear idea of what he wants to do and with an original voice. It requires the determination to stick with it over the course of a number of books. It also requires—and here's where the editors become very important— a publisher who's willing to support an author while the audience is finding the author and doing the word of mouth that makes a career grow.

It really takes five books just to establish the presence of a novelist out there among consumers. In my first book, *The Career Novelist*, I talk about what I call the five-book threshold—it takes a while for people to become aware of a writer. When they do, and when a certain critical mass of readers develops—and if the author continues to write well and grow—the audience grows, too. There's a snowball effect. But it takes a while to get that snowball rolling down the hill. It rarely happens in one book. If the author's good, over the course of five books it probably will happen.

Q Is it still possible to grow a novelist's career today, with big publishing's emphasis on large advances and best-sellers?

A Is it still possible? Yes. Is it easy? No—it's more difficult than ever. The mechanics of publishing today require that an author find a substantial following very quickly. That snowball must be of a certain size and already be rolling down the hill almost from Book One. It's very difficult to do, and it's incumbent on novelists who are serious and really want to have a career to start to push themselves hard from the very beginning, to write as well as they can and tell the biggest stories that they can. And by "big stories" I don't mean epic in scale;

I mean deep, large-feeling, committed, passionate, craftsmanlike on every page. It's incumbent on writers to do that, with the first book, with every book.

I think most novelists are not prepared for how much work that really is. Everybody thinks they work hard as a novelist. Most do not know how hard they really have to work to succeed. It is not an ivory-tower fantasy. The life of a working novelist is very, very time-consuming. Very labor-intensive. Very stressful. It's hard, hard work. Very few writers put in that kind of effort. And consequently, many wash out.

Q. What's the best way for a fiction writer to approach an agent, particularly a first-time novelist?

A Conferences are a great place to meet agents. I think the single biggest piece of advice I can give writers is: When pitching your story, be succinct. The number one drawback to the approach I get from most novelists—whether in person, at a conference, in a query letter, or what have you—is this anxiety-driven need to tell me everything about their stories and why they wrote them. Truthfully, I need very little to know whether a story is worth pursuing.

For instance, at writing conferences, frequently they have these one-on-one meetings, during which an agent or editor talks with an author for ten minutes. As a writer, you have just that much time to pitch your book and to tell the agent or editor a little bit about yourself. And those ten- or fifteen-minute meetings just feel incredibly short and rushed, impossibly difficult for most authors. It's a punishing exercise for them to get everything across in ten minutes. The truth is, I get everything I need in about the first thirty seconds.

Q. And what is it that you're looking for?

A I'll tell you exactly what I need, and I can get this information after just a few questions.

First of all: *What type of novel are we dealing with here?* Mystery? Mainstream? Young adult?

Second thing: *Where and when is it set?* Contemporary? Historical? Magical place? A real place?

Third: *Who is the main character?*

And lastly: *What is the basic problem that the character faces?*

Those things wrapped up together are the premise of a novel, and I know right away if it's the kind of work I handle, if the idea sounds original, if the main character is sympathetic, and whether I care about the problem. That's all I need. If all those things are a go, then I want to read the work. It's as simple as that.

Most authors might perceive this as additional pressure. It's exactly the opposite. What it means is that their job is much, much easier than they think.

Q You attend a lot of conferences. Do you actually find new clients there?

A Of course. Absolutely. I just signed up a new client this weekend whom I met at a conference exactly a year ago. We corresponded, I read a manuscript of her new novel last week, we met again at the same conference last weekend and shook hands on a deal. I wouldn't have met her save for the conference—last year we happened to be standing in line, waiting to get into the hotel restaurant, we started talking, her book sounded really interesting, and that was it.

Q We were talking earlier about the influence of "big publishing" on writers. In late 2001, novelist Jonathan Franzen made headlines when he found himself caught in a controversy with one of the most powerful forces in publishing today: Oprah Winfrey. What do writers have to learn from all this?

A I think one of the lessons in that whole story is that an author's idea of his audience and the reality of who actually reads him can be very different. I see the Franzen thing happening in smaller ways quite often. Authors, for instance, sometimes want a very classy all-type of photographic look on their novels—a very literary look. And that frequently is not what's right for their books. I think the lesson, if anything, is: Leave the packaging and marketing to the professionals. Let them decide what it is, who's going to enjoy it, and how to present it to them. Unless authors happen to have some expertise in marketing and an objective eye, they can no more make those judgments than they can make editorial judgments about their own work. Everyone, after finishing a novel, thinks one of two things: It's either the best thing the person's ever written or the worst thing he's ever written. And it's rarely either one. You need an editor. You need a critique group. You need an agent. These people are a mirror to you. So why would it be any different in the selling and packaging?

I think that's where Franzen went wrong: He perceived his book as a more rarefied and elevated type of book than Oprah would like. Empirically, he was wrong. Oprah picked his book. Readers are reading it. He's got a wider audience than he thinks. What is wrong with that? I think who your audience is can be a surprise. It's incumbent on authors to be open to that surprise. And to enjoy it! If you try to define your audience, you're probably going to miss the mark.

Q What's something you wish you could impart to all writers?
A That the so-called midlist is a very difficult place to be. There's really no place to hide from weak sales figures anymore. Your sales are too closely tracked by retail book chains, and too readily available to book publishers—your sales history follows you. You cannot hide it; you cannot get away from it. It's going to have an impact on your career going forward. Today it's not about survival—there's only growth. If you're not growing as a writer and growing an audience, then you are on your way out. It is incumbent on novelists to work hard, tell the best stories they can, and do it again and again and again.

CHAPTER 11

What Are Children's Book Editors and Agents Looking For?

For years, children's book publishing was regarded a little differently from the rest of the publishing world. At best it was seen as a sleepy backwater enclave—a quieter, slower-paced version of adult publishing. At worst, those writing and publishing children's books found themselves struggling for the same respect and recognition as their counterparts in the adult publishing world. "I think all of us have probably been asked, 'Oh, when you get really good, will they let you edit adult books?' says Scholastic editor Joy Peskin.

But these days, children's publishing is finally being recognized as being just as lively and dynamic as the rest of the publishing world. With agents proliferating, the creation of a *New York Times* best-seller list devoted to children's books, and (of course) the Harry Potter phenomenon, the children's book publishing industry has finally come into its own. With sales of $1.95 billion in 2000, books for young readers have become big business.

With these changes come challenges—and opportunities—for children's book writers. Agent Steven Malk discusses the changing role of the agent in children's book publishing and what it takes to "grow" a healthy, long-lasting career as a children's book writer. And a roundtable discussion with three editors at Scholastic reveals what a writer can do to make herself as appealing as possible to children's book editors, and what these editors are looking for in the post–Harry Potter world.

An Interview With Steven Malk, Literary Agent for Writers House

Steven Malk has children's book publishing "in his blood"—his grandmother started one of the first children's bookstores in the world in South Africa in 1952, and when she moved to the United States, her business moved with her. Today Malk's parents own two children's bookstores in California called The White Rabbit, one in San Diego and one in Orange County.

Malk started working at The White Rabbit at the age of sixteen, but after college he took a job as a literary agent rather than carrying on the family bookselling tradition. Today he's an agent with Writers House, specializing in children's books and representing some of the top authors in the field, including Elise Primavera, Jennifer Donnelly, Franny Billingsley, and Jon Scieszka.

Q So what drew you to the agenting side of children's publishing, as opposed to following your family into bookselling?

A Well I really loved the bookselling a lot, and I miss that to a certain extent. It's an incredible experience, and it's very rewarding, especially in an independent bookstore where you have the real interaction with customers and you build up a rapport with them. But I really saw myself going into the actual book business. I definitely knew by the time I went to college that I wanted to be in books, but I wasn't sure if I wanted to be an editor and work for a publisher, or be an agent. While I was in college I started working for an agency, and I really liked it—I think these days, agents are doing a lot of editing, so I get to be involved in the whole process.

I really do like the editing and the creative stuff, but I like the business side of it, too—being a career manager for my clients. For me, agenting is the best of all worlds. It's a lot of direct interaction with the authors, and it's also about being able to cultivate talent and strategize with people about their careers—whether it's bringing up new writers and really helping build their careers or strategizing with authors who are more established and being able to bring them to the next level.

Q **Let's talk about the author-agent relationship you cultivate with your clients. It sounds like you do a lot of work with your authors, helping them with their work even before you send it off to editors.**

A I don't want to discount editors at all—the editor-author relationship is a different one, one that I don't want to step in the middle of. But it is true that the nature of that relationship is changing. Back as recently as ten, twenty, or thirty years ago, authors would have editors who were like rocks. Editors never left a house, and authors would be with these editors for years and years, almost a career in some cases. Publishing has changed, and editors do move around more. If an author can find an agent whom she really trusts and clicks with, someone the author feels she's working toward the same goals with, the author-agent relationship can really last and be ongoing.

I think that these days the role of an agent has changed and become a bit more comprehensive. It's not just a business thing anymore. Agents have to have a really good eye to be able to offer some editorial advice to their authors—that's a really big part of the business, too.

Q **How do you see the role of an agent in children's book publishing? In years past, there was a perception that having an agent was less necessary for children's book authors than it was for writers in the adult market. What's changed? Why do so many children's book authors have agents today?**

A It *has* changed, and I've seen it change even since I've been in the business. In years past, a lot of authors in the children's business did not have agents. This was different from the adult publishing business. In adult books, you almost *have* to have an agent—maybe less than 1 percent of authors in the adult business do not have agents. A lot of publishers of adult fiction do not accept unsolicited manuscripts at all, so just to get through the door you need an agent. But in children's books, this wasn't always the case—some publishers did accept unsolicited manuscripts.

But recently, a couple things have changed. First of all, many children's publishers will now take only agented submissions. But I think, too, that a lot of writers are realizing that there are so many things an agent can do for you. For example, a new author who wants to try publishing without an agent is limiting herself to only those publishers who accept unsolicited manuscripts. She can go to conferences and research what editors are looking for, and if she does it thoroughly, she can probably do a good job. But without an agent, an author doesn't really have a large view of the industry. An agent knows all the different houses, knows all the different editors within those houses, and knows what editor would really be best for a particular author's work.

Beginning authors make the mistake sometimes when they're starting up of getting really excited and just wanting to get their books published, somewhere, *anywhere*. Sometimes they sell their books and then they realize later that they were just trying to sell to *any* editor and not really the *right* editor. I think a good agent can direct you to the right editor for your work, and it's different for everyone.

Q What about helping with contract negotiations?

A Actually negotiating a deal can be tough for writers. Some authors are savvier than others, but without an agent, a writer isn't going to have a lot of information to work with. Negotiating is what agents do. We know what offers are reasonable, what a publisher paid for a similar deal—we just have much more to compare it to, and a better idea of what's going on in the market. It's really hard for someone without an agent to stay on top of all that.

Q You mentioned earlier the idea of being a "career manager" for your clients. How can agents help their clients in this way?

A I try to always have a long-term plan in mind for my clients, and I try to make moves that reach a goal that my author and I set. For example, selling subsidiary rights—it's difficult for an author to do that on his own. Most authors without an agent really don't have any reason to retain their subsidiary rights, because they don't really have the means to sell them on their own. Whereas a good agent has the contacts and can explore those avenues for additional sales for you that most likely an author is not going to be able to do on his own.

Everyone has different goals; it just depends on where you are in your career. I like to set out a plan with my clients, and that's different for everyone. For example, for my client Elise Primavera . . . when she came to me, she'd never had an agent, and she was really interested in taking her career to the next level and exploring different avenues for her work. She came to me with this book *Auntie Claus*, and she was smart enough to realize that it had opportunities beyond the book market. It was a special project and it's a great book, with lots of possibilities. We had the idea of going to Saks Fifth Avenue with it before the publication of the book, and we also had the idea to try to get a movie or TV deal before the book was published—all of which we felt would generate a lot of excitement for the book. And it did. The book was a best-seller. It was a best-seller because it was a great book, and because the publisher was behind it—but it certainly didn't hurt that there was a lot of buzz surrounding the book, too.

Q **That was all "ammunition" for the publisher, information to get the stores and the sales reps and the public excited about this title.**

A Exactly—if you go into a bookstore, it's so daunting. Especially in the kid's marketplace, you're competing with so many other diversions: TV, movies, video games. I'm really looking to try and set my books apart. I'm really interested in trying to get extra attention for my books to get people interested in them early in the process, before they even get to the bookstores.

Publishers have become pretty centralized—there are not as many publishers as there used to be. And some of their lists are just absolutely enormous. You're competing with so much stuff. Sometimes getting the publishers really excited about the book, and about the *possibilities* for the book, will get them to put a little more effort behind your book. So I'm very interested in trying to take books to different places, to maybe where they haven't been in the past. I'm really interested in exploring different avenues for books, trying to get attention for books in new areas.

Q How do e-books factor in to all of this? Have you worked much with setting up e-book deals for your children's book authors? Are you trying to retain your clients' e-rights?

A It's really hard to say now how this will all play out—it's so early. E-books and e-rights are issues that everyone is talking about, but no one quite knows exactly where it's all going to go. I think the possibilities are exciting, but some people think it's going to be the next big thing, that books are going to start phasing out, whereas some people think it's going to be like the CD-ROM thing played out. When CD-ROMs came out, people thought this was going to be the "end of books," and clearly it wasn't. I think it has affected the way we negotiate contracts—we have to watch out, with the "out of print" clause particularly. If you have an electronic version of a book, that book could in effect never go out of print. It's important to be aware of that and protect yourself in that way.

But it's hard to say. Some publishers are exploring it, but no one has really been able to see exactly how it's going to affect business, if it is, in what way it will. It's still I think kind of early on, but everyone's watching carefully.

Q What specific material do you like to see from authors when they're contacting you through the mail?

A I really like to see a query letter. I'm pretty particular about query letters—I pay a lot of attention to them, and it really makes a difference to me if they're well done, professional. I like to see a letter in which someone really put thought into it, and that's very apparent. Too often I get letters and it's so clear that really no thought went into it, and that could be because they misspelled my name, because they addressed it to a completely different agent, because there are tons of misspellings or grammatical errors. I get stuff addressed to "Dear Agent"; I get stuff that it's very clear that all the writer did was change the name at the top of the letter.

I think a really good letter should establish the person as a professional; it should be well done, it should explain who the author is and what the book is about in a concise manner, and it should definitely include an SASE. That's just industry standard.

Obviously I'm not going to judge a project solely on the query letter, but when I get a query letter that's really nicely done, and I can tell a lot of time and thought went into it, it's going to make me maybe pay a little more attention to it. When you decide to approach an agent, that's a huge step, one that shouldn't be taken lightly.

Q What should a children's book author look for in an agent?

A An agent is a very important part of an author's career, and it's someone the author is hopefully going to be working with for a long time. I always think it's a good idea for authors to take some time to decide why they want an agent, and then think about what kind of agent they want, because all agents are different. Some are more hands-on; others work more independently. No one way is better than another, but authors need to decide what works for them and what kind of an agent they want.

And then I think authors should spend a little time researching agents, and try to decide what it is that they want in an agent. Then try to find someone who fits that mold, and then approach that agent. It's such a big decision that it's really important that authors take the time and care that they should. If they're serious about their careers, they'll realize that publishing is a long, long process. It's important to get the right person.

Q Conversely, what qualities are agents looking for in new authors?

A First and foremost, it's the writing. I'm really looking for something that speaks to me, something with a voice; I really look for something that moves me, for the stuff that stays with me. I'm very selective—I have about fifty-five clients right now, which sounds like a lot, but it's actually a relatively small number compared to a lot of agents. I try to keep it that way because I like to work closely with my authors, and I don't want to get to the point where I can't work closely with them. I see agenting as a very collaborative relationship.

Aside from the writing, I look for people who are serious about their careers and what they are doing. I don't want people who just wrote a book on a whim. I want to work with people for a long time, for years and years, and I want people who are serious about this business. I want people who appreciate children's books. And obviously people I can work well with; it's important that we have a rapport and that we have the same vision for the work.

I like people who are writing about stuff that means something to them, who are writing from someplace within themselves, as opposed to just writing about something because it's "hot." I'm really not interested in trends. I'm interested in people who write stuff because that's what they feel compelled to write. And it could be funny, or more serious, or thought provoking—as long as there's a voice there and it's something they feel compelled to write. People come to me a lot with projects that they're working on because they feel it's a "hot" part of the market, and I'm just not really interested in that.

Q **You've seen more than enough Harry Potter knockoffs lately?**

A As a result of Harry Potter, there have been a lot of people trying to get on that bandwagon. Those are great books, and when J.K. Rowling wrote them, you can tell that it's obviously what she wanted to write. I don't think she wrote them because she felt they would be more marketable than the next idea. I think a good book will succeed independent of any trends in the market. A good book will do well no matter when it's published. The quality of a book comes through.

Q **You attend a lot of writing conferences. Should children's book**

writers be attending conferences to meet agents and editors?

A I think conferences are great, and I think they're really important for new authors. They're a place to meet some people in the business, to really find out what different agents and editors are looking for, and to do some networking (though I hate to use that word). I like meeting new authors, and I've been lucky enough to find some really great authors at conferences.

Q More and more, we're hearing that it's not necessary for literary agents to be working out of New York to be successful. You're actually based in San Diego, as the West Coast arm of Writers House, a very well-established New York agency. Tell me about your experience working outside of New York City.

A I really like working out here. Definitely with e-mail, fax, and phone, location doesn't matter as much as it did in the past. I do go to conferences a lot, and I see the editors there; I'm always in very close touch with them. And it is great to work with Writers House, one of the bigger New York agencies—it's been around for more than twenty-five years—so it's helpful to have that base there.

But it's been great for me to be out here in San Diego. It allows me to think very freely. Obviously if I'm working in publishing in San Diego, it means I really love it and it's something I love to do. It keeps my perspective very fresh. . . . I feel like the New York publishing community can sometimes be a little bit stifling, because there's such a set way that things are done out there. I feel being out here allows me to be a little bit more creative and think a little more freely. It's never been a disadvantage, and in some ways I feel it's actually been an advantage—it sets me apart in some ways.

Q Where does children's publishing go from here?

A I do think that children's books are doing really well. The Harry Potter phenomenon changed things a lot, and I think people who hadn't been paying as much attention to children's books started looking at it. A lot of people, the Powers That Be, saw children's books as an area where they could make a lot of money, and they hadn't necessarily seen that before. It's opened up new avenues for children's books, and a lot of people are looking at children's books who maybe didn't before.

And I think the success of children's publishing will continue. The really nice thing about the children's book industry is that the publishers are really dedicated to building authors, to building people's careers. You don't really want to get into this mode in which publishers are so concerned with producing blockbusters (which I think is part of the problem in adult books). That can be a little bit dangerous—it makes it so much harder to cultivate new talent.

An Interview With Three Scholastic Editors

David Levithan worked his way "literally from the ground up" at Scholastic, starting his career with an internship during college and progressing to work on best-selling series such as The Babysitters Club and the Star Wars. Today he's a senior editor at Scholastic, specializing in series fiction, both hardcover and paperback. In January 2002, he launched his own imprint for teens called Push (www.thisispush.com).

Joy Peskin joined Scholastic as an editor after several years working with the Puffin imprint at Penguin Putnam books. She edits trade paperbacks for younger readers, including third-grade series and picture book series.

Kristin Earhart spent several years in the media group at Scholastic, working on licensed books such as Teletubbies and Mary Kate and Ashley, "unauthorized biographies" of stars such as Hansen, and the best-selling Magic Schoolbus series. Today she's an editor in Scholastic's trade division, creating original series books for middle-grade and younger readers.

Q Do children's book writers need agents to get published today?
Levithan: It's a mix. Certainly many agents bring great writers to

the table, and when they do it's a wonderful experience. But at the same time, I know I personally work with a lot of writers who do not have agents—whether I know them through other authors, or other activities, or some other link. It's very rare that we take on a writer totally unsolicited; there usually has to be a connection. But absolutely that connection does not necessarily *have* to be an agent.

Earhart: It has to be somewhat personal—if you just get something in the mail with your name on it and you've never heard of the person, it's just a harder route for the writer to take. It's not the most advised.

Levithan: It's important to note here that Scholastic has for the past eight years had a policy that we do not accept unsolicited manuscripts. If somebody just mails something in to us and we don't know the person— if there's not a connection there, if they don't have an agent, if they haven't been previously published—then we do not read it, and we do send it back unread. We get thousands of submissions a year, and we just don't have the staff to look at everything.

So for writers who are just starting out and don't know somebody who's an author or somebody who works in a publishing house, the agent is their best way.

Q **What should authors who do not have an agent keep in mind when they're preparing to submit a proposal?**

Peskin: I think the biggest trick if you are going to go the nonagented route is doing your homework. That was the biggest problem I had at Puffin in terms of getting submissions—we did almost exclusively reprints, so probably 99.9 percent of the submissions we got weren't appropriate for what we did.

I empathize with people . . . it's very complicated, even if you work in publishing, to figure out what each house does and what each imprint does. But that's the most important thing. You're shooting yourself in the foot, and you're wasting your time and your postage if you don't. It's a lot of research to do up front, but it will really pay off if you end up getting published. The advantage of an agent is that he or she has a much better sense of what goes on at each house. You can educate yourself, but it's a little bit tougher.

Levithan: My new imprint Push is a good example of that. It's a teen imprint for first-time authors. We're getting submissions that are just not appropriate at all—people who have published many books before, or from people who have written a middle-grade book. You wonder, did they read what this is really about? A lot of people just throw everything against the wall and see what sticks. That's not the right way to do it; it's a waste of your time—it's a waste of the editor's time.

Earhart: The other advantage about agents is that they can help you shape your book to be more appropriate for the market you're trying to hit, whether that's a certain age level or a certain publishing style. And it's good to have someone essentially "edit" the book before the editor even sees it, to help you have a solid proposal and deliver what the publisher really is looking for.

Q So what *are* you looking for? What kinds of proposals and authors do children's book editors want to publish today?

Levithan: In a general sense, you're looking for something that blows you away. You're looking for someone whose writing is good. It doesn't have to be great right off the bat—that's what editors are for—but it has to be at a level that you think, *This can go somewhere. This can do something.* It has to tell a story that hasn't been told before. It's not a rehash; it's not a copycat. It says something new. We're looking for exciting voices, people who are going to tell you a story in a really interesting way.

And for me personally, in cover letters and in authors' presentations, I'm looking for authors I think I'd want to work with on a purely personal level. Most of us, because we get so many submissions, get to choose who we want to work with. We can be picky. I've definitely had proposals in which the writing was good but the project wasn't right . . . and yet the person themselves came across so interestingly that I was intrigued. In some cases I've gotten back to their agent or to the person themselves and said, "This doesn't work, but maybe we can come up with something that does."

Earhart: I think the hardest thing about children's books is that you can never predict how people are going to react to it or what's going to work. It's an unpredictable industry. So many things have to come together—the writing has to be good; the idea has to be good. It's a lot of instinct.

Peskin: Also, one of the greatest things you can do for yourself when you're starting out is to be *extremely easy to work with*. It sounds like such a simple thing, but it's true. For instance, I'm working with someone now on a new series. A couple of years ago, this author was just trying to get into the business and sending me lots of ideas—some of them were good, some of them weren't great—but we established a good working relationship. She's not demanding. She gets stuff in on time. She doesn't take bad news in a bad way. I don't feel nervous about giving her feedback. She's not pushy. And that's why, when I proposed this new series, I had her name on the list. And now she's writing it.

Conversely, I just worked with someone who really shot themselves in the foot. They were pushy, came on really strong, were ultra demanding, wanted to meet every week. That's a bad idea! Of course, we're not going to turn talent away, but if you like somebody and their writing, and they're easy to work with, you're going to really want to put the time in to them and their writing.

Q How important is it to establish a good working relationship with authors?

Levithan: It's important to clarify that "easy to work with" doesn't necessarily mean that authors should agree with you on everything. But it does mean that all their questions are well thought out. I would say there are people who I would term "easy to work with" and who I love working with, and yet there's this huge give and take. But it's a respectful, trusting give and take. It's having a professional outlook.

Earhart: There's nothing better than a great relationship in which you're learning from an author, and the author's willing to take a little from you as well. That's when you hang up the phone and think, *I love working with him. What else could we publish together?*

Levithan: The word "relationship" is a great one to use. As an editor, I am going in there hoping that I will work with an author for a long time. Speaking for myself, most of the authors I work with now are people I've been working with for a number of years. We work great together, they're wonderful writers, and I want to keep that going. Of course, I'm still looking for new writers and constantly adding to that stable, but you want the people who are coming in to be just as much of a joy to work with. It's not a quickie; it's a relationship.

Q You all work for Scholastic, publisher of one of the biggest phenomena to hit the publishing world ever—the Harry Potter books. How have these books affected the children's publishing world?

Levithan: There is what we call "the halo effect." Harry Potter has shone this light around children's books. Children's books are a much bigger deal than they were before. And now national media outlets like *USA Today* or *Time* are much more willing to look at children's books. That does spill over to authors of every level. Certainly Harry Potter isn't solely responsible for that, because obviously it happened way before Harry Potter. But those books took this phenomenon to another level.

For writers, the Harry Potter effect has been twofold. On the one hand, it has been encouraging. The increased sales of children's books have been good for them, and there's more of a sense of value for children's books. But the downside to this has been that a lot of people have thought, *I could write Harry Potter. They must be looking for another Harry Potter.* It is so untrue. I will go on the record as saying: We won't see another Harry Potter for fifty years. If then. The success has been unparalleled; it's an aberration. And if people start trying to gear their writing toward being something like Harry Potter, that's where the effect can be really bad.

The amazing thing about Harry Potter and the primary reason it's done so well is that it's a story she worked on for five years. It's a story she totally invented in her mind, felt passionate about, got down on paper, and it was a wonderful story. The writing is wonderful. She didn't look and try to copy Goosebumps—she was truest to her heart, and the writing came out. If writers can take one lesson from that, it should be to follow that model. See what she did, rather than try to emulate what she has. There has never been a successful knockoff series in children's publishing.

Earhart: The next big thing in publishing is going to be nothing like Harry Potter. It's going to be so off the note of what everybody's been trying for that it's going to ring very true. One of the big hits that happened between the Harry Potter releases was The Series of Unfortunate Events, which picked up on some of the dreary tones of Harry Potter's early life, but was very much its own voice. There are similarities; there probably was a little filter effect. But it was its own thing.

Levithan: The best thing that happened with Harry Potter was that fantasy as a genre became highlighted. Did we start publishing a little more fantasy? Yes, but not significantly more, and nothing that we wouldn't have published in another time. Did our fantasy submissions increase a hundredfold? Absolutely.

We're looking for the next big thing, and we don't know what it is. It could be Westerns. It could be romance. Mysteries. It could be some other genre that has just lain dormant. That's what's so great about kids—you just have no idea what it's going to be. But when something strikes a chord, suddenly that's it.

Q Do you think children's publishing is even more unpredictable than adult publishing?

A *Peskin:* As kids are growing, their interests are changing so quickly. Every six months, they could be into something totally different. There's some hot new thing all the time. As an adult, if I liked to read a Bridget Jones–type book a few years ago, I'd probably pick one up now. I'm not suddenly going to be into science fiction.

I don't think it's a matter of trying to "keep pace with" kids, but rather a matter of trying to put fresh things out there. Kids who are into Harry Potter now didn't necessarily have a void in their lives before him. They just read it and got into it.

Earhart: I think so, because the people writing for kids, and the people who are marketing for kids . . . we're not kids! But at the same time, there are some kinds of "tried and true" topics that never seem to go out of style. Horses, for example. The fact that horse books are still being published and that kids are still reading them—it's amazing!

Q When *The New York Times* created a separate list for children's book best-sellers a few years ago, it was the subject of much contention. Should Harry Potter be allowed to sit atop the adult best-seller list, or do children's books need their own chance to shine?

Levithan: I think it's been a mixed blessing. On the one hand, a lot of books that are really good sellers but would have *never* made the adult best-seller list have made the children's best-seller list. It's exciting to be able to say that they're *New York Times* best-sellers. For example, the Star Wars series that I edit is constantly on the children's list, and it would definitely not be as present on the adult list. But on the other hand, you do have books like Harry Potter that are phenomenal sellers, and it is sort of unfair to sort of kick them to another category. But there are other best-seller lists, such as *USA Today*, that don't separate the two, so you can still gauge what the adult and children's are on one page.

Earhart: I think from the standpoint of the consumer, having the separate lists is a good thing. The children's list gives someone in a bookstore a better sense of what the recognized children's books are.

Peskin: I think it draws more attention to children's publishing in general when someone is reading *The New York Times Book Review* and sees the children's list. It adds a level of importance to children's publishing. I think all of us here have probably been asked, "Oh, when you get really good, will they let you edit adult books?" I think the separate list adds a certain legitimacy to children's publishing.

Q What information do you wish you could share with people who are submitting materials to you?

Peskin: Something that's hard to explain to people who are waiting to hear back from us about submissions is what a long process it is. The reason for that isn't because we're trying to torture you. It's because every proposal has to go through a series of hurdles. The editor has to like it. The editorial director has to like it. Then it goes to a senior editorial level. Then the numbers have to work on it. It has to pass a number of stages before it even gets acquired. And then the contract process is long. And then, it might get put on a list a year or two ahead of time! I think it's hard for people to understand, but it's a long process.

Q All three of you have extensive experience with series books. Let's discuss some of the special demands for children's writers working on series.

Levithan: Series writing is really a different kind of publishing—it's an author writing a book every two months or every three months. And we look for some different things in a series proposal. Obviously it has to be a really compelling situation. And the characters have to be compelling enough that you'll want to read about them for more than one book. There has to be a vision for the series so that Book 2 and Book 3 and Book 4 will be as compelling as Book 1. In order for us to commit to many books, we have to make sure that it'll just get better and better as time goes on.

In addition to original series, I get a lot of queries about writing for series that already exist. And the truth of the matter is, don't bother sending those queries. When we look for writers to carry on an existing series, we always look for people who we've worked with before or who are recommended by another editor or an agent. I discourage people from doing that.

What's worse is when we get ideas for new books in an existing series—that happened a lot with The Babysitters Club books, the Star Wars books, and some of the other popular Scholastic series. Legally, we can't look at those. The last thing we want to do is read somebody's idea for a series book and have to reject them because we already have a similar book in the works. They might think we stole their idea! I just don't look at those—I have to send them back unread.

Earhart: There's also a difference between hardcover novel writing and series writing. Someone can be a fabulous, solid novelist and not be able to pull off series writing. You have to really consider your talents and your strengths, and think about whether your ideas will last that long and whether you're willing to stick through that kind of commitment to a series. You have to know where the characters are going. They all have to be able to build and go through their own issues throughout the entire series. You need fresh conflicts.

Peskin: Also, if you have an idea that you think could be a series, an important question to ask yourself: Is this a series, or is it a long book that I've broken up into four sections? A series needs to have a reason to be a series. For example, The Babysitter's Club has a reason to be a series—it's a great idea, the writing is great, the characters are real, and you really want to read all 200-plus books.

Many writers have a great idea for a series, but the follow-through on the characterization is not there. I've read series that I've been really excited about the idea, but then the characters are coat hangers for the concept.

Q. What's on the horizon for children's publishing?

Levithan: We're trying some new things. With Push we're trying to reach the teen market, which has been largely untapped for the past few years. And some of our series, we're trying to return to some classic forms—things that are tried and true, like dolls and horses, but putting new spins on them. Not breaking the mold entirely, but refashioning it for the new century.

But I think really, we are open to anything. That's what's so great about children's books—we're not as locked into genres; we go across the board. It's fun to see what our authors can come up with.

PART III:

Publishing 101— What You Need to Know *After* Your Book Is Sold

CHAPTER 12

What Happens to My Book Once It Reaches an Editor's Desk?

If submitting a manuscript to an editor or agent is a confusing and bewildering process to writers, what happens to a manuscript once a publisher accepts it can be a virtual mystery. Once you turn over your completed manuscript to your editor for safekeeping, you'll probably see only a few infrequent glimpses of it over the next several months—a corrected manuscript here, some cover copy there. It's only when you hold the completed book in your hand, many months later, that you see the result of all your hard work—and the hard work of all those people behind the scenes at the publishing company.

It's an exciting time, but it can also be a frustrating one for a writer who doesn't understand what happens in the interim between submission and publication. In this chapter, editor John Scognamiglio attempts to demystify the process, walking you through every step of the process from manuscript to bound book.

The Making of a Book
BY JOHN SCOGNAMIGLIO

My job as an editor at Kensington Publishing is a simple one: I have to find manuscripts to publish. My publishing house publishes books in both hardcover and paperback in a variety of genres, including mystery, romance, suspense, health, humor, and true crime. And every day manuscripts arrive on my desk in one of two ways.

1. The Mail Arrives

One way your manuscript gets to me is through a literary agent—one who usually knows the types of books I look to acquire for Kensington. Over the years, through lunches, telephone calls, and negotiations for projects, the literary agents I deal with know my likes and dislikes. For instance, when it comes to mysteries, I prefer cozies over hard-boiled; if it's a suspense novel, I lean more toward domestic suspense rather than a serial-killer thriller. Of course, my personal tastes can't dictate everything I buy. For instance, if a certain type of book is selling well for another publisher, our sales department might want us to sign up a book that's similar. Remember when Grisham's *The Firm* (Doubleday) hit it big in the early 1990s? It helped propel a new genre—started by Scott Turow in the late 1980s—called the legal thriller. Soon every publisher in town was looking for legal thrillers.

As an editor, I need to be aware of what's selling and how I can find it for my publisher. And that takes us back to agents. They know what my current needs are in servicing my house's publishing program and won't waste my time in sending a manuscript they know I can't buy.

The other way manuscripts arrive is through unagented submissions. Here, aspiring authors might find my name in the acknowledgments of a book I've edited or call me directly. Or they might get my name out of the most recent edition of the *Literary Market Place.*

2. The Manuscript Is Read

Once a manuscript lands on my desk, I give it to my reader, who will be the first person to look at it. As much as I'd like to read the manuscript myself, I simply don't have the time: I'm usually in meetings or on the phone or doing one of the many tasks that leads to a manuscript becoming a finished book. My reader, however, knows the types of books I look for. For instance, my reader knows that any science fiction manuscript gets an automatic rejection because my publishing house doesn't publish science fiction—no matter how great the story may be.

Usually I'll give my reader two weeks to read a manuscript. When the manuscript comes back to me, attached is a reader's report that includes a summary of the plot, along with a paragraph of the book's strengths and weaknesses. My reader will love a manuscript, hate a manuscript, or suggest that a manuscript has potential and needs some revising. If the book's plot summary appeals to me, I'll start to read the manuscript. But if I'm not hooked by page 50, I'll send the manuscript back to the agent with a detailed reject letter. In that same letter, I'll also tell the agent about the types of books I'm still looking to acquire. Even though I haven't bought this manuscript, I do want the agent to keep me in mind for future submissions.

3. Selling the Story In-House

But say I do like the manuscript and I want to buy it. What happens next is that I introduce the manuscript at our weekly editorial meeting. Held every Tuesday, it's attended by the entire editorial department, our publisher, the publicity department, and the sales department. As we go around the room, each editor brings up the projects that he or she is interested in acquiring. Basically, what we're doing is auditioning the books and hoping that others in the room share our enthusiasm. Or we might have a project that we're excited about but not sure if it fits on our list of the other books we plan to publish, say, a quirky humor book or a nonfiction project geared toward a specific audience (like a diet book). By having the sales and publicity departments at our meeting, they can tell us if they think the project has potential in the marketplace. Will the bookstores want to stock this new revolutionary diet book, or are there just too many diet books out there? Will magazines and newspapers want to review it? If the sales staff and publicity staff give a book a vote of confidence, it makes the acquisition process much easier. But if they're lukewarm on a project or feel that there isn't an audience for it, then the book will not be bought by Kensington, no matter how passionately an editor feels about it.

4. Getting the Green Light

But let's say the project—your book!—gets a green light. What happens next? Well, a number of questions are then asked. Is this a first novel?

Is the author previously published? If the author was published by another house, what are the previous sales figures? How will we publish this book, hardcover or paperback? How much do we think we'll have to pay to acquire this book?

If the author has been published by another house but is looking for a new home, the most obvious question is: Why doesn't that house want this author? There could be a number of reasons: The author's books weren't selling, and his previous publisher dropped him; the author was unhappy with his previous publisher and didn't feel his books were getting the attention they deserved. (This can sometimes be the case. An author's books can be performing well, but the author doesn't believe his publisher is giving him enough support and helping his audience grow. This could be because there are better-selling authors on the house's list and they're getting all the attention, or it can be a smaller publishing house that doesn't have the resources to help the author grow.) Sales needs to know the back story because when it comes time to sell our new book by this author to the bookstores, the author's previous sales history will come into play. After all, we don't want to acquire an author whose books aren't selling. The person who buys books for a chain like Barnes & Noble (called "the buyer") looks to see how well an author's previous book has sold when our sales rep goes in to sell the new one. If sales figures are going down, then the number of copies that the buyer is willing to purchase for her stores will be small, and this will result in Kensington publishing a small print run. A small print run means less profit for both the author and the publishing house.

Conversely, if it's the case of an author who's been selling well but wants out of his old publishing house, Kensington can take advantage of the author's popularity by authorizing a large print run.

Here's a bit more on print runs and how they're figured. Let's say I've introduced a suspense thriller by a new author that I'd like to publish in hardcover. Let's say everyone in the weekly editorial meeting loves the plot. I will then get permission to do a profit and loss statement (P&L). A P&L gives us a projected summary of how much money both the publisher and author can expect to make from the book based on an estimated print run. For instance, a hardcover mystery by a first-time author usually has a print run of 5,000 copies in hardcover and 25,000 in paperback. The profit generated can go up or down based on how high or low the print run is. Sometimes, though, a profit and loss statement doesn't show any profit, and if that's the case, then I can't make an offer. But that doesn't happen too often. When it does, an editor will sometimes try to substitute different sets of numbers into the P&L so that it "works." It might result in the editor being able to buy the manuscript, but if the sales department can't deliver the print run that's been promised, then the finger of blame will be pointed back to the editorial department.

It's not often that a P&L is "cooked." Usually, it's in a case where we're publishing a kind of book that we've never published before—a multicultural novel, for instance. Sales will give us a print figure typical for a first novel, and that's the number that department will try to get. However, if the book is published at a special time of year, like Black History Month, the numbers might go up because a lot of bookstores will do special displays and order more copies than they usually would. Also, a spectacular cover can result in orders coming in above the target number. This happened with a gay romantic comedy we published in June in conjunction with Gay Pride Month—our target number doubled based solely on the cover. Now, when the P&L is redone, the book works and makes money! Sometimes a leap of faith can pay off.

5. Making the Deal

Once I know what I can spend on a book, I'll then call the author's agent and offer an advance and royalties. I will also offer splits on subsidiary rights, which include book club sales, first serial, second serial, and foreign sales (the author always keeps movie rights). An author will be paid royalties once the advance she's been paid has been earned back—that is, once the book begins to earn for the publishing house a sum greater than what it gave to the author as an advance.

After I make my offer, the agent consults with his client. Usually they'll come back and ask for more money. Or they might ask for better royalty rates or cover consultation (getting to see the cover before it's actually printed). If I can agree to that, I will. It's called negotiating—both the agent and the editor want to feel that they're making the best deal possible. There's usually room to maneuver, but sometimes there isn't. Then, too, the agent might have the manuscript submitted at other publishing houses (when a manuscript by the same author is submitted to more than one publishing house at the same time, this is what's known as a "multiple submission") and will want to call the other houses to let them know there's an offer. This can result in the other houses either passing on the manuscript or offering for it. If the other houses make offers, then you're in an auction situation and whoever offers the best deal gets the book.

Here's how the auction works. When I'm involved in an auction, I'm always on pins and needles because I don't know how high the bidding is going to go and at the end of the day, I don't know if I'm going to own a book that I really, really want. Auctions can be good and bad. They can be good because once you've bought that project—and usually for a large amount of money—the publisher must really get behind it to insure that the house is going to earn back the money the editor (me!) spent. The drawback to an auction is that everyone gets caught up in a bidding war, and you then overspend on a book that might not be worth the price you've paid.

6. Making a Book, Part 1

But let's say the manuscript has come to me only and the agent and author accept my offer. The author gets a contract and I now have a book to publish! The first thing I do after putting through the contracts paperwork is schedule the book. Kensington has a publishing program that works two years into the future. Looking at our schedule, I'll see where we have holes to fill and schedule the book accordingly.

Next, I put together an art sheet. The information that I include on my art sheet is a brief summary of the book along with any cover ideas I might have. If my editor in chief approves it, I pass it to the art department. We work fifteen months ahead of schedule on all cover art.

A few months later, the book's cover is discussed at an art meeting (another Tuesday meeting). At this meeting are our art director, our publisher, and the sales department. We talk about the ideas I've listed on the art sheet and look at any sketches the art director might have commissioned for the cover. Cover type for the book will also be shown, and we'll discuss what kind of special effects we might add to the cover. Will the type on the jacket be foiled and embossed? Just embossed? Do we want to use a matte and gloss finish to give the book a shiny look? Each type of "special effect" has a certain price, and the art department has a budget it must stick to. Naturally, the designers want to come up with a spectacular design package, but sometimes they're limited in what they can spend. (Of course, if the book we're publishing is by one of our authors who sells extremely well for us, then money is no object.) If everyone in the room likes the sketch that's shown, then artwork will be started (usually it's a painting the art department later scans into its computer). If not, then it's back to the drawing board. Those present at the art meeting might come up with cover ideas after listening to me describe the plot of the book in more detail. Or we might bring in books from other publishers and try to come up with a cover design that's similar in appearance, especially if the book is in a genre that's selling particularly well. Once a cover idea/sketch has been approved by everyone, the cover will be presented weeks later in a more finished form.

While the art department is working on the outside of the book, I'm working on the inside. Usually what I'll do after buying a manuscript is write a detailed editorial letter to the author that points out revisions she'll need to make. I'll list page numbers and share my ideas. If the author is able to accomplish the changes I'd like via her own writing solutions, that's fine—in fact, most writers will want to solve their own problems. After I've approved the revisions, I'll do a line edit. Essentially, all I'm doing is smoothing out whatever kinks there are in the manuscript, making sure that everything reads well. Once I'm finished with line editing, the manuscript goes to the production department for copyediting. Copyeditors are freelancers who work outside the publishing house, and it's their job to check for typos, grammar, and punctuation and to make sure the story is consistent. When a manuscript comes back from a copyeditor, it will usually have an array of yellow flags, each one with a query for me from the copyeditor. The copyeditor, for instance, might catch an error in which the author's heroine is wearing a red dress at the beginning of a scene but by the end of the scene her dress has turned green. Those are the types of catches we pay them for. The copyedited manuscript will then be sent to the author so she can address those questions, as well as check the line editing I've done.

This is the author's last chance to see the manuscript in this "raw" form. Any additional changes that the author wants to make must be done now—once the manuscript is returned to me, it will be in production and will be set into galleys. Galleys are the page proofs set into "book" form. I'll send these to the author, but all she can do at this point is check for typos and printer's errors—no rewriting is allowed.

Making a Book, Part 2

While the author is proofing galleys, the final round of work for the outside package starts up. By now, the cover copy department has a copy of the manuscript, and its people will write the copy for the back of the book. I have to make certain to provide some direction here.

There might be several plot developments I don't want revealed to readers, or I might want the copy to have a specific tone or focus on just one character. There may be certain elements of the story that I want highlighted or an introductory paragraph comparing this author to another who writes a similar type of book. Cover copy is usually worked on nine months before the book's actual publication date. Once both the editor in chief and I have approved the cover copy, it's then sent to the art department.

The art department now has the copy for the back cover and the finished artwork for the front cover. What the designers do next is put

Terms of the Trade

Advance: A sum "loaned" to an author before her book is published. The actual figure is based on what an editor thinks the book will likely earn in the marketplace.

Auction: A bidding war between two or more publishing houses for an author's book.

Buyers: The bookstore employees—for chains and single stores—responsible for ordering books from publishers.

Chromalin: A color version of a soon-to-be published book's cover that's circulated throughout the publishing house for approval.

Galleys: A prepublication copy of a book that's been set in book form. The galley is sent out in advance of publication to drum up publicity and to the author to catch any final errors.

Mechanical: The black-and-white version of a book's cover that precedes the Chromalin.

Multiple Submissions: Copies of the same book that are sent by an agent to more than one publishing house. The goal is to fan the flames of interest in a project and force an auction.

Print Run: The total number of books a publishing house will print. This number is determined by several factors, including an author's previous sales history, similar books in the marketplace, and numbers presold by the publisher's sales force to bookstore buyers.

P&L: Short for "profit and loss." A business plan created by an editor for a particular book title. It helps to determine if a book will be bought by the house and what the print run might be.

Royalties: A percentage of each book sold that's paid by the publishing house to an author. Royalties are paid on a sliding scale and aren't paid until the publishing house earns back the advance the author was paid up front.

Subsidiary Rights: The publisher doesn't "buy" a book outright; it "buys" the right to make money from it in various ways. This term applies to some of the other ways a house and an author can profit from a book, and includes things such as selling a portion to a magazine (serial rights), selling the book to an overseas publisher (foreign rights), etc.

Unagented Submissions: Proposals for books that come into a publishing house without an agent's representation.

together a mock-up of the cover, called a mechanical. This mechanical is a black-and-white printout that shows what the cover will look like. It's circulated to the editor, the publisher, and the sales department. If any of us have concerns about the mechanical—be it with the image or the words—now's the time to voice them. But if everything's okay, the cover is sent to the printer, who next produces a color version, called a Chromalin. We circulate this, too, and it's absolutely the last chance to fix any errors.

7. The Final Step

While the cover is off at the printer, the sales department gears up for its launch meeting. At a launch meeting, the sales, publicity, and editorial departments get together to discuss all the books that are being published in a particular month. In preparation for the meeting, editors write a tip sheet for each of their books. A tip sheet provides the following information: plot of the book, where the author lives (so we can make sure books are in the author's area, for the local appearances and signings), previous sales history, and comparisons to other books in the market.

As we go through each title on the list, we'll determine a target number that we want to print. It's then up to the sales department to meet that number when they go out to sell the book. The sales force tries to remember the number they committed to when they did the P&L and will use that as the target number. By this point, there could have been changes in the market, so maybe sales feels it can get out more copies. Then, too, we might have a terrific cover and sales will feel the print run will go up. The reverse can happen if the cover isn't very good (yipes!). After Kensington's sales reps visit their bookstore accounts, they come back to the office and enter their orders in a master file. After this "sell in" period is complete (it usually lasts three months), all the orders are added up and a print run is determined. Sometimes the print run is below the target number, sometimes it's above it, and sometimes it's right on the mark. Orders are determined not only through the author's sales history but by what the buyer in the bookstore thinks of the cover. If the buyer likes a cover, he might order more copies than the sales rep expected. Or, if the buyer hates the cover, he might take fewer books. Naturally, we always try to come up with the most striking cover possible. So although you can't judge a book by its cover, book buyers often do!

With the print run in place, it's time to send the galleys and the Chromalin off to the printer. We usually receive finished books about a month before they hit the stores. This is a special time for me—there's nothing I like better than opening my box of editor's copies and seeing the finished product of all my months of hard work, and all the author's hard work, too.

Now the only thing left to do is watch the book climb the best-seller charts.

John Scognamiglio is the editorial director of the fiction program at Kensington Publishing and the author of the young adult novel *Where the Boys Are,* published by Scholastic under the pseudonym John Hall.

CHAPTER 13

How Do I Work With My Editor Throughout the Publishing Process?

As we've discussed in earlier chapters, the relationship between writer and editor has been mythologized throughout the years—the writer and his editor-mentor worrying over every comma and word choice, striving together to create a lasting masterpiece. It's an appealing picture, to be sure. Today, say many people in publishing, editors are too busy buying books and dealing with corporate concerns to spend much time actually, well, *editing*. Conventional wisdom says that the role of career advisor, line editor, and confidant is more often filled by an author's agent rather than his editor.

But all of the editors we spoke with were steadfast in their commitments to their authors, and most relished the opportunity to delve into a writer's work and forge a strong working relationship. In the last chapter, you learned what happens to a writer's work once it reaches an editor's desk. Now we'll examine the process more in depth—specifically the working relationship between author and editor. Jerry Gross speaks with editor Beena Kamlani, who discusses the delicate process of line editing an author's masterpiece. Then author (and editor) Robin Hemley identifies the different types of editors you're likely to run across in your publishing career and how to work with each of them.

What a Good Editor Will Do for You
BY JERRY GROSS

Beena Kamlani brings a worldly perspective to the editing profession. Born in Bombay, India, Kamlani went to a boarding school in the foothills of the Himalayas, was then educated in England, and has worked in book publishing in New York for more than twenty years. She's spent the past eleven years at Viking Penguin, where she is senior editor.

Kamlani has edited a wide range of books, working closely with literary heroes like Saul Bellow (whose *Herzog* she read when she was ten); classicists like Robert Fagles (*The Iliad*'s and *The Odyssey*'s translator); popular writers like Jacquelyn Mitchard, Terry McMillan, and Joanna Trollope; biographers like Robert Kanigel and Leon Edel; and recently published writers like Nora Okja Keller, Ruth Ozeki, and Peter Sheridan.

Kamlani also knows the other side of the desk: She's a fiction writer herself and is just completing her first novel. When asked how she'd respond to editing, she says: "If I know I'm dealing with an equal mind, a sensibility that genuinely understands what I'm trying to do, I'm eager to play. I feel truly challenged by good editorial feedback. When an editor gets my work—and I suppose I know what it takes to really get what a writer's trying to do—I'm exhilarated. It's thrilling to know you've got that kind of ally for your work.

"When the feedback is off course, you know the editor's read the book she wanted to read, not the book you wrote. Then you do the only sensible thing: You just ignore the feedback. You can't always ignore it, it's true. But sometimes you may feel that you're making a compromise you can't live with. In that case, don't cut your cloth to suit. Wait for the right editor for your book."

Q How does "line editing" differ from and/or resemble "developmental editing" and "copyediting"?

A Actually, the term "line editing" covers the entire gamut of the editorial process, from the big, conceptual picture to line-by-line editing. In reference books and in college textbooks, the term "developmental editing" is used more, and I think it's slightly different. In trade editing, we call the actual editing process "manuscript editing" or "line editing."

Copyediting is very different from line editing. A copyeditor does not have much flexibility. The manuscript is already in its final form when it gets to the copyeditor, and there isn't very much she or he can do with it other than make it grammatically sound; watch out for errors in syntax; catch repetitions in words and in phrases; pick up inconsistencies in ages of people, chronology, physical characteristics; make sure the spelling and punctuation are right—that kind of thing. There isn't the reshaping of a manuscript and taking it through several drafts as you would if you were line editing it. Sometimes I go through several drafts before a manuscript is ready for copyediting, and that could take a year and a half, maybe more.

So that's the big difference between copyediting and line editing.

Q **So line editing is the process of going through a manuscript's different drafts and shaping it and reshaping it until you and the author are happy with it.**

A That's it, although sometimes one thorough revision could do it.

Q **Is this type of line editing a fading art in modern book publishing?**

A I think editing is a dying craft, and it really is a craft. I teach it—not instinct, not discrimination, not good taste, which are inherent or developed through experience—but the technique and the craft of narration, of writing, and, therefore, of editing. All editors should know the craft of writing backward if they want to be good editors, and that is how I approach it in the class I teach—through narrative technique itself. Ironically perhaps, because it is dying and authors are really beginning to feel it now, there is much more interest in the craft. Once learned through apprenticeship, through osmosis as it were, smart editors now come to a class like mine in order to learn it. That is a huge change in the state of editing.

Q **Is there time now in a publishing house for an editor to get this kind of training from a senior person?**

A Rarely. People aren't editing in quite that way, and editorial assistants are worked to the bone, as are editors. Editorial assistants don't really have the time to learn how, just as editors often don't have the time to edit manuscripts the way they'd like to. The very principle on which acquiring a book was dependent—the editor's ability to edit it— is no longer really as central to the job as it once used to be.

Q **In an average calendar year, how many manuscripts are you working on at any given time?**

A Sometimes it could be one a month, sometimes it could be several, because different drafts of different manuscripts overlap; it's very hard to actually pin that down. I'm constantly editing, though.

As soon as a manuscript comes in that needs the kind of in-depth, roll-up-my-sleeves-and-edit job that I do, the publishers sort out which ones I should be working on and in what order.

Working With Author and Manuscript

Q **How do you approach a manuscript that you'll be helping an author shape and sharpen?**

A As a fresh challenge, a totally new experience. It's exciting when someone walks into my office with it and puts it on my desk. Sometimes I know a little bit about it beforehand, sometimes not. I read it through; I see what the author's trying to do. No editing at this point. I take very extensive notes; sometimes these run into fifteen, twenty pages of very tiny handwriting. I also put down my overall impressions, my thoughts as I'm reading.

Then I begin the actual line editing. By the time I begin, I've been through the manuscript at least once very meticulously, sometimes twice. I'll go back and reread portions of it to reconfirm my impressions and have a very carefully calibrated sense of what the author's trying to do and what she needs to do to get there before I actually start the editing process.

Q **How do you actually work with an author? What's the day-to-day give-and-take?**

A In terms of the principle behind editing, it's essential to have a good sense of strategy, of negotiation. I pick my battles very carefully. You give some; you win some. You don't win them all, but it's important to know what's bottom line for you and what you can live with if you have to. If you begin with that, it's negotiation all the way, and you're going to be diplomatic, you're going to be tactful, because you see it as a two-way process that can be only a win-win situation for the book.

The book is very much the author's work. You're trying to make it as good as it can be, but you need the author's cooperation. Without it, nothing can be done.

Q **How does your editor choose the books that need you?**

A What I often get—and I don't choose them—are manuscripts that need solid reshaping and/or very thorough attention. That's the single most important criterion: These manuscripts need careful editing. In one case, the author was too close to his novel. It was a 2,000-page manuscript that I cut down to 800 pages, and I managed to preserve the main story intact. The author worked with me on it, was in fact very pleased with the changes. That's the kind of editing one has to do sometimes: literally go through three and four drafts of it until it's down to a very clear and coherent version.

The other kind of book that comes to me is when the author has somehow managed to write several books in one and a sharper focus on story line and clearly subordinate subplots are required. I help the author refocus so we have one beautifully honed story as opposed to several that go all over the place and in the end lead nowhere.

Often I work with first drafts. I'm trying to determine how much of the material is really essential and how much merely digressive. Is the author showing off? If a passage is, in the end, just verbal pyrotechnics, it should be taken out.

It's very clear when an author hasn't really thought through what he's trying to do, or if it's a hasty job, or if it's sloppy. I hate to see that. I think that it's important to do the best you can. Put your best foot forward, whatever that might be. I don't think you can afford to let the editor think that your book is a little like a neglected child. It shows, you know—both the care and the neglect.

Q **What does a line editor fear to find in a manuscript, and what does she hope to find?**

A I dread allowing myself to feel the impression that this is a lazy author, that there's no sense of a real focus in her work. Repetitions, sloppiness, names, physical characteristics, etc., change halfway through the book; plot lines are left dangling and aren't really linked to the main plot; obscure language—these are all signs of laziness.

I don't want to have to go back to an author with the most basic question of all, which is, "What's your story?" That's very different from saying, "What are you trying to do?" That's saying, "Let's work with what you have." But trying to figure out what the story is makes you wonder whether this author actually thought her book through properly.

The things I hope to see are a love of language, careful phrasing, a playful yet clever use of metaphor—an unusual way with metaphors is, as Ford Madox Ford said, a true sign of originality. I love dialogue that shows a good ear for the way people actually speak; a vision, a focus, an earnestness in trying to get that world to be seen, felt, heard, smelt by the reader. When I feel that the manuscript has been a well-tended, well-nurtured child and is really bright, I'm in awe of the writing process.

Q **If you and an author hit an impasse, will you rewrite a passage and show it to the author as an example of what you're looking for?**

A I think there's no problem with that, but you'd better be sure you know what you're doing. With fiction, especially, authors would much rather be asked, "Are you trying to say something like. . .?" and have the editor attempt a version of what the author is trying to do. Then they have something to work with, instead of just receiving something that's been done for them.

It's all a dialogue. And part of an ongoing dialogue is to put something out so you can get something—hopefully a lot better—back. An author might say, "But that's not the way I want to say it," and then go ahead and do it exactly the way he wants to do it. That's the point. I would actually rewrite only when the author's given up—if he says to me, "Why don't you have a shot at it?" Even then I would say, "This is the kind of thing I thought you were trying to do here."

The way you preface something is so crucial; trying to be the book's author, or even a coauthor, however heavily you may have edited it, is not the point of editing.

As long as you justify everything in the margins and you say, "You're repeating yourself here; you've said something identical through such and such character," no question to an author is out of bounds. But you've got to provide a very strong basis for doing it, whatever you do. Whether it's rewriting a paragraph, or finding fault with a word somewhere, or problems with an entire chapter, you'd better justify it.

The Publishing Process

Q Manuscripts come to you from an acquisition editor, the person who actually bought the book from an author's agent. How does your position interact with the acquisition editor's?

A At Viking, we've worked it out beautifully. The acquiring editors know what their responsibilities are, and they leave me to mine, and it's quite clear-cut. After I've read through the manuscript, I sit down with the acquiring editor; we talk about the initial problems I have with the manuscript. I share the drafts of my letters with her, and ask for her comments and feedback. Then it goes off to the author.

Nothing in publishing is done in an isolated way—everything is interdependent. No part of this industry could exist without the other. As a line editor, however solitary my craft is with the work itself, I'm dependent on the acquiring editor for feedback, for a certain amount of sound-boarding, for the very wonderful experience that editing a book can be.

Q What's the process for getting back to an author with suggestions for revision?

A Sometimes the acquisition editor does it with a phone call, and then I follow it up with a letter that explains everything very clearly. Or sometimes I might just call the author up myself and discuss it, and say, "I'm sending you a letter that the acquiring editor and I have worked on together." It's always a unified thing that goes out so that the author's never confused about what the editors want. The acquiring editor and I will agree on what should be done with the manuscript before a letter, whether it's from her or him, or me, to the author.

Q What's next?

A The manuscript first goes to the acquisitions editor. The acquisitions editor looks at it and says to me, "This is what I think. Let me know what you think." Most of the time we agree; sometimes we disagree. In one book I worked on, I wanted historical material about a certain place up farther. I didn't want it halfway through the manuscript because I felt I needed the historical background to understand the evolution of this place. The acquiring editor felt slightly differently. We put both points of view to the author. And the author decided.

We work things out.

Q How can the writer have a happy, creative relationship with the line editor?

A This is actually a very important question, and I think it needs to be done justice to. My feeling is that authors, when they come across an editor who really cares—really, really cares—they should treasure him or her.

It takes a lot to really care in the changing environment of publishing today. If you have it, don't, for the sake of your book, blow it.

I have two examples of bad behavior. One is an author who might have been having a bad hair day when she wrote this, but a perfectly reasonable comment in the margins—something to the tune of, "Would So-and-So be likely to think this so soon after meeting this person?"—elicited "Bullshit" scrawled like mindless graffiti, in red, across my query. It irritated me so much, I felt myself shut off deep inside. It felt as if the author didn't care, so why, I felt it necessary to ask myself, should I?

The other example is an author who clearly wasn't prepared for the kind of editing I do, and his irate comments throughout were overtly offensive. I felt again the same sense of undeserved abuse. He was extremely relieved to know that I had reacted in a completely professional way and ignored his comments throughout. Again, trying circumstances in his life had provoked them, and once this was explained to me, coupled with his genuine appreciation of my work, it made it possible for us to become very good friends.

That's really it. It's crucial to know what you've got and to appreciate it. I think a good editor is not trying to tread all over your toes; a good editor does not want your book to be her book; a good editor is not going to try to be your coauthor. A good editor is acutely aware of the nuggets of gold in your manuscript, and when she comes across dross in it, she helps you to convert it to gold, metaphorically speaking. It's Rumpelstiltskin without the catch! That is what a really good line editor is trying to do.

I think of myself as the spa treatment for authors. What I mean is that a tremendous amount of care is lavished on their manuscripts, there's a good amount of nurturing and of hand-holding, and I love what I do, so hopefully that shows. My gratification comes when the author sees this and is deeply appreciative of it.

The best way to answer your question is with a quote from a letter from one of my authors. I don't want to say who it is, because I haven't asked if I can name the person, but this was the final paragraph of his letter. He said, "All through this revision process, I felt you beside me. I found these cuts and changes difficult and time-consuming, but not agonizing. I felt that through your comments, we were communicating, that you cared about this manuscript, that you wanted only good for it, that I had an equal partner on the opposite side of the page, and that I enjoyed the encounter with your mind." The care showed, the manuscript benefited—that's what I care about.

Jerry Gross is a book doctor in Croton-on-Hudson, New York, and was a frequent contributor to *Fiction Writer*. His books include *Editors on Editing* (Grove Press).

Editors: Can't Work With 'Em, Can't Work Without 'Em

BY ROBIN HEMLEY

In the early 1980s, I worked as a kind of glorified shipping clerk at a major men's magazine, and I was acquainted with the fiction editor. She told me once that she almost always preferred working with established writers rather than first-time authors. The new writers, she said, tended to be opposed to anyone touching their immortal prose, while the seasoned writers tended to act professionally—not only agreeing to changes but encouraging intelligent editorial input.

Of course, there were exceptions. The magazine was publishing at the time a 50,000-word excerpt of Norman Mailer's *Ancient Evenings* (Little, Brown). The fiction editor had tried to edit Mailer, but he wouldn't allow her to touch a word. The manuscript was a mess, according to the editor, and Mailer was being paid a fortune—not because the work was good, but because he was Norman Mailer.

There are many reasons why a book is or isn't successful, and it's impossible to say whether a good editor might have made a difference with *Ancient Evenings* (not generally considered one of Mailer's strongest works). Sometimes, though, writers do their work and reputations harm by refusing to heed to advice of an experienced critic whose ego is less involved than the writers'.

Over the course of your writing career, you'll deal with many different types of editors. If you understand the working styles of the various types, you're more likely to know when to push, when to stay silent, when to revise. After all, it's to the benefit of both of you to have a successful, friendly, and perhaps even profitable relationship.

The Old Give-and-Take

I've had my own experiences—both good and bad—with editors, and I've learned from each. My first collection was a small chapbook from a small press. The editor of the press didn't ask me for changes on any of the stories included in the collection, and I thought this was only proper because the stories had already been edited—through workshops and by the editors of the various magazines in which they had originally appeared. I figured the stories were about as good as they would ever get.

Then a lucky thing happened. My story collection was accepted by Atlantic Monthly Press. Normally, one wouldn't publish the same stories twice, but I had added a stipulation to my small-press contract that I could publish these stories with a mainstream press.

My new editor, Anne Rumsey, told me that they were going to suggest a few changes to the stories. Fine, I thought. I'm sure there can't be many. All of these stories have been published and edited already. When I received the manuscript from her, every page, every paragraph had red-pencil line edits through my immortal prose. I think I experienced the seven stages of dying right there. But I accepted the fact that not only were my stories imperfect but they'd *always* be, no matter how many versions there were.

I think of Raymond Carver's many versions of the same stories that he published throughout his life, and W.H. Auden's admonition, as true for fiction as it is for poetry: "A poem is never finished, merely abandoned." I saw that I couldn't simply trust editors to tell me what needed improvement—they could help me, certainly, but I couldn't expect them to fix my stories for me.

In the ten years since, I've had almost every type of editor imaginable for my books and magazine stories. Overall, I think I'm pretty easy to work with: open to suggestions, but not always willing to take a suggestion simply because an editor makes it. I've published two books with Graywolf, and my editor there, Anne Czarniecki, likes to remind me of the snide comment I wrote in the margin after she edited my first novel: "You want to take out all my best lines!"

In general, I've found that editors fall into one of five categories, and all of these categories have writerly versions of the same. In other words, what can be said of editors can also usually be said of writers. And of course, there are many editors who are a combination of the following categories, or who can be different types of editors on different days. (And good luck figuring *those* editors out.)

1. Editor as God

There are some editors whose word is law, and every word must be obeyed. I've run into very few of these types. Recently, when a large-circulation magazine took a story of mine, it came back copyedited in such a way that it affected the style and meaning of the story. I let most of the changes go. The magazine gave me only a couple of days' turnaround time to make any revisions to the editor's revisions. One line had been removed at the end that I wanted restored. When I called back, I was made to justify why I wanted this line restored, and then the copyeditor told me he'd get back to me if that wasn't okay with the editor. In essence, I felt that I'd lost control of the story—but I choose my battles carefully, and in this case I decided I'd change it back the way I wanted if it ever appeared in a book.

I know other writers, one I respect and admire, who might have withdrawn their stories. One famous writer told me recently that he doesn't send out stories until he believes they're publishable, and he simply asks the magazine to accept or reject, not to edit. I used to feel, as in Norman Mailer's case, that such writers were acting like children, but I've come to see that some writers feel quite strongly that what's on the page should reflect their own consciousness entirely, flaws and all.

If you find yourself dealing with an Editor God, you have several choices. You can act as I did, choosing your most crucial battles, but maybe giving in a little more than you'd like. Or you can stand your ground and risk losing the publication. Sometimes, you have no choice if the story is going to be completely compromised by the suggested changes. Know the word *stet*. This means, "No, you toad, I want the words to read as I originally had them." Editors generally respect this.

2. The Hands-Off Editor

More and more, people say, editors are becoming acquirers rather than editors in the true sense. That is, they spend their days looking at manuscripts to buy, not poring over manuscripts already bought. Personally, I haven't found this to be true, though I know that marketing reigns supreme these days, and in some houses, editors do spend much of their time acquiring books that will please the marketers rather than editing. Editors like this are full of enthusiasm but fall short on suggestions. Some writers might prefer this type of editor, but I'd feel a little lost, I think, and nervous. If your editor doesn't care enough to carefully go through your work, how committed will she be in the future to you? What if your book isn't a smash success? This type of editor picks authors like lotto numbers, and lets them go just as easily.

If you find yourself with such an editor, resist the temptation to think all is lovely with your work. In the long run, you're much better off making revisions before the book is published than suffering the attacks of reviewers who will gladly point out the flaws in your prose. Show your work to various critics you can trust (former teachers, your workshop group, other writers), and ask them to look at your book with an editor's eye. Obviously, you don't have to accept all their advice, but you'll get some gems. Of course, make your editor aware early on that you expect to do some revising and agree on a date at which you'll return those revisions.

3. The Inexperienced (or Just Plain Dumb) Editor

Sometimes, an editor will remark on something so odd that you wonder if he's on the same planet. Maybe he's inexperienced. Maybe he's dumb. My agent once sent a story set in Japan to an editor who wrote back,

"We'd like to see more stories set in China, but not this one." Well . . . okay.

Rick Bass tells about the time a story of his was accepted by a major magazine and the editor said she loved it but didn't like the fact that the main character died in the end. "The main character doesn't die," Bass told her. "Yes, he does." They argued about this absurdly for a while; it was his story, but she thought she knew it better than he. Bass took the story to *The Paris Review* and George Plimpton accepted it. The other editor's reaction to his story so angered him that he rewrote his story and, indeed, made the character die in the end—not once but three times. Later, the story appeared in *The Best American Short Stories* (Houghton Mifflin) anthology.

4. The Ruby-Throated, Rat-Toad Editor

Very rare, almost extinct. Twice, I have dealt with editors who could only be considered mad and vicious. Early in my career, an editor at a well-known publishing house accepted my first book of stories and then ten days later unaccepted it, dashing off a note to my agent: "The fever of last week has died off. Thanks for sending this but my fall list is too full with short story collections." Not only was this unprofessional, but it had a devastating effect on my morale for a couple of weeks until, thankfully, Atlantic Monthly Press picked up the book. I had previously published some of these stories in a small-press chapbook, and the editor of this press also gave me trouble. Even though I had attached a rider to our publishing agreement that stated I could publish the stories in a larger collection, he started calling my editor at Atlantic Monthly and making trouble, nearly squelching the deal. Luckily, Atlantic Monthly's lawyers said that I was well within my rights to publish a book with them. Finally, to be rid of him, I paid him five hundred dollars. I hope you never have to deal with either of these types, but be careful. Don't celebrate until the ink is dry on the contract and the check has cleared in the bank. Most important, make sure you have everything in writing.

5. The Hands-On Editor

Happily, most editors fall into this category. This type of editor thinks of him- or herself as your advocate and another set of eyes to help improve your work. My own feeling is that I'm grateful for such attention. Sometimes, editing comes down to the personal preferences of the editor, but I find that as long as the editor explains his or her reasoning rather than simply expecting blind obedience, the relationship remains a healthy give-and-take.

I once had an editor who didn't like to use the work *asked* in dialogue, as in *"Can I go to the store?" she asked.* He argued that the word *asked* is redundant when one includes a question mark in the dialogue. The sentence should either read, *"Can I go to the store?" she said* or *"Can I go to the store," she asked.* This might seem like a minor point, but I liked his explanation and have since followed his advice.

You should count your blessings with such an editor. Most of them are underpaid and definitely overworked and stressed. They often neglect their own work to deal with yours. My father was Isaac Singer's editor and translator for many years, and I still have many letters from Singer to him thanking him for all his hard work. I also have letters from the publisher to my father berating him for not being quick enough with the translations. Singer gave my father rough translations from Yiddish to English, but my father spent long months turning Singer's words into polished prose.

At the *Bellingham Review*, I've seen the other side of this. On occasion, I've had to deal with intractable writers, but for the most part, my dealings with writers are on the level of mutual respect and professionalism. I make suggestions and sometimes my suggestions are followed, sometimes not. Even if the writer doesn't follow my suggestions, I'll often publish the story, but sometimes not, and in that case we simply go our own ways, no rancor on my part at least.

Personally, I prefer being a writer, partly because I'm probably a little too selfish to be the best kind of editor. Such editors are remarkable for their own unselfishness, and while they are able to separate their own egos from the work of the writer, they still seem to take a kind of familial pride in the work. Of course, it's not only unselfishness that makes a good editor but also an ability to enter into the writer's work fully, to know what she is attempting to do, and help her do it. Some editors have an uncanny knack for articulating your work better than you can, and no matter how good you think you are, they'll end up humbling you. And for writers, that's not altogether a bad thing.

Robin Hemley teaches creative writing at the University of Utah. His short stories have appeared in *Story* and other magazines, and his work has been anthologized in *The Pushcart Prize XV* and *XIX* (Pushcart Press). His short story collections include *All You Can Eat* (Atlantic Monthly Press) and *The Big Ear* (Blair). His novel, *The Last Studebaker*, was published by Graywolf, as is his memoir, *Nola: A Memoir of Faith, Art, and Madness*. He's also the author of *Turning Life Into Fiction* (Story Press).

CHAPTER 14

What Do I Need to Know Before I Sign a Contract?

For many writers, dealing with contracts is a necessary evil—a distasteful bit of business to get out of the way at the start of the publishing process. For others, haggling with editors can actually be kind of fun, like an afternoon spent bargaining at the flea market. No matter which camp you fall into, there are some basic things you should know about contracts, negotiating, and rights before you sign on the dotted line.

As we've discussed throughout this book, one of the most important roles an agent can play for a writer is that of negotiator—agents know who's buying what and how much to charge for it. They're also skilled negotiators, adept at retaining as many rights as possible for you (and getting as much as possible for the rights you sign away). But not all writers have agents, especially those authors who are just starting out or those trying to establish themselves through publication in smaller journals or magazines. For those writers, and even writers with literary representation, knowing the basics of contracts and negotiation is imperative.

In this chapter, Timothy Perrin discusses how to be smart about your rights and offers a five-part SMART test to evaluate whether a contract is fair or foul. And Donya Dickerson guides us through an in-depth discussion of rights to your work: which rights the publisher keeps, which rights the writer keeps, and which rights are definitely negotiable. Whether you've got an agent or you're going it alone, when it comes to contracts and negotiation, knowledge is definitely power.

An Offer You *Can* Refuse
BY TIMOTHY PERRIN

In 1995, Dallas writer Sophia Dembling was pleased with the progress of her new freelancing career. She'd already managed to become a regular contributor at Condé Nast's *Bride's* magazine. When the publisher wanted her story on the U.S. Virgin Islands, she was thrilled.

There was only one wrinkle. Condé Nast was offering a "work for hire" contract. The publisher would own all rights to Dembling's story just as if she'd been a staff writer; freelancers normally only license limited rights to publishers. Dembling thought about the offer and decided she could rework the material into another piece if she wanted to resell it. Rather than argue, she just signed the contract. "Because I was starting out in my career, I was signing blindly," she recalls. "They said their contracts were nonnegotiable."

A year later, Dembling was surprised to find her article appearing in a brochure put out by the Virgin Islands tourism agency. The photographer for the same piece—who had held on to his rights—got paid, but not Dembling. "It didn't occur to me that my story would become a brochure for the tourist board," she says. "No doubt the publisher made more money on the story than I did!"

Dembling fell victim to her own eagerness to make a sale, something that happens to many writers when confronted with a contract negotiation. Her mistake is typical of the contract problems that plague writers at all levels—in magazines, books, and online.

You need to be smart about contracts. And any contracts you sign need to be "SMART"—Specific, Measurable, Achievable, Relevant, and Time-Limited.

Specific . . .

Where many contracts fall down is that they aren't specific. They don't designate the details of a deal sufficiently narrowly. As Atlanta writer Maxine Rock advises, "Assume nothing. Spell out exactly who does what and who gets what."

Sometimes the problem originates with the client. "All too often these days, clients want to throw things at you without really thinking it through themselves or giving proper direction," says Toronto writer Newman Mallon. "They just want to pass [the problem] on so you can think it through, and you can bet there will be many variables they never told you about and you never considered."

Regardless of where the problem originates, it becomes your predicament when you take on a poorly specified job. "Beware of saying 'yes' to a contract without making sure that all three elements of the projects are well-defined: scope, time, and money," says Bill Johnstone. The Victoria, British Columbia, writer found himself caught in a vaguely defined project for a nonprofit society. "I'm only now finishing the second draft of a 200-plus-page report, more than a year after the initial projected delivery date."

Protect yourself by making sure a contract specifies exactly what's your responsibility and what isn't. You can then decide whether or not to take on additional work and at what price. For magazine work, the "specification" is often the query. Make sure that your story answers the promises made in the query. The same goes for a book based on a proposal. For corporate work, use a detailed estimate as the basis of the contract. Be sure to include review dates, what happens when the client doesn't give you the required feedback when promised, and how many rewrites the corporation gets for the specified price.

Measurable . . .

By creating a series of milestones that can be objectively assessed, you can also make your job measurable.

When writing for books and magazines, it's possible to build yourself a checklist of client expectations. Go back to your query. List exactly what it promised. Carefully review the notes of your conversations with your editor. (If it's legal in your area, I suggest you tape all your conversations with your editors; it avoids arguments later.) Exactly what was said? Reduce it to a list of goals for the story, not just word count and deadline but what elements you promised would be in the story.

What did the editor say she was looking for? Then you can compare your finished story against the promises you gave and the expectations she expressed.

Achievable . . .

Perhaps the most important criterion is that your contracts be achievable. Even if your assignment is specific and measurable, it may still be more than you can achieve in the time and on the budget the client has in mind.

Santa Clara writer David Snellbacher recalls one project that was to be a four-month job: "They told me what they thought it would consist of. I told them how long I thought it would take, and they didn't have the budget." By working with the client, Snellbacher found parts of the project that could be delayed and parts that could be done by existing staff. Together they reduced the scope of the job to fit the available resources.

It's up to you to be clear on your abilities and how fast you can work—because the client won't be. "Most of the time, I don't think people have a really good understanding of how long it's going to take to do something," says Snellbacher.

One of the best things I ever did for my career was to set some financial goals that gave me guidelines by which to measure whether an assignment is achievable. For example, this year, my goal is to bring in $72,000—that is, $6,000 per month, or almost $1,500 per week. Since I get to spend only about two days a week actually writing—the rest is selling, administering, and all the other things I need to do to keep my freelance business afloat—I have to make about $750 per writing day. So, when a publication and I settle on $2,000 for an assignment, my question to myself is whether I can do it in three days. If the answer is yes, I take the job. If it's no, I graciously decline and devote my time to selling to better markets. The job may have met the publisher's spending budget, but it fell short of my sales budget.

Relevant . . .

When you're looking for your next assignment, do you consider whether the job is relevant to your career plans? Is it going to help you go where you want to go? Being in business for yourself—and that's what you are, if you dedicate yourself to writing full-time—is a delicate balancing act between satisfying your customers' needs and meeting your own.

I failed to keep this rule in mind myself a few years ago. I contracted to write the documentation for what can best be described as a low-tech local-area-network for running factories. The product was dull, the company was dull, and, to make things worse, the managers insisted that I report every day to a cubicle in their offices so they could keep an eye on me. That kind of job wasn't why I went freelance and certainly wasn't a credit that would help me get more of the kind of work I wanted. I suggested they might want to find someone else to take over the project and got back to assignments that were more to my liking.

Time-Limited . . .

Finally, life is limited. There are only twenty-four hours in each day, and I don't know about you, but I like to spend a few of them having fun! So remember to put time limits on your projects.

There are two kinds of time limits. First, how many hours, weeks, months are you willing to invest in this project? When are you going to be free to move on to the next assignment? Right now, I am facing a second rewrite from one magazine that seems to change its mind with every version I file. Now, for version number three, the editors are asking me to put back material I took out at their request in version two. Enough is enough. I'm through. I'd rather take the kill fee and fight them in small-claims court for the balance than invest more time in an apparently hopeless cause.

Second, don't forget to address the time limits on how long the client can use your work. Remember, what you're really doing is creating intellectual property and either assigning (selling) it or licensing (renting) it to your clients. Your agreements need to address what happens to intellectual property rights and for how long.

In particular, do your contracts specify a publication deadline? For example, if you have a magazine article with good resale value, it's important to specify the date by which the publisher must get the work on the street. After that date, the publisher can still run your story but you no longer guarantee it will be the first publication to do so. With a book, late publication means you're losing sales. Smart contracts can protect you: Los Angeles freelancer James Joseph, for example, received an additional $15,000 from a book publisher who didn't publish by the deadline specified by Joseph's contract.

. . . SMART

Finally, don't forget to be smart in the normal sense of the word. Use your head.

On important projects, particularly books, always have a professional review the contract. "Most writing contracts, especially for books, motion pictures, and TV, are booby-trapped," says Joseph. "If you don't know the traps when you read them, hire someone who does—not just any lawyer, but a lawyer specialized in literary contracts." The Authors Guild has a free contract review service for members; if you've been offered a mainstream book contract, you probably qualify for membership.

Alternatively, The Authors Guild, the American Society of Journalists and Authors (ASJA), or a writer's group in your area can refer you to a lawyer who understands contracts. The ASJA also posts a searchable version of its Contracts Watch bulletins on its Web site at www.asja.org/cw/cw.php. These provide up-to-date information on what various publishers are really doing, not what they say they're doing. At the very least, check your contract against the publishing contracts checklist I've posted at www.writingschool.com/checklis.htm.

And never let your eagerness to make a sale make you shortsighted. As Buffalo, New York, writer and lawyer Sallie Randolph notes, "Sometimes the best contract is no contract. There are snakes in the grass out

FIVE TIPS FOR SMART NEGOTIATING

Negotiation is a learned skill, and even for professionals, it's still a challenging task. Here are five tips to remember in your contract negotiations:

Oh, Is That All?

Whenever you're negotiating, let the other side make the first offer, then, no matter what the offer, pause about five seconds and say, "Oh, is that all? I was thinking more like . . ." and triple whatever they offered. Make sure your voice drips with disappointment. I can virtually guarantee they'll boost their offer substantially.

Time Is on Your Side

According to writer-lawyer Sallie Randolph, "The party not in a hurry generally has an advantage. Always say, 'I'll think about it and get back to you.' " Randolph suggests ignoring artificial deadlines, particularly ones imposed by the client's failure to get to the project in time.

Don't Take It or Leave It

When editors tell you a contract isn't negotiable, ignore them and start negotiating. "They've already invested time and money in your idea," ssays Randolph. "You being businesslike and reasonable in your requests for changes in contract position won't drive them away." Writer Sophia Dembling says she "goes for the ideal. I take out everything I don't want and put in what I want. Then I throw in a few things I can give away later."

It's Not About Price

Editors aren't buying what you think you're selling. You think you're selling your delightful writing, your sparkling idea. But like anyone else, they're buying a solution to a problem and the good feeling they get from solving the problem. So, ask questions of your customer (the editor) and of others who have dealt with your customer to find out what problem you can help solve.

Pressure Is Mutual

You're not the only one feeling pressure. The magazine editor has a publication to fill with quality material on a budget that is undoubtedly too small. A book editor has to buy enough profitable books to hang on to the job. Don't let yourself be intimidated.

there. When you get an indication someone is unethical, it's hard to protect yourself, even with a good contract."

Silicon Valley lawyer Cem Kaner agrees, saying much of his business comes from people who don't listen to the little voices in their heads that tell them particular contracts are bad news. "They know the situation is impossible," says Kaner, "or the person they are working with is unethical in some way—and they they take the job anyway. Then *I* get to make money from it."

That's money some SMART dealings could have left in your pocket instead of your lawyer's.

Timothy Perrin is a writer and former lawyer in Westbank, British Columbia, and the author of five books and several hundred magazine articles for such markets as *Science Digest, Omni*, and *Continental*. He is the newsletter editor for the ASJA, an advisor to the ASJA contracts committee, and a past director of the Periodical Writers Association of Canada.

Subsidiary Rights: Much More Than a Book
BY DONYA DICKERSON

Most writers who want to be published envision their books in storefronts and on their friends' coffee tables. They imagine book signings and maybe even interviews on *Oprah*. Usually the dream ends there—having a book published seems exciting enough. In actuality, a whole world of opportunities exists for published writers beyond seeing their books in print. These opportunities are called "subsidiary rights."

Subsidiary rights, or sub-rights, are the additional ways that a book—that your writing—can be presented. Any time a book is made into a movie or excerpted in a magazine, a subsidiary right has been sold. If these additional rights to your book are properly "exploited," you'll not only see your book in a variety of forms but you'll also make a lot more money than you would derive from book sales alone.

Unfortunately, the terminology of subsidiary rights can be confusing. Phrases like "secondary rights," "traditional splits," and "advance against royalty" could perplex any writer. And the thought of negotiating the terms of these rights with a publisher is daunting.

Although there are many advantages to working with agents, the ability to negotiate sub-rights is one of their most beneficial attributes. Through her experience, an agent knows which publishing houses have great sub-rights departments. If she knows a house can make money with a right, she will grant that right to the publisher when the contract is negotiated. Otherwise, she'll keep, or "retain," certain rights for her clients, which she will try to exploit by selling them to her own connections. In an interview in the *2000 Guide to Literary Agents,* writer Octavia Butler said that working with an agent "is certainly a good thing if you don't know the business. It's a good way to hang on to your foreign and subsidiary rights, and have somebody actively peddling those rights because there were years when I *lived* off subsidiary rights."

If you want to work with an agent, you should have a basic understanding of sub-rights for two reasons. First, you'll want to be able to discuss these rights with your agent intelligently (although you should feel comfortable asking your agent any question you have about sub-rights). Secondly, different agents have more expertise in some sub-right areas than others. If you think your book would make a great movie, you should research the agents who have strong film connections. Knowledge of sub-rights can help you find the agent best suited to help you achieve your dreams.

An agent negotiates sub-rights with the publishing house at the same time a book is sold. In fact, the sale of certain sub-rights can even determine how much money the publisher offers for the book. But the author doesn't get paid immediately for these rights. Instead, the author is paid an "advance against royalties." An advance is a loan to the author that is paid back when the book starts earning money. Once the advance is paid, the author starts earning royalties, which are a predetermined percentage of the book's profit.

The agent always keeps certain rights, the publisher always buys certain rights, and the others are negotiated. When an agent keeps a right, she is then free to sell it at will. If she does sell it, the money she receives from the purchasing company goes immediately to the author, minus the agent's commission. Usually the companies who purchase rights pay royalties instead of a onetime payment.

If the publisher keeps a particular right, any money that is made from it goes toward paying off the advance more quickly. Because the publisher kept the right, the company will keep part of the money the right makes. For most rights, half the money goes to the publisher and half goes to the writer, although for some rights the percentages are different. This equal separation of payment is called a "traditional split" because it has become standard over the years. And, of course, the agent takes her commission from the author's half.

Most agents have dealt with certain publishers so many times that they have preset or "boilerplate" contracts, which means they've already agreed to the terms of certain rights, leaving only a few rights to negotiate. The following describes the main sub-rights and discusses what factors an agent takes into account when deciding whether or not to keep a right. As you read through this piece, carefully consider the many opportunities for your book, and encourage your agent and publisher to exploit these rights every chance they get.

Rights the Publisher Always Keeps

The following sub-rights are always kept by the publisher and are often called "nonnegotiable rights." Money earned from these rights is split between the publisher and the author, and the author's share goes toward paying back the advance. Selling these rights helps the advance earn out faster, which hopefully means the writer will receive royalty checks sooner.

Reprint Rights

In publishing, a "reprint right" refers to the paperback edition of the book. When a hardcover book is reprinted in paperback, the reprint right has been used. According to agent Donald Maass, of the Donald Maass Literary Agency, "In deals with major trade publishers, it's a long-standing practice to grant them control of reprint rights. However, in some cases, a small-press deal for instance, we withhold these rights." Traditionally, if a hardcover book sold really well, paperback houses bought the rights to reprint the book in a more affordable version. Any money earned from the paperback was then split fifty-fifty between the publisher and writer. Paperback houses often paid substantial amounts of money for these reprint rights.

But the recent consolidation of publishing houses has changed the value of reprint rights. "In the old days," explains Maass, "most books were hardcover, and paperbacks were cheap versions of the book. Today, so many paperback publishers have either merged with hardcover publishers or begun their own hardcover publishers that the business of selling reprint rights has diminished." Now, many publishers make what is called a "hard/soft deal," meaning the house will first print the book in hardcover and, if the book sells well, reprint the book in paperback. This type of deal can still benefit writers because they no longer have to split the money earned from reprint with the publisher. Instead, they earn royalties from both the hardcover and paperback versions.

Book Club Rights

These days it seems that a book club exists for every possible interest. There are the traditional book clubs, like Book-of-the-Month and its paperback counterpart, the Quality Paperback Book Club. But there are also mystery book clubs, New Age book clubs, book clubs for writers and artists, and even online book clubs. And many major publishers, like Scholastic or Doubleday, have their own book clubs. Most book clubs are very selective, and you should be flattered if your book is chosen for a book club. Like reprint rights, any money made from book club rights is split fifty-fifty between the publisher and the writer. If an agent believes a book will appeal to a certain book club's audience, she will target the manuscript to publishers who have good relationships with—or who own—that book club.

Serial Rights

A serial is an excerpt of the book that appears in a magazine or in another book. To have your book serialized is wonderful because excerpts not only make additional money for you, but they also provide wonderful publicity for your book. There are actually two types of serial rights: first serial and second serial. First serial means the excerpt of the book is available *before* the book is printed. A second serial is an excerpt that appears *after* the book is already in bookstores. First serial rights are actually negotiable—sometimes the right to use them is kept by the agent. Usually an agent's decision is based upon her knowledge of the publications available in the book's subject. If she doesn't know the various magazines that focus on the book's topic, she will let the publisher have this right. Second serial rights, however, are almost always granted to the publisher.

Nonfiction books are more commonly excerpted than fiction. Nonfiction usually stands alone well, and magazines are always eager to use these excerpts because they usually cost less than hiring a freelancer to write original material. Recently, though, serialized fiction has regained popularity. John Grisham's *A Painted House* (Doubleday) made a giant splash by appearing, in six installments, in *The Oxford American*. According to Marc Smirnoff, editor of *The Oxford American*, response to Grisham's story has been "overwhelming. I've heard from several people who think it is the best writing John has done. John wanted to challenge himself, and we're always looking for exciting work to publish." Grisham's success will certainly create opportunities for other writers who want to have their novels serialized.

Rights Negotiated Between the Agent and Publisher

The owner of these sub-rights is always determined when the book is sold. Often an agent and editor must compromise for these rights. In other words, an agent may agree to sell foreign rights if she can keep electronic rights. Or, an editor will offer more money if he can obtain the audio rights to a book.

Foreign Language Rights

If your book might appeal to audiences in a non-English-speaking country, then you'll want an agent who has good connections with foreign co-agents. According to agent James Vines of The Vines Agency, Inc., a "foreign co-agent is someone who specializes in the sales of foreign publishing rights and who has good relationships with the heads of publishing houses throughout the world. These agents work on behalf of a New York City agency and approach the foreign publishers with manuscripts and proposals. They will typically have appointments booked at big trade shows like Frankfurt, London Book Fair, and BEA. That's where a lot of the big foreign deals happen." Usually an agent charges a 20 percent commission when a foreign co-agent is used, and the two split the earnings.

"All of my clients have benefited from the sale of foreign rights," continues Vines. For example, "*Kokology*, by Tadahiko Nagao and Isamu Saito, started as a big phenomenon in Japan, selling over four million copies there. Kokology is a game you play about psychology, it's one of those ideas that crosses all languages and cultural boundaries because it's uniquely human—we all want to know more about ourselves." Vines sold the book to Simon & Schuster, then worked with a co-agent to sell it all over the world.

When agents are considering how a book will do abroad, they must be aware of trends in other countries. "Most agents try to stay on top of the foreign markets as much as possible and listen to what foreign co-agents have to say," says Vines. "Trends vary from territory to territory, and I try to keep those trends in mind. For example, in the United Kingdom the Bridget Jones phenomenon is still in full swing. In Germany, historical novels are popular." Vines also points out that writers can benefit from different sub-rights over a period of time depending on how well a sub-right is selling. "Three or four years ago we were selling more film rights than we are now—studios are not as hungry as they were. Interestingly, as their interest tapered off, the foreign interest increased."

Many publishing houses have foreign counterparts, and often an agent will grant the publisher these rights if she knows the book can be printed by one of these foreign houses. If the publisher has foreign language rights, the author receives an average of 75 percent of any money made when the book is sold to a foreign publisher—minus the agent's commission, of course.

British Rights

Like foreign language rights, the owner of a book's British rights can sell the book to publishers in England. Australia was once included in these rights, but Australian publishers are becoming more independent. If an agent keeps these rights, she will use a co-agent in England and the two will likely split a 20 percent commission. If a publisher has these rights, the traditional split is eighty-twenty with the author receiving the larger share.

Electronic Rights

Recently Stephen King caused a big commotion in the publishing world first by using an electronic publisher (Scribner) for his book *Riding the Bullet* and then by using the Internet to self-publish his serialized novel, *The Plant*. Many publishing professionals worried that King would start a trend drawing writers away from publishers, while others claimed only high-profile writers like King could ever compete successfully against the vast amounts of information on the Web. Regardless, King's achievement showed that readers are paying attention to the Internet.

Basically, electronic rights refer to the handheld electronic, Internet, and Print-on-Demand versions of a book. This right is currently one of the hottest points of contention between agents and publishers because the potential for these rights is unknown—it is quite possible that electronic versions of a book will make a lot of money one day.

This area of publishing is changing so rapidly that both agents and editors struggle with how to handle electronic rights. Many publishers believe any version of a book is the same material as the printed book, and, therefore, they should own the rights. Agents worry, however, that if the publisher lets the book go out of print, the rights to the book will never be returned to the author.

Audio Rights

Before people feared that the Internet would cause the end of traditional book publishing, people worried that audio versions of books would erase the need to have printed books. In actuality, audio books have complemented their printed counterparts and have proven to be a fantastic source of additional income for the person who owns the rights to produce the book in audio form—whether through cassette tape or compact disc.

Many publishers own audio imprints and even audio book clubs, and if they are successful with these ventures, an agent will likely grant the audio rights to the publisher. The traditional split is fifty-fifty. Otherwise, the agent will try to save this right and sell it to a company that can turn it into a profit.

Rights the Writer Always Keeps

When a book is sold, an agent always reserves two rights for his authors: performance and merchandising. Some books are naturally more conducive to being made into films or products. And when those subrights are exploited, there is usually a lot of money to be made. And a smart agent can quickly identify when a book will be successful in these areas.

Performance Rights

Many writers fantasize about seeing their books on the big screen. And a lot of times, agents share this dream—especially for best-selling titles. If your agent feels your book will work well as a movie, or even as a television show or video game, she will sell these rights to someone in the entertainment industry. This industry works fairly differently than the publishing industry. Usually a producer "options" the right to make your book into a movie. An option means the producer can make the movie only during a specific amount of time, like a year. If the movie isn't made during that time period, the rights revert back to you. You can actually option these rights over and over—making money for every option—without the book ever being made into a movie. Keep in mind, however, that once your book has been optioned, you'll likely lose any say over issues of creative control until the option expires.

As with foreign rights, an agent usually works with another agent to sell performance rights. Usually these agents live in Los Angeles and have the connections to producers that agents outside California just don't have. A 20 percent commission is the norm for performance rights, and the money is split between the two agents who partnered to sell these rights.

Commercial/Merchandising Rights

Merchandising rights create products—like calendars, cards, action figures, stickers, dolls, and so on—that are based on characters or other elements of your book. Few books transfer well into such products, but they can be successful when they do. Keep in mind that if a producer options the performance rights to your book, the merchandising rights are usually included in the deal.

Agent Steven Malk, of Writers House, made wonderful use of these two rights for his client Elise Primavera and her book *Auntie Claus* (Silver Whistle/Harcourt). According to Malk, "When I first read the manuscript of *Auntie Claus* and saw a couple of Primavera's sample illustrations, I immediately knew the book had a lot of possibilities in the sub-rights realm. First of all, the character of Auntie Claus is extremely memorable and unique, and, from a visual standpoint, she's stunning. Also, the basic concept of the book is completely fresh and original, which is very hard to accomplish with a Christmas book.

"The first thing I did was to approach Saks Fifth Avenue with the idea of featuring *Auntie Claus* in the stores' Christmas windows. In addition to using the book as the theme for window displays, the retailer created some merchandise that was sold through Saks. It's a perfect project for Saks stores; the character of Auntie Claus is so sophisticated and refined, she seemed ideal for their windows.

"Shortly after that, the movie rights were optioned by Nickelodeon with Wendy Finerman attached as a producer—she produced *Forrest Gump* and *Stepmom*. Nickelodeon is currently developing the project, and, when it's released, more merchandise will likely follow."

Like Malk did for Primavera, many agents successfully exploit subsidiary rights every day. If you want the most for your book, look for an agent who has the know-how and connections to take your publishing dream beyond the book and to its fullest potential. And use the information in this article to help your agent make the most of your subsidiary rights.

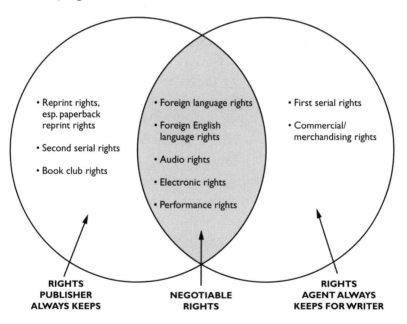

CHAPTER 15

How Will My Publisher Promote My Book—and How Can I Help?

Good publicity can turn a just-published book with good reviews into a best-seller or give new life to an already published title. As many of the agents and editors we've talked with have already said, the publicity and promotion a book gets is just as important as what's between its covers. Today, authors are called upon to take a larger role than ever in a publisher's marketing and publicity efforts—and increasingly, to supplement those efforts with their own.

In this chapter, you'll get some helpful tips for getting exposure for your book in bookstores, in your community, and online. Author Patricia L. Fry offers advice for conquering your shyness and getting the word out about your writing. And Fauzia Burke, president of FSB Associates, an Internet marketing firm that promotes authors' work online, discusses why publishers hire her to publicize their new books and what writers can do to help.

 ## Speak Up for Your Writing!
BY PATRICIA L. FRY

As a serious writer, you probably emerge from your office each day only long enough to raid the refrigerator and check the mail. But, there's another good reason to leave your inner sanctum—to promote what you write. No matter how distasteful the idea of marketing seems, if you want someone to read your book, you have to put it before the public eye.

There's more to selling books than placing them in the megabookstores and sending out a few review copies, which is often the extent of your publisher's promotional efforts. "If I had to guess, I would say that better than half of all books published are never promoted beyond a catalog listing," says Richard F.X. O'Connor, an executive editor at Renaissance Books and the author of *How to Market You & Your Book* (Coeur de Lion Books).

What sells books? Exposure. Who is most qualified to give your book adequate exposure? You. Think about it: No one knows your book like you do, and no one else cares as much about its future. Sure, the concept of marketing and promotion can be daunting to someone who just wants to write. Start your promotional journey by doing something else that comes naturally—talking.

Talk about your book everywhere you go. I've sold books to beauty shop patrons, grocery store clerks, the receptionist at my veterinarian's office, neighbors, members of my civic organizations, and people I met on the Internet. More than once, while giving directions to tourists in my hometown, I also sold them copies of my local history book. Do book signings. Schedule speaking engagements. Get booked on radio and TV shows. When I suggest this to my clients, they often say, "Whoa, I'm a writer, not a speaker."

If you shudder at the thought of standing before an audience, but you want to sell more copies of your book, it will behoove you to hone your speaking skills.

Master Your Fear

If you resist getting up in front of people even when you have the opportunity to talk about your book, you probably lack confidence in your abilities. The best way to gain confidence is to improve.

• Have someone videotape you speaking for fifteen minutes. Watch the tape, and note each area where you need improvement. Maybe you speak too softly, tend to mumble, or avoid making eye contact or using gestures. Once you've isolated the problems, practice correcting them in your everyday communication.

• Seek out role models or mentors to help you become a more confident and effective speaker.

• Improve the quality of your speaking voice. "Breathing is the biggest factor in giving the best voice possible," says voice coach Susan Colla. "We tend to hold our breath, and, when we try to speak, we feel strangled and tight." She recommends a simple exercise: Recite the ABCs in a singsong manner holding the sound and the breath as long as you can. "This and other similar exercises will encourage better breathing awareness," she says. "It teaches us to breathe into our sounds more while speaking rather than trying to squeeze our sound out through a tight throat."

To experience proper breathing, lie down and notice how the abdominal muscles help with each breath. When we stand up, many of us tend to take more shallow breaths and this can, as Colla points out, affect the quality of our voices.

• Speaking in monotone is another common habit. To encourage vocal variety, practice reading to a small child. Exaggerate your voice, using your highest and lowest pitches.

Watch Your Language

Many of us use nonwords like *uh*, *er*, and *uhm* when speaking. Listen for these filler words in your everyday speech, and eliminate them. Avoid overusing words and phrases such as *you know*, *clearly*, *know what I'm saying?*, and *yadayadayada*.

Be Prepared

The best way to calm those speaking butterflies is to be prepared. Plan your speech well in advance of the event and then practice. Write out your speech, create an outline, or jot down some notes—it doesn't matter. Just don't try to cover too many points in one talk, and don't withhold good information. For example, Mary Embree, author of *The Author's Toolkit* (Seaview), uses her table of contents as her outline.

Another method of squelching jittery nerves is to know what to expect. Find out ahead of time about the size of the room and the availability of a microphone, podium, and overhead projector. Ask how many people are expected, the time allotment for your talk, who will publicize the event, and how far reaching this publicity will be. Volunteer to help with publicity.

Find the Right Venue

Who wants to hear you speak? Bookstores love having new authors talk about their books. Civic organizations always are looking for interesting programs. Also contact clubs, associations, and specialty stores related to your topic.

I sometimes speak to visiting Elderhostel groups about grandparenting, and I always sell copies of my book *Creative Grandparenting Across the Miles* (Liguori). Some authors attract sales through demonstrations. Teddy Colbert visits nurseries throughout the state and demonstrates how to make succulent and fresh flower wreaths. Folks clamor to buy copies of her book, *The Living Wreath* (Gibbs Smith).

Debbie Puente has sold more than sixty thousand copies of her book, *Elegantly Easy Crème Brûlée & Other Custard Desserts* (Renaissance Books). Her most successful sales tool is the demonstration. She has whipped up her famous crème brûlée at Williams-Sonoma stores and bookstores throughout the United States, as well as on the sets of the Howie Mandel and Martin Short shows.

Promote Without the Hype

When you have the opportunity to talk about your book, avoid giving a sales pitch. Your goal should be to pass along information in an entertaining way. Focus on educating the audience, helping them overcome a problem, or teaching them a new skill. If members of the audience benefit from your presentation on how to take better vacation pictures, for example, they will most likely purchase your book featuring photography for the shutter impaired.

The idea of public speaking may not appeal to you. As an author, however, good speaking skills may be one of the most effective tools you can use in promoting your self-published and traditionally published books. Remember, two of your greatest marketing assets are your knowledge about your project and your enthusiasm for your book.

Patricia L. Fry is the author of *Over 75 Good Ideas for Promoting Your Book* and *A Writer's Guide to Magazine Articles for Book Promotion and Profit* (both Matilija Press). For more information, see www.matilijapress.com.

An Interview With Fauzia Burke, President and Founder of FSB Associates

Fauzia Burke had years of experience in book marketing and publicity, working at publishers such as Henry Holt and Company, John Wiley & Sons, and Springer-Verlag. But in 1995, sensing the promise of the emerging online marketplace, she opened her own marketing and publicity agency specializing in promoting books over the Internet. Today, FSB Associates has hundreds of successful Internet campaigns under its belt, including promotion for the best-selling books *The Corrections* by Jonathan Franzen, *A Man in Full* by Tom Wolfe (both published by Farrar, Straus and Giroux), and *"O" Is for Outlaw* by Sue Grafton (Henry Holt). Fauzia Burke tells what it takes for a publisher to launch a book online—and what authors can do to help their books succeed.

Q It's becoming more important—and more typical—for publishers and writers to enlist the help of marketing and publicity professionals to generate buzz about books. Why is this? Why do publishers call upon a company like yours to supplement their in-house efforts?

A FSB Associates promotes books and authors on the Internet. We have been doing just that since 1995, and those years have given us unparalleled experience in Internet marketing. Some of our clients feel that it is more cost-effective to outsource their Internet marketing to us than to develop those resources in-house. Other clients use our services to supplement their own efforts during particularly busy times, or for books that need specialized attention.

Q **Are you typically hired by the publishing company? By writers? By literary agents?**

A Usually the publishers hire us, but we work closely with the authors. Some agents have used us as consultants to discuss the Internet marketing strategies for their authors.

Q **Let's talk about exactly what a marketing or publicity firm will do to promote and market a book.**

A FSB specializes in promoting books on the Internet—through on-line marketing campaigns as well as Web site development. We promote the books through author chats, e-mail/phone interviews, book reviews, excerpt placements, newsgroups and mailing list postings, sending e-kits and e-releases, and working with online booksellers. We also develop Web sites for authors (such as Jonathan Franzen, www.jonathanfranzen.com; Scott Turow, www.scottturow.com; Gail Godwin, www.gailgodwin.com; William Steig, www.williamsteig.com; Sue Grafton, www.suegrafton.com) as well as for individual titles (including Farrar, Straus and Giroux's *We Were There, Too!* by Phillip Hoose, www.weweretheretoo.com; *A Density of Souls* by Christopher Rice, www.densityofsouls.com; *In Harm's Way* by Doug Stanton, www.ussindianapolisinharmsway.com).

Q **Perhaps we could talk about some examples from recent campaigns.**

A Of course. Two campaigns that I'd like to point to are those for *In Harm's Way* (Henry Holt) by Doug Stanton and *A Density of Souls* (Hyperion) by Christopher Rice. Both made *The New York Times* best-seller list, and both are first-time authors.

In Harm's Way is a historical account of the sinking of the USS *Indianapolis* at the end of WWII. We started to work on the book's campaign in January of 2001, and it was published in April of that year. The early buzz and reviews among history sites as well as WWII veterans was imperative in the success of the book. We launched the Web site on March 1, 2001. Both the site and the proactive online promotion started long before the tour and gave the book momentum right from the start, and we continued to work on the book right through Father's Day.

The campaign for Christopher Rice is also an interesting study in the marketing potential of the Internet. *A Density of Souls* was published in September of 2000. We launched the Web site as well as the campaign in June 2000. We created early momentum that went hand in hand with the publisher's successful publicity and advertising campaign. The book hit *The New York Times* best-seller list. The following year we updated the Web site and promoted the paperback, all the while creating early buzz for Rice's new hardcover novel, *The Snow Garden*, which came out in February 2002 from Hyperion.

Q What are some of the differences between promoting fiction and promoting nonfiction? And between established authors and emerging authors?

A Nonfiction is better suited for an Internet promotional campaign because we can target specific audiences. Genre fiction, such as science fiction and mystery, also does well, but general fiction is often a challenge. As for authors, established authors get attention quickly, but the Internet is accepting of new voices as well.

Q How do your efforts complement a publisher's in-house efforts?

A Internet marketing complements all traditional marketing efforts. For example, an ad with the URL of a Web site invites readers to continue learning about the book. It is also important to promote an author tour online, since it can get more people to the actual events. Also, book and news editors are always looking for story ideas online. Books that we have promoted have led to interviews and book reviews with major radio stations, magazines, and newspapers. In fact, last year we saw the synergy in action when Christopher Rice had an interview in *The Advocate* and the readers of the magazine came to *A Density of Souls* Web site in droves. The traffic on the site as well as e-mail messages to Christopher shot up dramatically, with many visitors claiming that they got interested in the book through the story in *The Advocate*, read the excerpt on the Web site, and were now hooked.

Q. Author legwork is important, too. How do you work in conjunction with authors to promote their books? What should all authors know about promoting their books online and about working with or hiring a publicity/marketing professional?

A The Internet is made up of communities. Our specialty is to promote the book to those online communities. Authors can be instrumental in that effort. They should learn about the communities online and get involved—participate in newsgroups, set up a Web site that genuinely provides something of value, and host online events through chats.

The most important advice I can give to authors is to find an online marketing firm that is trusted by colleagues. Just because something *can* be done online does not mean it should be. Renting a cheap e-mail list and sending out a message for thousands of people sounds good in theory but can do more harm than good. Authors should insist that the people who promote them online are representing them well. It is the author's reputation on the line.

Q. Where do we go from here? What's the future of online promotion?

A A: The Internet changes and evolves constantly. As new technologies and broadband connections emerge, we will see more streaming audio and video. We may have more Web casts of actual book events. We see some of that now. But through all the changes and evolutions, the essential elements of a good online strategy will remain the same.

The respect for community is essential on the Internet through all promotional avenues. The Net is the most powerful, cost-effective marketing tool we have. It offers us the ultimate in niche marketing, word-of-mouth promotion, and building author (brand) loyalty. Six years later, I still find the potential phenomenal.

CHAPTER 16

What Can I Expect After My Book Is Published?

Congratulations—your book is complete! You eagerly await the publication date, tell all your friends and family when to expect the book, and clear your schedule in expectation of Oprah's phone call. Is your life about to change? Or are your big dreams of bestsellerdom setting you up for a big disappointment?

After all the hoopla wears off, publication can be a strangely anti-climactic experience for some writers. Sure, your book got some nice reviews, and the sales are looking fine. But this is publication. This is *your book*. Isn't everything supposed to be different now?

In this chapter, publishing insider Betsy Lerner discusses her career move from editor to agent, her own experiences as a writer, and why her extensive editorial background is an asset in guiding her authors through the entire publication process. She'll also talk about how a writer can get realistic about the expectations for a book's publication while working to give that book the best possible chance of succeeding.

 An Interview With Betsy Lerner, Literary Agent With the Gernert Company and Author of *The Forest for the Trees: An Editor's Advice to Writers*

Betsy Lerner holds many titles in the publishing world: writer, editor, and agent—and that's a big advantage to the authors she works with. After receiving an M.F.A. from Columbia University, she worked in the editorial departments at Simon & Schuster, Ballantine, and Houghton

Mifflin, and finally as executive director at Doubleday before becoming an agent with the Gernert Company. But she was always a writer, too; Lerner is a recipient of the Wolfe Poetry Prize and the Academy of American Poets Poetry Prize, and she was named by American PEN as one of three emerging writers in 1987.

Lerner's book, *The Forest for the Trees: An Editor's Advice to Writers* (Riverhead Books), brought the different areas of her life together, offering witty and empathetic advice to help writers finish their books and get them published.

Q One of the most interesting aspects of your book, *The Forest for the Trees*, is the way it allows the writer to glimpse the editorial process from an insider's perspective—starting with the writing and editing process and continuing through to publication and beyond. Do you think the inner workings of the publishing business are still shrouded in mystery for many authors?

A Well, a lot of the writing books out there are not written by publishing insiders. And if they are, like Michael Korda's fantastic book, they're about people who are incredibly famous. While it's fun to read about, most aspiring writers don't feel they're in the same league.

I actually had thought about doing this book for a number of years. It started out as a parody of a book called *No Bad Dogs* by Barbara Woodhouse (Summit), which outlines the personalities of different dogs and their owners. Her theory is that there are no bad dogs, only bad owners. And as I was working with authors, I always thought it was so similar—that the "bad" authors, the nuisance authors, the bothersome authors really just didn't have good editors who helped them understand the process and work the system. As I grew up as an editor, I felt that this was in many ways as important as getting the book well edited.

I had been thinking about this idea, and thinking deeply about writers' personalities for a long time. And I'm not exactly sure what clicked when I sat down to write the proposal and made me actually do it—I think it was because I was pregnant and my hormones were racing. But I definitely had been thinking about it for at least six years before I did anything about it, and before I took the idea seriously.

Q **Now you're working as an agent, but you've got such a strong editorial background—many years spent working as an editor at some of the top publishers in New York. In addition, you're a writer and a poet yourself. This inside knowledge of all three roles in the publishing process—editor, agent, and writer—must be a real advantage for you and your clients.**

A Definitely. I'm very glad that I had as much editorial experience as I did before I started writing, and I'm glad I had as much editing experience as I did before I became an agent. These roles do work hand in hand.

Though I am jealous of people who are purely one thing. A lot of people say that they wish they could do all the different things that I do, but in some ways I feel that it would be nice to be purely a writer—to have that kind of drive and that kind of ability. But I don't have that. And while I think I could have just stayed an editor, I became frustrated about the way publishing worked. So it became more appealing for me to be an agent, where I had freer reign.

But all roles are interdependent on each other. And ultimately, we're all really dependent on the writer. Without books, without the material, there would be nothing to sell and nothing to publish. So the writer comes first—though sometimes I think that often writers feel they come last. And they do sort of come last, I suppose, until deemed "worthy" by the publishing system. But the writers really are the most important in the mix.

Q **Let's talk about what drew you to agenting after so many years as an editor. As you discuss in your book, you were part of a larger trend—a mass exodus in the 1990s of editors becoming agents. Is this because agents are doing more and more actual editorial work with their clients these days?**

A I think there are some agents who do tremendous editorial work. And some editors who do tremendous editorial work. But the real difference is when you're an editor working for a large publisher, you really aren't authorized to give anybody an advance; you always have to get the approval of either a committee or a publisher. You always have to get permission; you have a lot of responsibility, but you don't actually have the authority. But when you're an agent, a client chooses to come with you and you choose to work with a client. I am my own boss on that front. Now, I may not be able to sell the book, or I may sell it very well. But for me, having that freedom was what drew me to agenting.

And then, on another note: As an editor, sometimes you'll work for a publisher, and you'll have been working with an author there for years. Then that publisher doesn't want to continue with the author because he's not being lucrative, or his next project the publisher doesn't like as much, or whatever. Again, you don't have the power to keep that author. But as an agent, you can continue working with writers for their entire lives, even if they have to move publisher to publisher. The two things I most craved when working with writers were autonomy and longevity. Being an agent really gave me both.

Q **You're one of the few writing instructors who focus on what happens *after* the writing and publication of the book is complete. You discuss the great expectations many writers have about Publication Day and the almost inevitable disappointment when authors find that publication does not, in fact, usually change their lives in earth-shattering ways. How can writers prepare themselves realistically for publication?**

A There's a lot that writers can do, but the first thing is really getting realistic. If your publisher paid a modest advance for your book, the company is not sending you anywhere to promote it, and there's no ad money or anything like that, you have to understand that your book will have to make it on the strength of reviews. Now, if you're not satisfied with that and that alone, you have to ask yourself what you are willing to do. Are you willing to pack your car trunk with books, and create flyers, and knock on every door, and talk with every person at every Web site? Are you willing to speak about your book at sites other than bookstores—churches, synagogues, YMCAs? What are you willing to do? How much elbow grease are you willing to put into this venture? Some people have gone on to best-seller lists promoting books on their own.

Q So there are things that writers can do after a book is out, besides hope and pray and start the next book?

A Definitely—but it's a full-time job. Ask yourself how much work you're willing to put into it. You can't expect the publisher to publish your book and all you have to do is just sit back and reap the rewards. That happens to maybe a half a dozen books a year. So if you're not one of the chosen, how are you going to do that?

Q Is this disappointment particularly keen with first-time writers? What should they be thinking about as they prepare for publication?

A I know a lot of writers who expect to be "made" on their first books. And they're just devastated when that doesn't happen—when they don't get a National Book Award, when the book doesn't sell particularly well, when the publisher decides not to do the paperback. But you have to again be realistic. How many careers were built on one book? Very few.

Do you want to have your career as a writer? If so, what sacrifices are you going to make? Because you will have to make some. How will you supplement your income? Are you going to write fiction or nonfiction? What sort of career trajectory would you like to have? Now, you can't always plan for those things—books grow in organic ways— but those are all really big decisions. How much time are you going to give it? Some people give it a certain amount of time and then move on. Other people just can't quit.

Q What should writers be doing themselves to promote and publicize their books?

A I think writers can do a lot of guerilla marketing on behalf of their own books, especially if they're nonfiction. The more creative you want to be and the more willing you are to do the legwork, the more likely you're going to meet with some success.

Some authors set aside some of their advance money and hire a freelance publicist. That can cost between $3,000 and $30,000. And if you have the money, it's well worth it. You have to get a good one, you have to know what her plan is, and you have to feel positive about what she's going to do for you. Because publicity is like wind—it's very hard to quantify. But publicity is the best way to sell books. If you have the money, and certainly if you get a big advance, you should set aside money for that. It's a good investment.

Q I know that editors themselves take a large role in-house, too, to generate publicity and interest in a book among the sales force, the marketing department, the designers—before a book is even published.

A I always remember an editor saying to me, "I can't believe we have to sell our own books to our own sales force," and hearing his despair in that. And I thought, *You know, welcome to the real world.* There are sixty to eighty books in a large house's catalog. How many are the reps going to truly read? How many is any one rep going to truly focus on? So, an editor gets creative to make her author's books stand out. Perhaps instead of getting to all the reps, she gets to three key reps. Maybe an excerpt to those reps, with a special personal letter.

You know, the personal touch just works all the way through in publishing. The selling system is still very personal. One sales rep goes to one bookstore buyer and pitches the book, and that person makes the decision about whether the book is in Barnes & Noble. And it's completely based on gut, on feeling, on relationships—and yes, on sales track records. It's a combination of those things. It's still handled very personally.

There's a lesson in this to all writers: Jacqueline Susann used to write thank-you notes and birthday cards to every bookseller in America. And that to me is a reminder to *any* author who wants to be promoted. She cared about them. She knew they were her bread and butter.

Q Is there such a thing as "bad buzz" about a book?

A There's no bad publicity. I worked a long time ago in the theater with Charles Ludlum, and he always said, "The only bad publicity is no publicity." This recent Oprah vs. Jonathan Franzen dustup is totally brilliant—just *try* to get that kind of publicity on most books! It's not easy. And that really sells books.

I have three authors who have really made a living being the target of attack. And they've learned to live with it; they kind of see it as their role now. Deep down they'd probably still love to be loved . . . but they sell.

Q You're a big believer of writers building a "community" for themselves, such as writing groups or writing conferences—a support system of fellow writers who will offer advice, help, and encouragement. I'm sure this, too, can be a help when a writer is going through the publication process. How can writers find such a community?

A If you live in any decent-sized city, it's pretty easy. You can go to your local library, or the Y—anything to put together a writers group. Writers need feedback—a place where people are expecting you to show up, and show up with a few more pages than you had the week before.

You can also try to find a mentor by writing to a famous writer. Sometimes that has panned out for people. There's a fantastic set of letters in Flannery O'Connor's book *The Habit of Being* (Farrar, Straus and Giroux) in which she corresponded with a fan whom she eventually tutored. That can happen.

You go to a lot of readings. You buy books, you buy literary magazines. There are so many people who send their stories in to literary magazines that the writers have never owned. I think that's terrible. I think you should read the magazines you submit to, and you should subscribe to them and support them. You just get in the world of it.

Q Are workshops and retreats helpful to working writers?

A It all depends. Some people work really well being very closeted.

If that's not you, you need to make an effort to do a retreat like Bread-loaf in the summer, or go to a great summer workshop for a few weeks. I know someone who just got back from Yaddo, and it was a totally eye-opening experience. He'd never seen himself as a writer profession-ally, and everybody there pretty much had a book published already. And all of a sudden he began to see himself in a new light.

You're very "green" in this world when you first want to be a writer. At first it's overwhelming—you don't know whom to talk to or even how to present a manuscript. But the good news is that there are ways of becoming a professional, of getting ready to get yourself into the hands of an agent or a publisher.

Q You're a writer yourself, as well as a professional agent, wife, and mother. How have you been able to balance your own writing with the many aspects of your life?

A Well, I've given up a number of things. Like, I don't have a social life. I don't watch any television. And I often don't go to the gym. When I'm in the midst of writing, like I am now, I just don't do anything else except my job and my writing and my kid. I can't wait to finish my new book so I can just go out again and see people.

It's weird—I always thought writers were so lucky to be writing, that I never imagined them making any real sacrifices. But now that I'm writing again, I realize that if you want to have the time and the focus to write, you simply must make sacrifices. And if it feels like a true sacrifice, you probably don't want to be a writer that much. I'm just coming to the end of the writing process, so I'm ready to reengage again. But for most of the time, I'm much happier being by myself, working, than I am having a dinner party. I think it's sort of a matter of temperament, and will, and drive, all kind of coming together with knowing what it is that you want to do.

PART IV:

Trends in Publishing Today

CHAPTER 17

What Do I Need to Know About E-Publishing?

A ccording to *Entertainment Weekly*, Stephen King generated more than $720,000 in revenue from his six installments of *The Plant* when it was made available exclusively in e-book format in 2000. At the time, expectations were high for the new technology and the predictions were grand—publishing companies and books as we knew them would become obsolete, replaced by e-book readers and instantly downloadable titles on any topic imaginable.

That moment may have been the highpoint of excitement in the emerging e-book technology, at least for a while. As technology stocks tumbled in 2000 and 2001, many e-book companies scaled back or folded entirely, and many large publishing companies put their sweeping e-book publishing programs on hold.

For now, it appears much of the publishing world is taking a "wait and see" approach to e-publishing. But a few of the e-publishing professionals who are forging forward are starting to report some solid successes. In this chapter, you'll hear from two publishing insiders: John F. Baker, editor with *Publishers Weekly*, and Richard Curtis, president of Richard Curtis Associates and the e-book company e-Reads. Both discuss the challenges and opportunities for publishing companies and authors in the e-book arena.

A Mixed Review of E-Publishing: An Interview With *PW*'s John Baker
BY PAULA DEIMLING

When *Publishers Weekly*, the news magazine of book publishing and bookselling, ran its first reviews of electronic books in the summer of

1999, there was only a handful of responses from readers. "A few hailed the fact that we'd moved into the twenty-first century at last, and a few others deplored this thin edge of the wedge to the end of the book as we know it," observed John F. Baker, the magazine's editorial director.

Whether you agree with the former or latter take on e-publishing, or something in between, one thing is certain: E-publishing is something to be aware of in the months and years ahead. It's certainly a dynamically changing front *Publishers Weekly* editors are closely watching. The magazine recently added an e-publishing department to its pages. What started as a monthly department now appears regularly in addition to the latest news on e-publishing and e-book reviews. "That will grow slowly as I expect electronic publishing to grow slowly," Baker says.

A "PW Spotlight" in late 1999 said in part: "Loosely grouped under the rubric 'electronic publishers,' these companies have as their collective mission a better way of distributing books. Some fancy themselves software companies, others prefer to be called content managers, still others like to be known as digital distributors. If their means are different, their ends are, at heart, unified: to disrupt fundamentally the business of book publishing and bookselling—not the writing or editing of books, but everything that happens afterward, or, in New Media speak, the way it is distributed to, and consumed by, the end user."

We asked John Baker for his thoughts on electronic publishing: What impact will e-publishing have on the book publishing industry? How might today's fiction writers be affected? Baker is one of the book industry's most astute observers. The former Reuters News Agency journalist started at *PW* twenty-seven years ago as its managing editor, worked as its editor in chief for ten years, and for the past ten years has been the magazine's editorial director.

Want to know what agent just sold which author's book, and to what publisher, for what terms? Baker's "Hot Deals" column in *PW* is the place. In October 1999, Baker added another facet to his reporting: a twice-weekly e-mail-subscription newsletter, *Rights Alert*, on book, script, and licensing deals. His insight on the publishing world also extends into projects beyond his New York office, such as his 1999 book, *Literary Agents: A Writer's Introduction* (Macmillan).

Here Baker shares his views on the impact so far of e-publishing on traditional book publishing, where he sees the medium going, and what writers should consider before submitting their work to an electronic outlet.

Q Define e-publishing as you see it.

A Any book published in a way other than the traditional printed form. Something that could be read online or played on an e-book reader or could be encrypted in such a way that it could be printed on demand. Those are the three principal approaches to electronic publishing.

Q Is e-publishing a disruption, or is it the cutting edge of what you're going to see in the book publishing industry?

A It's a bit of both, actually. It's certainly the cutting edge in certain ways. I think obviously books that are searchable online are much more easily perused for key passages and key words. In other words, for scholars looking for references, instead of searching endlessly through indexes and so forth, they can search masses of material in seconds, and obviously that's an enormous advance.

In terms of actually getting material from authors to readers, it's a rather mixed bag. There's this machinery that's evolved over the years in effect screening out the publishable and the worthwhile from the enormous amount of material that is simply repetitive, imitative, inadequately expressed, badly written, badly thought out, banal, etc. It seems to me if widespread electronic publishing is going to take off, and authors can simply put anything they like up and hope that somebody will pick it up and read it, all those careful safeguards and screenings are going to go out the window. It would be as if you turned over publishers' slush piles to readers anxious to see what they were missing.

Q Publishers in effect have taken years trying to dissuade authors from sending unsolicited material to them so that it will not hang around in the slush piles.

A The agent community has been enormously built up and increased and grown in power simply because they act as an early line of approval, a screen if you like, through which the better writers' properties and ideas are passed. It's almost as if they're throwing all this away by saying anybody can publish anything anywhere. So from that point of view, it's a pretty chaotic prospect.

The other point of course is: How does anybody get paid? It's all very well to say that authors who publish online can get royalties of 40, 50, or even 60 percent, but of what? How are people paying for this? Are they paying at all? Most of what is read on the Internet these days is not paid for at all. Why are they going to read novels and nonfiction works by authors they've never heard of, who haven't been promoted, edited, or marketed, and pay for the privilege? I don't see it.

Q In your opinion, what impact will e-publishing have on the world of novels and short story collections?

A I can't really foresee it having any enormous impact on fiction at all, to tell you the truth. I could be entirely out of step here. It seems to me that reading fiction in any of the currently available electronic forms is simply inferior to the experience of reading it in the printed form. As I said, the chief virtue of electronic publishing is its extreme searchability, and that simply doesn't really apply to fiction reading. People don't need to search fiction; they just want to keep turning the pages. For nonfiction, for biography, for historical works, for important studies of this and that and the other, for reference works, of course it can certainly revolutionize that, and already has to a large extent.

Q Would there be certain types of novels that might eventually be better suited to e-publishing?

A Some children's works, particularly if they could be made interactive and if the children could interact with the text and make things move in different directions by pressing certain buttons at certain points in the story. The other kind would be, and for the same reasons, science fiction, where obviously you can play with the notions of reality, what's actually in print and what can be imagined on the page. You could play cybergames with science fiction concepts that I think would be interesting. There was an avant-garde novel published by Pantheon in 2000, *House of Leaves*. It lends itself to people who like playing fancifully with the medium, but there aren't a large number of books like that.

Q Will Stephen King's foray into e-publishing lend support and encouragement to other authors who might want to follow this approach?

A King is such a unique case. King has an enormous body of fans, not just readers—he's collectible as well as readable. They'll pick up anything he has written. Very few authors have that kind of following. Because of his subject matter—often with teenage or young heroes becoming involved in horrific situations—he has a much younger and more technologically hip readership than most authors do. Whereas he can do almost anything, the number of popular authors who could command that kind of loyalty isn't very great. I don't think the readers, say, of Mary Higgins Clark and John Grisham are going to dart automatically to reading anything that they write on the Internet.

Q Do you think that e-publishing will in any way affect the way novelists write their books?

A Only in the ways I've suggested. They may seek to make it interactive in various playful and not-so-playful ways, offering people in mysteries, for instance, ways of following up on certain clues or, at certain points in the action, choosing ways in which it might go in different directions, and I think that could be extended to certain kinds of fiction or narrative—science fiction, fantasy, and, in certain cases, mysteries.

I don't see how it would change things in other respects. Basically it's still a matter of putting one word after another; however, the words are read. Another aspect, of course, is at the moment the quality of the images isn't terrific. I think it will be quite a while before anything other than utilitarian illustrations will be an important part of an e-book.

Q. What other developments will authors be seeing on the business side of publishing?

A The electronics rights auction, conducted online, and several bodies, such as rightscenter.com, that exist for the exchange of rights information and rights dealings around the world with thousands of subscribers—that will certainly continue and persist, I would think. And with the new development that electronic signatures are now acceptable, I can visualize the time when book contracts will be sent and signed over the Internet as well. At the moment, people still require paper documents, but I doubt that they will for very much longer. That's an entirely new development.

There hasn't really been enough time to know if most books, published initially as e-books, eventually will be published in printed form. Oddly enough, even people wedded to the medium still prefer to see things in print. For instance, I put out a twice-weekly e-mail newsletter called *Rights Alert* describing those rights deals, and although I can get much more into that because there are no page restrictions and things like that so it can be as long as I like, really, everybody who gets mentioned in the e-mail always wants to say, "Will I get in the print version, too?" I point out to them that there is a lot of wasted readership in the print version whereas the e-mail readership is extremely focused and only people who really need the information are getting it. There's a sense of validation in seeing something in print, I think. That is still lacking in terms of the weight of the authority that e-publication carries. I think things on the Net are rightly or wrongly seen as evanescent. You can erase them at the press of a button, and you may well by accident, and they're gone. You can't do that with anything actually printed. These are people, many of them engaged in forms of electronic publishing anyway, who still want their doings described in print.

Q James Ellroy, author of *L.A. Confidential* (Mysterious Press), and his agent conducted an online auction among e-book publishers for the electronic rights to one of Ellroy's projects, while reserving the print rights for a later time. To your knowledge, how would Ellroy or other authors be compensated for their work?

A There are various ways in which authors are compensated for electronic publishing. In this case, he got an advance and was to get royalties on the use of the material. In any case, he was going to get paid a royalty on the basis of how many people hit upon his work when it appears.

But many electronic publishers don't pay anything. They say we'll run your stuff for free and will pay you on the basis of hits if it's a subscription thing, or some sites are supported by advertising. I think that's probably the most reliable source of support at the moment, and publishers are paid royalties on the basis of the advertising revenue that's generated by the site on which their work appears.

Then there is still of course a handful of electronic publishers who work on the old vanity principle, and actually charge authors to put their work online. They don't charge nearly as much as the old vanity print publishers did, who charged up to $5,000 or even $10,000 to do a very limited run of a small book. I've heard of fees of $250 or even $500 to put something online for an author. At first they [authors] paid more and then they became aware there were a number of sites that weren't charging them anything at all, and even a handful that were paying them small advances, and most of the vanity ones have probably disappeared by now. There's an enormous rate of flux and change among these start-ups. There are a half-dozen start-ups every week and some of them last a few months and most of them have been around eighteen months or, at the most, two years. For an electronic publisher, two years is really old and well-established—something to bear in mind.

The other thing authors should bear in mind is that e-publishers can be quite evanescent. They have been mostly funded by start-up capital by an IPO [Initial Public Offering of stock] or by some backer.

That kind of support is extremely volatile, especially these days. It can disappear and the stock can shoot down very rapidly or the backer can run out of money quite quickly, and off goes your publisher. It's not quite the same as a publisher that has a backlist of thousands of books and a warehouse and premises and a large staff to pay. Those publishers are not about to disappear overnight. They may be swallowed up by another publisher, but they won't actually go out of existence, whereas electronic publishers go out of existence all the time. Of the electronic publishers that have more than, say, two hundred or three hundred titles in their repertoires or inventories, there are very few that would have four figures worth of titles available. They're still building, growing.

Q **For e-publishers who have been in business for two years, are you seeing any patterns in terms of what they're doing right?**

A One of the problems they all have is how to promote the work, how to let people know that it's there. The very well-endowed electronic operations, we've all seen their extensive advertising, they spend literally millions on it. The big ones can afford to do that. The little ones can't, and how they make themselves known and make their authors known other than to a very, very limited readership of faithful cruisers of the Net, who are always looking for new sites and links to publishing or whatever they click on to, it's very difficult to see. How are they going to make known the availability of the various books they're publishing? I think the whole electronic publishing business is going to rise and fall on the basis of how thoroughly the marketing and promotion of the material available is. I think that's probably its weakest link at the moment for most of them anyway, the ones without deep pockets.

Q **For years we've heard how the lack of marketing and promotion can affect a print book, but it's ironic that electronic publishers face this same dilemma.**

A The machinery in place for the promotion of the print book is still infinitely more effective and efficient than anything that has so far come along for the electronic book—to say nothing of the fact that print books depend very heavily on major TV appearances by a handful of important and significant shows, and also some radio, and so electronically published authors have almost no clout at all in those areas. Bookseller co-op advertising; print advertising in newspapers and magazines; television advertising when you can afford it—all of those things electronic publishing lacks at the moment.

Q Do you have any long-term predictions for e-publishing for, say, the next five or ten years?

A Probably the area to have the most impact on authors will be the existing links between book publishers and e-publishing allies, such as bookstore links. E-publishers who don't have such alliances will have a harder time of it.

Q Is there anything you'd like to say further about e-publishing?

A It seems like a very exciting possibility for writers, the way of communicating directly with the author without all the intervening screens of agent, editor, publisher, printer, reviewer, etc. But somebody has to pay the bills in order for the authors to get anything at all out of the experience other than the thrill of seeing their work only rather transitorily in print and not really in a portable way. It's not quite the same thing, pressing a few buttons and seeing your words come up on a screen, as it is having a book you can carry around and show people. And therefore I think if they're aiming to make money on their writing, and get anything out of it other than the thought that a handful of readers may be looking at what they've written on their screens, they ought to look at all the alternatives very carefully. They should find out how and how much they're going to be paid, and what the outermost extremities of their likely revenues will be, and then make their decisions accordingly.

Paula Deimling is a full-time writer and former editor of *Writer's Market*. She is one of the authors of *The Writer's Essential Desk Reference* (Writer's

Digest Books) and has also interviewed Russell Banks, Jane Smiley, and Isaac Asimov.

An Interview With Richard Curtis, President of Richard Curtis Associates, Inc., and Founder of e-Reads

Richard Curtis has worked as an agent, author, and writers' advocate for more than forty years. After starting his career as foreign rights manager at the Scott Meredith Literary Agency, he launched a freelance writing career, publishing more than fifty books with several major houses. In the early 1970s, he began his own literary agency, and today Richard Curtis Associates, Inc., represents more than one hundred authors in a variety of writing genres.

In 1999, his interest in emerging media and technology led Curtis to start the e-publishing company e-Reads. A strong supporter of e-books in the publishing community, Curtis believes that e-books are the perfect tool to keep out-of-print books available, as well as to introduce original titles by new and established authors. He's also the author of *How to Get Your E-Book Published* (Writer's Digest Books).

Q We hear so much conflicting news about e-books—one moment they're the next big thing, the next moment they're merely a folly. What's the state of e-publishing and e-books today?

A It is certainly true that this industry is in a rapid state of flux. As a result of (in my opinion) poor business models, a number of companies that launched in this business at the same time we did have ended up on the rocks—or collapsed completely. Many of those companies started out with millions, in some cases tens of millions, of dollars in investment income. And they have failed, or turned away from their original business plans and gone into something else.

As a result, there's been a lot of negative publicity about the e-book industry in general. And (again, in my opinion) it's been fueled by a desire on the part of many people to see e-books fail. Their reasons may be jealousy, may be competition, may be a desire to see everything "stay the way it is" in publishing.

Q What makes some e-publishers succeed while others struggle?

A My company [e-Reads], I believe, is based on a sound business model. We have made the cut, and we've made the cut on next to no investment (outside of what comes out of my own pocket). I'm not the only company that's showing revenue, if not profit, in the e-book area. But I think it will be a while before authors, agents, and the consumer feel the confidence and security in the e-book industry for it to become as viable of a consumer technology as CDs became after several years.

A lot of people say e-books are another CD-ROM disaster. In the early 1990s, everybody thought CD-ROMs were going to be huge in book publishing, and they turned out to be a bit of a blind alley when the Internet came along as the main source of information for consumers. But we know what the revenues are for e-books—by the end of 2001, e-Reads will have paid out nearly $50,000 in royalties to authors, and the projections for 2002 are much higher. There are a few companies who are doing this right. But it does depend on good business models—whether their overhead and their expenses are so high as to make it doubtful that they will ever recover their money. This is not an issue for my company. People *are* buying e-books. And people are buying e-books to read on their PalmPilots, to read on special e-reading devices. We know that there's a market, but the general perception of the public is that it's a folly, but it's not true.

Q What about the big publishers? Some have entered the e-book business with a roar but exited with a whimper; for example, Random House announced plans in late 2001 to scale back its e-publishing imprint drastically. How do the big publishers fit into the e-publishing picture?

A A number of big publishers, like Random House and Warner, have gone into this business. But what it costs them to produce a title for e-books is prohibitively high, because they have so much overhead compared to smaller companies. If it costs them $1,000 to convert a title to an e-book and they only get $200 in revenue, they're going to stop doing it.

Q **What are the advantages that an e-book can present as opposed to a traditional printed book?**

A There are some obvious advantages, and some that are maybe not so obvious. The first one, and probably the foundation stone of the business, is that there are some books you can't find any other way. Period. Unless you go into specialized used bookstores and are willing to pay a serious price, some out-of-print books are available only in electronic format.

Also, when people think of e-books, they think of an electronic version of the book that's delivered online—and that is the major way that e-books are delivered. However, many companies use the digital files (the same digital files we use to make e-books) to make printed books as well. This allows us to have books printed on demand. And since at the current time the preferred method for reading books is still the printed book, thanks to digital technology people are now able to once again buy printed books (or e-books) that they have not been able to get for years, or decades.

In addition, other advantages to e-books include the portability—the fact that one device can carry many, many books. Students may no longer need backpacks to lug around ten or twenty pounds of books. Also, the fonts can be made larger for those who are sight-impaired. E-books are now being downloaded for the blind; they can be converted easily into audio text that "reads" the titles aloud. These are all people who benefit from e-books.

Q **You've been an agent for many years. What interested you in the e-book arena and led you to pursue this new technology?**

A Because of my interest in science (I have been an agent for science fiction writers for all my career), I have always been interested in technology. I follow trends, not just out of personal interest, but also because many of these technological trends affect writers. So when audio books became big, I was very interested and quick to point out the advantages (and disadvantages) to my authors. Same with CD-ROMs. I knew that a day would come—because science fiction writers had written about it for decades—when you would be able to download a book into a handheld reading device. So I began to prepare for it, and I began to prepare my clients for it.

We started a very aggressive campaign at my agency to recover the rights to out-of-print books. So when the e-reading devices were introduced in late 1998, we had hundreds and hundreds of out-of-print titles that the authors had recovered and were ready, willing, and able to put into an e-book program. I decided at that time that instead of just handling those books as a usual agent and selling them on behalf of the author for the usual commission, there was more money to be made and more trails to be blazed by becoming a publisher for those books. And after working out a model of business that I believed would be commercially successful, and working out some conflict-of-interest issues with my clients (and my own conscience), I started the business.

We had to learn publishing—I actually had very little direct publishing experience. I'm an agent, and most of what I knew about publishing I'd learned from lunches with editors. But it was no detriment to us, because we were kind of starting a new industry based on new technologies that really didn't exist in the twentieth century. So I was able to throw out all prejudices about how it should work and create a new model for business for the twenty-first century.

Q. Electronic rights have proven to be a thorny issue. Several recent court cases have pitted author against publisher (*New York Times v. Tasini*) and publisher against publisher (*Random House v. Rosetta Books*) in a battle to determine who owns electronic rights to a work and what each party is allowed to do with those rights. How can authors protect their e-rights to their work? How do you help them protect those rights?

A Well, you're talking to an agent as well as an e-publisher. As an agent, when I make a deal for an author to a publisher, the chances are that that the publisher will insist—take it or leave it—on purchasing the electronic rights to a book. Until there's a viable independent e-book market, such as there is a viable independent audio book market or a viable independent magazine serial rights market, we don't have any choice. All those other rights are separated now from the ordinary rights you give to a publisher. Any author who wants to publish in the traditional publisher today has got to kiss his electronic rights good-bye.

That's not going to last forever. As time goes on, writers will have the option of selling only print publication rights to a traditional publisher and reserving the electronic rights. Or even more importantly, the e-book publishers will be competitive in every respect to "the majors"—the Random Houses, the Simon & Schusters. There is no capability that a Random House or a Time Warner or a St. Martin's Press has that cannot be duplicated or sometimes exceeded by an e-book publisher. We're now printing mass-market paperbacks in some cases. Except for our size and our financing, there's nothing we cannot do that's being done by the larger publishers.

Q **Are there particular genres or types of books that are best suited to e-publishing? Where have you had the most success?**

A Right now the most responsive areas are science fiction, horror, male-action—which indicates to us that the early users, the so-called early adopters of this technology, are male. However, our next-biggest category is romance, and that is growing very quickly. Mysteries and certain areas of nonfiction are also selling, but only at a fraction of what we're selling in category fiction. But once you've cleared your costs for converting any book, it doesn't matter whether you're selling one or two or three copies; they all contribute to the money flowing into our royalty coffers.

The possibilities for travel books are phenomenal. There's no reason why someday you can't carry an e-book that will tell you where you are in Paris, how to get back to your hotel and what room you're in, and how to get to the Louvre and what exhibit you're seeing.

Q A few big-name authors (Stephen King, for example) have had very successful e-publishing experiences. And some authors, such as M.J. Rose, have parlayed their e-book success into contracts at traditional publishing houses. How can authors who publish e-books successfully promote their books?

A The promotional potential for authors is unlimited. Thanks to digital technology, every author can have a home page that links to his publisher, his agent, fans, user groups, so that all those components can work together in a coordinated effort.

Q Do e-book authors get the same respect as authors who publish with traditional houses? Do e-publishers get that respect?

A All the authors who are published by e-Reads are previously published authors whose books are being reissued online. These are not people who are publishing original books, although we are publishing a few originals. And most of the originals we are publishing are ones we were disappointed not to be able to sell to traditional publishers, so the authors said, "Okay, if I can't sell it to a traditional publisher, I'll sell it myself through your company." So they've got that going for them.

That said, I sometimes feel like I'm living on the moon. I know how much work is being done, money is being spent, effort is being made, and titles are being published in the e-book field. And yet the general perception in the public and the press and the publishing industry is that this is a flash in the pan. I don't know how I can help skeptics to see what I see: that this is a far more viable business than they might think it is.

Q One of the oft-cited advantages of e-books is their "instant" nature—there's no manufacturing time and usually very little cost in preparing e-book files. Have e-books proved useful in getting

information out to the public quickly, such as in the wake of a tragedy like September 11, 2001?

🅰 A number of publishers have done quickie e-books. Some others have discovered that books they already had suddenly became relevant to September 11 and quickly put them out in e-book format or repromoted them in e-book format. It does provide you with an instant way of tying your books into current events. We had a book about the firemen. We not only repromoted it, but we offered to contribute all of the revenue generated for a month after September 11 to charity.

🅀 **What's the future of e-books—where do we go from here?**

🅰 We need to create the same infrastructure for e-books that we have for the rest of the publishing industry. That's going to be very difficult to do, because we don't have yet the same filtering system, the same tastemakers we have in the old book business. We don't have critics and reviewers; we don't have editors and agents who can agree on what is good and what is junk. Anybody can publish his or her book online. How does a bookstore like Barnes & Noble or Amazon know if it's good? What criteria do booksellers use to accept a book for their stores or their sites?

There are other questions: What is a real publisher? Is it a publisher who publishes ten of his friends? Is it an author who publishes himself? Is it a company that publishes two thousand titles but all of them are vanity? These are questions without answers, but we're going to have to create a way to filter books, as we've been filtering them for years, through a network of tastemakers who all pretty much agree what is a good book and what is not.

I have faith that the same thing is going to happen with e-books as happened with other areas of the industry: Nobody knows what it is, and suddenly everybody knows what it is. Nobody's buying it, and then suddenly everybody is not only buying it but is completely comfortable with it. That happened with CD-ROMs, and it will happen with e-books.

CHAPTER 18

Do All the Mergers in Publishing Mean It's Harder for Me to Get Published?

You've probably heard a lot in the last few years about the seismic shifts in the publishing world: huge publishers merging into even larger megacompanies, editors hopping from one house to another. Or maybe you haven't really been paying attention: *Mergers and conglomerates—ugh. I became a writer so I wouldn't have to deal with this stuff. That's what my agent is for, right?*

Well, yes . . . all good agents are on top of these changes: They know which editor is at what house and what shifts are taking place within the business. But, as agents Mary Evans and Virginia Barber explain, the ever-changing face of corporate publishing has a very real impact on writers, too. Understanding what's going on in the business is an important step toward becoming a part of the business. In this chapter, you'll find a primer for the changes occurring daily in the publishing industry—and learn how these changes affect you.

 ## The Conglomeratization of Publishing: Two Agents Give Their Two Cents
BY DEBORAH WAY

It was a deal worthy of the Richter scale—if not The Big One, at least the biggest one yet: Random House (home of Crown, Ballantine,

Fawcett, Knopf, et al.) sold to German media heavyweight Bertelsmann for a reported $1.4 billion in 1998. When plans for the sale were announced, agents and editors reeled. Random already topped the charts in U.S. trade book publishing, and à la Bertelsmann would now expand to include the conglomerate's existing megahouse, Bantam Doubleday Dell. In terms of sheer magnitude, nothing—not even the 1996 merger that led to Penguin Putnam—had ever come close.

The deal solidified what industry watchers had known for some time: The industry is consolidating. And as the ranks of independent houses shrink, many agents are worried about the fate of smaller books in a corporate culture that seems to think bigger is better, and about the diversity of who and what gets published.

For an insider view on the effects of conglomeratization, I spoke with veteran New York agents Mary Evans of Mary Evans Inc., and Virginia Barber of Virginia Barber Literary Agency, Inc. Evans's clients include Michael Chabon, Robert Ferrigno, and Abraham Verghese. Barber, who has served several times as a board member of the AAR and was its president when the Random House deal took place, represents, among others, Peter Mayle, Anne Rivers Siddons, and Alice Munro.

Q What do you see as the conglomeratization's impact on the kind of books that do get published?

Evans: I think there's going to be less diversity. And even more of a search for the book that's easy to market, the book that brings in the big numbers. But to me, the really significant change with conglomeratization is the consolidation of hardcover and paperback deals. When I started in publishing in the middle 1970s, most books were initially sold hardcover only—which meant that what was in the book mattered. If the author did a good job, there could be excitement. There could be buzz. You could go around and auction paperback rights to a bevy of paperback houses, all of whom would bid against each other. For example, when *Ragtime* was sold in hardcover—to Random House, I believe—it was bought for a low advance because no one had any idea of what the book would become. Then when Doctorow wrote the brilliant novel he wrote, everyone could respond; I believe it sold for a million dollars in paperback to Bantam.

But today, since so many houses have paperback arms, almost all books are sold hard and soft simultaneously—often on just the basis of a proposal. And if you buy a first novel for half a million dollars, your paperback arm is really going to push the book no matter if the writing turns out to be good, bad, or indifferent. Meanwhile, the paperback editors' slots are so full, they don't have room to discover the wonderful book that missed out on a really big deal. There are, of course, exceptions. Places like Norton and Grove don't have paperback arms, so something like Charles Frazier's *Cold Mountain* could have an early preempt by Vintage. And that caused some excitement; it helped the industry notice that book. But sadly, it's a rare occurrence.

Barber: It's more difficult to find publishers for serious books, unless the topic has very broad appeal or the author already has a good readership. I fear that with some publishers, "What does the public want?" is becoming a guideline much as it has with Hollywood studios. It's fine to know the tastes of your generation, but to publish only what is known and expected stifles us, and doesn't work for very long.

Q Beyond altering the conditions in which manuscripts are sold, does conglomeratization affect writers' writing?

Evans: Writers see that their chances are better if they can write *about* something. The question today is which type of book is going to further an editor's career, and if a book doesn't do the cancan plotwise, it's very hard. You know, an editor would rather buy Caleb Carr's *The Alienist* (Random House) than a tender coming-of-age novel, however brilliantly written it might be. We've become a plot-oriented, an *Is this a movie?*–oriented culture. I think we're going to lose a lot of good writers.

Barber: Publishers are becoming impatient with late books and even canceling contracts they would formerly have extended. They want their money back, too, even if the author has spent it financing his research and supplying his kitchen. Everybody knows authors are notoriously optimistic when it comes to due dates, but it takes a Morgan Entrekin (of Grove/Atlantic) to wait—how many years was it?—for Gary Kinder's *Ship of Gold in the Deep Blue Sea.* Simon & Schuster would have canceled the contract, no doubt.

Publishers also become impatient waiting for authors' sales to grow. We used to have publishers stay with authors they thought highly of, through one small book after another until the author "hit." Now they bow out. Of course, that's not only their fault. The bookstores will buy only as much by the author as they actually sold the last time around, making it difficult to increase the author's sales.

Q Does your job as an agent change as the number of independent houses decreases?

Evans: It's harder to justify a literary novel that you hope might sell seven thousand copies when you're competing against agents who have first novels written by movie stars. I would be willing to sell a literary novel for $10,000, but the houses just aren't interested.

You try to figure out anything—besides the book being really good—that will catch the publishers' attention. You don't give up. I had a first novel I thought was brilliant yet needed work. When the major houses wouldn't take it, I ended up selling it for less than I usually sell a magazine article for. In a sense, I lost money; there was no way my commission even paid the photocopy bill. But I believe in the book, and I believe that when edited, it will find its audience and perhaps be one of those Norton or Grove/Atlantic paperback successes.

It's important to pick your causes. I sold a literary first novel—Michael Blaine's *White Outs,* [published as *The Desperate Season*] to Rob Weisbach Books—for into six figures, but it was the first first-novel I'd taken on in almost two years.

Barber: Agents have always understood that their favorite manuscripts may be big yawns to some editors. We try to match a manuscript to the right editor and house, but that requires a wide variety of tastes and interests. We need many places to try, many editors to approach. If Bertelsmann keeps all the imprints it has acquired independent, alive, and well, then perhaps we won't suffer so much. But it can't do that forever, anymore than Harper and Row remained so with Lippincott as part of the same house. Row and Lippincott are gone, along with many other publishers that were bought and eventually "disappeared" by the new owners.

Q. Does conglomeratization work against certain nonfiction books—books whose publication might entail stepping on someone's or something's toes? In other words, by complicating corporate affiliations and allegiances, do mergers and acquisitions undermine a house's ability to publish disinterestedly?

Barber: I don't think a book about the effects of DDT on bird eggs would immediately attract conglomerates, but such a book—Rachel Carson's *Silent Spring* (Houghton Mifflin)—turned out to be a classic. It's more difficult to publish controversial books now. Not only do big conglomerates have many special interests, but they also tend to feel more comfortable sitting in the middle of the road. They're looking for the safest subjects, the biggest authors, and the fattest profits.

Evans: I don't think it's so much a question of stepping on someone's toes. The issue with nonfiction books is the increasing insistence on, "What is this author's platform?"—platform meaning radio show, infomercial, Web site, self-published book. It doesn't seem to be enough these days to write a good book and have some credentials. Authors need some sort of media-related connection for the houses that are part of conglomerates to get excited. There is no level playing field anymore.

Q. Where do readers fit in? If there is a market for the kind of books that even now seem threatened, won't that market eventually even out?

Evans: To some degree, but something else has happened in our culture. Reading as a form of recreation has definitely been downsized. When I was growing up, television was the big competition. When my mother was growing up, it was movies and radio. Now we have a multitude of diversions, and books just aren't as important.

Also, it's harder for people to know which books are really good. I grew up in the Midwest, and every week to my parents' home came the *Saturday Review of Literature, Commonweal, The New Yorker,* the Sunday *New York Times*—and back then, I think there was much more of a consensus as to which writers were the ones to notice. Now, much of what's called literature is dependent on marketing. I've seen really wretched writers being marketed as "literary." And people buy it.

The other point about book reviews is that newspapers are struggling with readership, too, and if they need to make budget cuts, guess what's going to go first? Not television or movies; the papers would lose the big ads from the studios. So it's not surprising if readers aren't particularly well informed. They go for the books that have the marketing muscle, the books the marketing people call literature, when anyone with any sort of education or discerning eye would know otherwise.

Barber: How will the readers find us with a small-press publication? True, miracles happen. I love the success of Soho Press with Edwidge Danticat. I have a writer published by a small press who got a rave front-page *Los Angeles Times* review and is being reviewed in *People* next week. I'm grateful the small publisher accepted the manuscript. The large ones rejected it. But how will anybody find the book? There are very few copies in only a few stores.

Q What about the contention that merging the business aspects of publishing frees up more resources to devote to writers?

Evans: I would like to think that—if I put on my Pollyanna cap. But I just can't see the heads of these big conglomerates saying, "We want to give more money to writers, so let's lay off half the sales force!" Weirdly, conglomerates have been overpaying for some books for years, but I don't think they're going to overpay even more. They're going to cut and consolidate, because it helps the bottom line and improves their stock and their bonuses.

Barber: Merging the back offices seems to free up resources to steal successful authors from smaller publishers. The gap between the top authors and the smallest ones grows as rapidly as the gap between the rich and the poor in this country. It's nearly obscene. How can we compete a $5,000 offer versus a $10 million offer to a top author? Yet the $5,000 author could someday grow into a big one, if there are publishers willing to keep trying.

Q. Where and how do you see your predictions already playing out? Can you point to specific changes?

Barber: One big change with merging is meetings, meetings, and more meetings. Several levels of management. More people to be ignorant of what actually is happening in the trenches. More and more callbacks required. We rarely reach an editor on our first try. They're in meetings. Then they have trouble reaching us because we're fielding ten callbacks from editors we left messages for. Telephone tag ensues. I wonder how much time is lost in those games.

Evans: Even though at this point I believe Random House can bid against Bantam for a book, I don't know how true that's going to be down the road. Fundamentally, with the merging of sales forces, it's going to be the same people selling the books, and books that used to be on completely different lists are going to be competing for the attention of the same buyer.

Q. Supposing that conglomeratization represents merely an evolutionary moment, what might be the next big publishing world trend?

Barber: I think we'll see significant reductions in the costs of producing books by using technology better. If that happens, and if we can also improve the distribution system, then you may well see smaller publishers springing up. Currently the distribution system penalizes small publishers, who can't get enough of their books into the chains or wholesalers and can't pay the costs that chains such as Barnes & Noble require of publishers in order to get their books up front or in special promotions.

Then, too, booksellers seem to expect more co-op advertising (essentially, publishers paying the stores to advertise the books). As Pat Schroeder, president of the American Association of Publishers, once said, publishers guarantee everyone's salary except their own. There's something to that. But to be honest, my crystal ball is cloudy. I remember some twenty years ago when "computer-assisted instruction" was the rage, and publishers lost fortunes believing in it. We're only now beginning to reach the point they thought was around the corner. And recently we've seen the huge push for the electronic book, but now there's a big pullback in interest on that.

Evans: People talk about self-publishing—you know, "I'm going to put it on the Internet"—but I don't think we're quite ready for that. Because again, how do you find the good things; how do you differentiate? For better or worse, agents and publishers perform some sort of screening function. Without that function, well, all Americans think they have the great American novel in them. And with the word processor, it's become a lot easier to try. I'm just a small business, but you wouldn't believe the volume of queries I receive every day. If all these people were to post their books on the Internet, I think readers would read two of them and give up reading. And libraries don't want to order a book from a publisher they don't know. So I think there needs to be some sort of branding. A Knopf book now is not what a Knopf book was, but the name is still important.

Deborah Way has profiled numerous authors for *Fiction Writer* magazine, and her short stories have appeared in *The Missouri Review* and *American Short Fiction*. She is the executive editor for *Indianapolis Monthly*.

CHAPTER 19

Are All the Good Agents and Publishers in New York City?

For years, the terms "New York" and "publishing" were inseparable. All the industry's movers and shakers—the editors who bought the books and the agents who sold them—were located in the Big Apple. Sure, a writer could live on a Montana ranch or in the Florida Keys or in the south of France, but his agent had better be available to have lunch with the publisher tomorrow in Manhattan.

But today, things have changed. Though most of the big-time publishers (Random House, Penguin Putnam, Simon & Schuster) and many top agents are still firmly established in New York, good agents and successful publishing companies are now located all over the country. Technological advances such as the telephone, fax machine, computer, and e-mail have lessened the need for the entire industry to be located in a single city. In fact, some editors and agents located away from New York cite some distinct advantages to their "outsider" status.

In this chapter, we'll talk with Linda Mead, a former New York-based publishing professional who has spent the last twenty years living and agenting from northern California. She finds the collegial community of literary agents and the thriving community of artists in San Francisco to be a source of inspiration—and clients. And Duncan Murrell, editor with Algonquin Books of Chapel Hill, North Carolina, has helped his company grow into one of the most respected literary publishing houses in the world, with books such as Robert Morgan's *Gap Creek*.

An Interview With Linda Mead, Literary Agent With LitWest Group, LLC

Linda Mead founded LT Mead and Associates in San Francisco in 1983, after leading a successful career in New York publishing at Crown, Simon & Schuster, and Schocken Books. Specializing in prescriptive nonfiction titles, she served as the agent (and co-writer) for Suze Orman's first book, *You've Earned It, Don't Lose It,* and represents authors such as chef Martin Yan, back surgeon Dr. Arthur White, WFN.com founder Jennifer Openshaw, and business guru Larraine Segil. Today Mead is one of the five member agents of LitWest Group, a consortium of San Francisco Bay Area agents.

Q Let's talk a little bit about your path in publishing. How did you decide to become an agent? And how did you end up agenting in California?

A Well I started out in publishing back in the day when women weren't allowed to wear pants to the office, if you can believe that! My first job was at Dell Publishing back when Helen Meyer was the head of the house there. I basically fell into publishing. I originally worked in the cover art department doing pasteups and mechanicals. Then seven months later I became the assistant art director at Fawcett. After that I went to Bantam to work on promotion, then on to Crown Publishers as promotion director. And I was at Crown for four-plus years as head of promotion and advertising.

Each step I took added on to my publishing education. I learned about promotion, and I learned about advertising. I worked on Judith Krantz's first book, *Scruples.* I worked on the *Joy of Sex* series that Crown had a lot of publicity for. From there I went to Simon & Schuster as the marketing director of trade paperbacks, then to Schocken Books. That's where I worked on Harold Kushner's book *When Bad Things Happen to Good People.*

Then I decided to move out to California, and I made the transition into agenting because of my background in subsidiary rights at Schocken. That was in 1983, and I've been agenting ever since.

Q One of the things that's interesting to me is the apprenticeship aspect of publishing—for editors, agents, and even writers. We all know that it takes writers time to hone their craft. But it seems like good agents are grown/cultivated, too, and that many work in publishing houses before they begin agenting. Did your background in the big houses help you?

A I felt like every position I had was an adventure—there was something new and exciting to learn. I feel really strongly about the learning aspect of things. And I recall when I was offered the director of advertising at Crown, I almost didn't take it I was so nervous about it. Then I stepped back and said to myself: That's so crazy. Everything you've done has been different and new, and you really didn't know, you learned. And it was the same thing. Being at Crown in those days was probably the best learning experience. It was a very tight-knit group. There was no such thing as e-mail. And you literally walked out of your office and into the president's office. Or downstairs into the production office. There wasn't the formality there is now.

Q Let's discuss your experience working as an agent in California, outside of the traditional New York publishing scene. Was it difficult to make that adjustment, after so many years in New York? Do you still manage to feel connected to the larger publishing community?

A We actually have a really strong writing and publishing community out here. In the San Francisco Bay Area, we have a group of agents and we all share information and socialize. It's a time for us to come together and see each other face-to-face and schmooze.

What's interesting is that we do come together in a very supportive way. Whenever anyone here needs information or is stuck on something or needs help with something, all he has to do is put an e-mail out there. We're there to help and support one another. This happened recently with Kimberley Cameron—she got in a project that she didn't feel that she could handle. She told the author to come to me, my group of people at LitWest Group, because she really felt it was the kind of project that needed more than one person devoting time to it. And she was right. And so we ended up selling it and getting a two-book contract out of it.

Q **Sounds like that kind of cooperation is good for the agents and the writers.**

A Certainly. And if something comes across my path—really strong narrative nonfiction, for example—and I don't feel as comfortable with it as someone like agent Amy Rennert would, I would suggest that that writer speak to Amy. It's that kind of a community. We compare notes on publishers, we compare notes on authors, we compare notes on a lot of things.

Q **In that way, being an agent outside of New York sounds like it's been a real advantage for you.**

A I don't believe they have anything like this in New York, where the agents there are going to come together and help one another. It's more competitive there. It's not that the people here aren't competitive, but they're not *not* going to help one another. If you help your fellow agent, you'll get it back in some way, you'll get help in some way.

When you're in New York and you're working in an office with five other agents, or you're in New York City and you're in your apartment working as an agent, you have the ability to meet someone for lunch, or have coffee with others in the afternoon, or whatever it is. We're so separated here that we don't have that ability as easily. I'm forty minutes from downtown San Francisco, for instance. It's a lot more difficult to do that. So getting together and being able to support one another, even online, is really helpful.

Q **And I'm sure technology—phone, fax, e-mail—helps keep you in touch with not only other agents but also the editors and writers you're in constant contact with.**

A Exactly. It's so easy, especially these days. You can get a pitch or an overview to an editor almost immediately, and she can decide if she wants to see the whole proposal. It's instantaneous. Yes it's still nice to talk to someone over the telephone, and yes it's still nice to meet the editor in person, which is why I do go to New York several times a year. But for all those other times, it's just as easy to pick up the phone or go over the Internet. In fact, a lot of times people *prefer* to be e-mailed.

Q Tell me about the role attending conferences plays in your business. Do you attend conferences to keep in touch with editors and writers?

A As a group, the agents I work with attend an awful lot of them: Maui, San Diego, Santa Barbara, Big Sur, Fresno, Pikes Peak, Austin, Willamette Writers Conference, Pacific Northwest Writers Conference, Iowa Writers' Workshop. I speak at UC Berkeley. It's interesting—I hadn't gone to them for a very long time, but once I started again recently, I realized how much I liked it.

I know that a lot of writers are at conferences to meet with editors and agents, or just to get help on their work. But believe it or not, it also energizes us. It's so refreshing to see people enthusiastic about writing. It really, I think, brings out the best in editors and agents in terms of that need to nourish. And I love the enthusiasm. The very first time I came back from the Maui Writers Conference, I was so energized. I was flying for a month. It was great! And they're all that way.

And I realized that this was a great place for editors and agents like me to meet with our colleagues. It's a different venue, and it's helpful for us to meet in a different way, not from behind a desk. And it's a lot of fun. It's hard work, but it's a lot of fun.

Q Does an author's location have any bearing on whether you will represent him? Do you tend to represent clients who live on the West Coast, closer to you?

A I've had authors whom I've never met. I've had authors from other parts of the world. Some authors feel like they want to be near their agents, but it's really not necessary. Ultimately, it's up to the author and whom they feel most comfortable with. Authors can feel comfortable only meeting their agents on the telephone if they're getting the right kind of service. I don't think it matters, not in this day and age. It's really up to the writers, whatever they're most comfortable with.

Having a Bay Area agent certainly hasn't hurt anybody. We've got a lot of really good agents out here, and some of the oldest agencies out here, like Larsen and Pomada, have been around for years.

There's also a lot of local writing talent out here, and we get to see that firsthand. I think that's one of the things that's very attractive to New York editors, too. Since they don't get to be out here and see that talent for themselves, we're here to tap into that for them. We're another resource for them.

Q Looking into the future, do you see more agents, and possibly more editors and publishing companies, moving outside of New York? Is the New York location becoming less crucial?

A I think they're already there. I think for many years, when most agents and publishers were in New York, many of the smaller presses outside the city weren't seen as particularly important or outstanding because New York kind of had its own mind-set for a while.

But now there are so many places where I can sell a book—it doesn't have to be to a humongous house in New York. There are so many small and wonderful publishing houses that have actually been around for a long time. And now people are really starting to recognize that. And perhaps there will be more. Perhaps people will move away from having to be in New York. I think some of the publishing houses are even starting to move out a little bit.

Q As publishing houses merge and grow larger, perhaps the appeal of a smaller or midsize publisher grows—for both agents and writers.

A It really does. I acted as the agent for the first book by Suze Orman, called *You've Earned It, Don't Lose It,* with a small publishing company called Newmarket Press. I had known the publisher Esther Margolis for many years, and I knew of her ability to promote a book. That was her background: publicity. And she did a fabulous job of making Suze a household name.

When you go to a small press, you're not a number. Everybody is at the top of the list. Small houses are not willing to take on anything that they don't think will do well for them. And the way it will do well is by putting effort behind those books. And the truth is, there are a lot of talented people at small presses, just like at the big houses. They're just as capable of seeing the potential of something. Sometimes it's worth it to me to take a project to a small house, to be the "big fish" in a small house.

An Interview With Duncan Murrell, Editor With Algonquin Books of Chapel Hill

Duncan Murrell will tell you up front: He's had exactly one job in book publishing, as an editor with Algonquin Books. But augmented by a background in journalism and a lifetime "obsession" with books, he's developed a roster of best-selling and acclaimed authors that includes Robert Morgan (*Gap Creek*) and Derek Lundy (*Godforsaken Sea*). Murrell is dedicated to discovering new voices—he's one of the few editors who admits to reading the infamous "slush pile" of unsolicited manuscripts that publishers are deluged with.

After college and a four-year stint in the military, Murrell went back to graduate school and became a journalist. When his work took him to North Carolina, he got a part-time job reading manuscripts for Algonquin in the evenings, finding it a "delightful break from covering politicians." A job opened up at Algonquin a few years later, and he made the leap to book publishing. He hasn't looked back since.

In 2000, Murrell got the phone call that all editors (and authors) pray for: Oprah Winfrey had picked one of his projects, Robert Morgan's *Gap Creek*, to be the selection of the month for her TV book club. He discusses how the relatively small Algonquin Books of Chapel Hill dealt with the deluge, and discusses some of the advantages of working outside the traditional New York publishing scene.

Q A lot of people would say you have the perfect job—reading books all day.

A That's one of the most common notions, and I hate to disabuse people of it. But I would say that of my time spent at work, maybe 30 percent is spent actually reading something. Most of the rest of that time is spent composing letters, on the telephone with agents and other people, writing copy for the jackets and the galleys, and also trying to manage the inflow of manuscripts that come in here. We have a small staff and a lot of manuscripts. I do most of my editing work at home.

Q In early 2000, Algonquin Books was thrust into the spotlight when Oprah picked *Gap Creek* by Robert Morgan to be one of her book club selections. How did your relatively small house deal with that tsunami? How did it affect you as the editor?

A I was the acquirer and editor of *Gap Creek* and *This Rock* [Robert Morgan's latest book]. I remember getting the notification from Oprah's people that we were being picked, and then walking down the street (you can still do that in this small town) to the little pub and just *shaking* while I ordered a drink. And then staring at the mirror behind the bar and just thinking, *What the hell does this all mean?* Well, it meant that Bob got a lot of new fans, and we got a lot of money, and so did he.

Before Oprah, the print run for that book was 10,000-12,000 copies, and we had almost sold it out. Which was good; we were happy! That's not bad for literary fiction. Bob had a critically acclaimed career as a poet and novelist and was happy being a teacher with a small, loyal audience, writing work that he really cared a lot about.

Then when Oprah called, we jacked the print run up to 525,000 copies. But the funny thing was, Bob didn't really know who Oprah was and was not really familiar with Oprah's Book Club. He knew it was a good thing, but he didn't really know what it would mean. He thought that being picked for her club meant he would sell an extra 30,000 or 40,000 copies. Which he thought was amazing! We finally made him understand that it was a whole different order of magnitude. It's been fun the past couple of years.

Q Algonquin has a really diverse list—lots of fiction, many first-time novelists, but some serious nonfiction, too. Is there a theme to your company's list, other than eclecticism?

A I think we're always looking for books that we like first of all, and second, ones that we think we can sell. I think we're a little closer to the bottom line around here than perhaps other publishers are, because we're small. We have to make all of our books "work." When a good book comes along, the question is not, "Have we published books like this before?" but "Could we publish this book?"

Q Publishing is such a risky business anyway; are the stakes even higher at a smaller publishing house?

A Certainly one book that fails at a smaller house like Algonquin is a bigger failure than that same book would be at, say, Random House. It's a lot harder to write it off here. So we've always said that we don't have "star" books, not in the way that a large publisher does. There they really pick a book: They put the money behind it, promote it, and do what it takes to pop it onto the best-seller list and see where it goes. We don't do that as much. But there are times when we think we have a big book. But the small book on the list doesn't suffer as a result.

Q How do you find your authors and your projects at Algonquin?

A I pay a lot of attention to the slush pile. Which we don't call the "slush pile," by the way, out of respect for it—because we've gotten many books off of it. We call it the "submissions shelf." I've gotten several books from that, books that do well and that I can be proud of. Some of the biggest books in Algonquin's history have been un-agented and unsolicited books.

I think that if you're a publisher like us, one of the tons of small-to medium-sized publishers outside of New York, we know that we're not seeing the best of the agented projects all of the time. Agents might not think to send a hot manuscript our way first. But how does the agent come across those great projects? Well, he reads his slush pile. So we take the approach that we're going to read our slush pile, too, and see if we can find those gems.

Q How do agents fit into the mix?

A I have *great* relationships with agents. If my sister or my friend came to me tomorrow and said, "Duncan, I've written this book. Should I try to get an agent?" I would say yes. I think that an agent can help you. If you find the right agent, one who understands your work and what you hope for it, someone like that is invaluable.

And then from an editor's point of view, when it comes down to negotiating a contract, I would much rather negotiate with an agent than with a writer directly. First of all, the contracts are complicated, and a writer could use that advice in understanding a publishing contract. But most of all, reading a book and loving it is one thing. Negotiating for it, figuring out how much you're going to pay for it, figuring out what rights you're going to get or not get, what percentages . . . that's business. And talking business with a writer and then trying to turn around and be a collaborator in an art form is hard. You've talked about that book as a commodity to her instead of as a work of art. You do it sometimes, but it's not comfortable.

Q What's your ideal relationship with an author?

A When I am working best with a writer, that's the kind of relationship we have, where we're only talking about it in terms of the art of it, in terms of making the book better for what the author intended.

My relationship with authors varies from book to book and author to author. We as a house tend to be hands-on; that's our editing style.

I've learned that from working right next to some great editors. We're not afraid to say what we think about a book, and also not afraid to suggest revisions that might strike someone as major. But with an emphasis on the word *suggest*.

And that gets to the root of the kind of relationship you have with an author: Some people love for you to roll up your sleeves and get right into their books and move stuff around and cut and suggest new scenes. Other people don't. Other people would rather come to the conclusion about what needs to be fixed and how to fix it themselves. There's an art to figuring out what kind of person you're dealing with.

Q So that's your role, to offer an impartial eye?

A When writers get to the level of writing well enough that their books are being published, they have friends, family, students, and colleagues who love them and give them positive feedback about their books. The job of an editor is to be an unbiased, good reader of the books and not be afraid to point out where the authors have stumbled.

Q Do smaller houses like Algonquin offer more stability for writers in terms of editors staying put?

A It does seem like we're more stable here. I've had only one job in publishing, but I've been at this job for four years, not counting the year and a half I spent reading manuscripts for the house. And my understanding is that four years is a long time relative to a lot of the career paths of my colleagues up in New York at the larger houses, particularly for a younger editor. So we do tend to stick around here, and not just on the editorial side—also on the marketing side, the publicity side. There's a certain esprit that derives from that.

I think that there's a homey feeling here. If you're a certain kind of author, and you want to feel that you have a collegial, collaborative relationship with an editor whom you can call all the time, at home and at work, who will call you back and have dinner with you whenever you're in town . . . we have the luxury of being able to do that here. Some authors really groove on that. Some people that doesn't mean anything to—great writers, too. They have other things that they're looking for.

Q Algonquin is known for launching first-time authors, which is a remarkable feat for any house but particularly for a small publishing company. What does it take to debut a new author successfully?

A We *do* like to work with first-time authors. I think we're really good at it. Of all my peers at all the other publishing houses, I think that we're as good at launching a new novelist as any publisher in the country of any size. We've developed a reputation as people who are on the lookout for new writers. And it doesn't hurt that we publish an annual anthology (now going into its sixteenth year) called *New Stories From the South*. We all subscribe to all the literary magazines, and we all read them. And we correspond to those authors whose short stories catch our eye. We've developed a reputation, and booksellers like to hear that we have a first-time novelist on the list, or a couple. They're excited about that!

When we get a new young author who's promotable, who's written a wonderful book, there's nothing like it. Every day is the author's birthday when you're publishing someone like that. He loves going to readings and giving interviews; he gets teary-eyed when he looks at the book for the first time. He's excited about it, and I think that's infectious. Readers love to discover new writers. And we love publishing them.

Q Is it difficult to sustain a successful first-time author's career?

A Well, we also love publishing those authors in their second and third and fourth books and sticking with them. We've had a good record of keeping authors around for a long time. Some big ones, too—Julia Alvarez, Larry Brown, Clyde Edgerton, Jill McCorkle. These are people who have not gone anywhere, and who might have gone off to a bigger publisher if flat-out cash was the most important thing to them. So there must be something here.

Q Your house really seems to emphasize readings, particularly in smaller and independent bookstores, as a way to build support and interest in your authors. What part does publicity play in your plans to publish new books? And does a smaller house need to be more innovative or aggressive in its publicity efforts?

A We've been fortunate to have talented and aggressive publicists who have probably gotten us more than our share of publicity, both as a house and for our books. Our books get reviewed in *The New York Times* and other major papers regularly, and that's not an easy task.

But that's only a small part of it. We put people on tour. We've been thinking up all sorts of ways to drive people into the bookstores, like linking writers with certain musicians to play and read together. We pay attention to the small bookstores, too. That's smart business on our part, and an acknowledgment that when we were starting out as a publishing house, we relied on independent bookstores. We have great relationships with them now, and they're very loyal to us.

We've done all sorts of crazy things to promote our books. We've put authors on CDs reading their work and sent those out to reviewers. A few years ago we noticed that we had three authors from Virginia all on the same list, so a few of us piled into an SUV and handed out galleys to more than one hundred small bookstores in the state over a three-day period. I think we have to maybe be a little more creative than some of the larger publishers do. For the most part, our authors haven't felt the need to hire their own publicists.

Q What part do authors play in promoting their own books at a smaller house?

A Authors should always be doing their own publicity. Any author who can promote herself well helps the book. If authors are reluctant to tour, if they don't give very good interviews and don't like to do it, they give off this vibe, and it gets picked up somehow. But the author who hustles, who goes to meet bookstore sellers on her own while on vacation or something like that, who's willing to do anything and even goes beyond what she's asked to do (sending postcards to lists of friends or e-mail messages to lists of acquaintances, just being happy to be there) makes a big difference.

I don't think you have to be beautiful, which some people think. But I do think you have to really want to publish your work well, and be really appreciative of people who buy your book or come to see you. Because they didn't have to. No one knows he needs your new book until you tell him he does.

Q Is there still room for more new authors and new books in the crowded publishing world?

A Ultimately, I still think that editors at any size publishing house, located anywhere, publishing anything can still recognize people who have done something of great quality. And books like that are written without respect for what's selling. It's about familiarity with books. I want to tell people to just go home and write. If you get published, it will be because you wrote a good book.

CHAPTER 20

Should I Consider Self-Publishing My Book?

Publishing contracts are a hot commodity—and there are never enough to go around. According to the online book publisher Xlibris (www.xlibris.com), more than 500,000 books are written each year in the United States. And the chance of having one's first novel published through traditional publishing channels: one in four hundred.

Throughout this book, we've offered you advice, pointers, and tips from publishing insiders about how to navigate the sometimes confusing channels of traditional publishing. Following this advice will increase the odds of your book finding a home. But it's still a competitive marketplace out there. What's a writer to do with a great book idea if nobody's buying? Or if a publisher or agent suggests changes to your manuscript that you're not willing to make?

Think carefully about what you want out of the publishing experience. There are benefits and disadvantages to both routes. For some writers, being associated with an esteemed publishing house means a lot—but they may fear being small fish in a big pond. For others, having complete control over the look and contents of their books is paramount—but by self-publishing, they lack the marketing savvy and distribution know-how offered by a larger publisher. When making the decision of whether or not to self-publish, you'll have to evaluate what's most important to you.

Self-publishing can be challenging, but in this chapter you'll hear from Tom and Marilyn Ross, a pair of successful writers who literally wrote the book on self-publishing. Then there's an interview with Betty J. Eadie, whose story is every self-publisher's dream: She couldn't find a publisher who shared vision for her book, so she and some friends started a company and published the book themselves. A few years later, her book *Embraced By the Light* was on *The New York Times* best-seller list, and it has sold nearly six million copies to date. They all impart their stories and share the anxiety—and exhilaration—that self-publishing can bring.

Self-Publishing: Take a Chance and Change Your Life
BY TOM AND MARILYN ROSS

Are you the type of person who wants to be behind the wheel rather than go along for the ride? Then you have the stuff self-publishers are made of. They choose to control their own destinies. The feeling is exhilarating, the rewards are great, and the process is a lot simpler than it may seem. Not necessarily easy, mind you, but simple.

Self-publishing offers the potential for huge profits. No longer do you have to be satisfied with the meager 6 to 15 percent royalty that commercial publishers dole out. For those who use creativity, persistence, and sound business sense, money is there to be made. Self-publishing can be the road to independence.

Coming Up Daisies
What motivates entrepreneurs to launch their own businesses? They want to be their own bosses. More personal freedom was the second most important reason. Most people dream of becoming self-employed.

Aside from being their own bosses and being self-employed, self-publishing offers many other advantages.

• After forming your own company and meeting certain requirements, you can write off a portion of your home and deduct some expenses related to writing and to marketing, such as automobile, travel, and entertainment costs. Always check current tax regulations and restrictions. Hence, self-publishing becomes a helpful tax shelter.

• Begin your business on a part-time basis while keeping your current job. Why risk your livelihood until you've refined your publishing activities and worked out any bugs?

• You guide every step. You'll have the cover you like, the typeface you choose, the title you want, the ads you decide to place. Your decision is final. Nothing is left in the hands of an editor or publicist who has dozens (or hundreds) of other books to worry about. You maintain absolute control over your own book.

• Privately publishing your work gives you speed. Big trade houses typically take from a year to a year and a half to get a book out. Self-publishers can do it in a fraction of that time.

• If your venture blossoms and the company expands by publishing others' work, you have fresh opportunities to join the growing small-press movement. You can set policy, serve as a spokesperson, and bring deserving writers to the public's attention.

Overcoming Obstacles

Of course, like any business, self-publishing has some stumbling blocks you should be aware of. Contrary to what Mama always said, you must become a braggart. You'll need to learn to toot your own horn. Since you—and you alone—will be promoting this book, it is up to you to tell anybody and everybody how great it is.

It is an investment, an investment in yourself. As in any business, you will require start-up capital. There must be enough money to print the book, send out review copies, sustain a promotional campaign, and so forth. How much depends on many variables. How long will your book be? Will it have photographs inside? Will the cover be full-color? The costs vary drastically. Generally speaking, to produce a professional-quality book and promote it properly, you'll be in the range of $12,000 to $20,000 in today's marketplace. But be forewarned: Lack of market analysis, careful planning, budgeting, and persistence has caused some people to lose their investments.

You should be willing to devote a substantial block of time to your publishing project. While this can be spread over a long period, there is no getting around the fact that to have a dynamite book, you must spend much time writing it, revising it, producing it, and promoting it.

Finding That Spark

Not everyone self-publishes for the same reason. Most, however, choose this alternative for financial gain. They recognize that here is a potential for much greater returns than any other publishing avenue offers.

Literary contribution is an important facet of self-publishing. As trade publishers become more and more preoccupied with celebrity books and sure bets, good literary writers turn more and more to self-publishing. Here they find an outlet for their novels, poetry, and other serious works.

Many are not concerned with making a profit. Instead, they need to see their work in print—to hold in their hands the books with their names as authors. Some have spent arduous years submitting and having manuscripts returned, cutting and rewriting and sending again, vainly trying to please an editor, any editor. Often those few who do sell find their work whittled and changed beyond recognition. To some, self-publishing is simply fun. They embark on kitchen-table publishing like kids with new toys. Their motive is simply to enjoy themselves. Alas, some end up making money, too.

Another less widely admitted reason for producing your own book is for ego gratification. It's downright satisfying to see your name emblazoned across the cover of a book.

For those more practically minded, publishing your own book can be a springboard to other revenue-generating activities. Many authors discover paid lectures and seminar programs open to them once they've established their expertise between book covers.

Choose a Subject

The first and most important step any potential businessperson takes is to decide what product or service to offer customers. Whether you've already written your book, know what you are going to write about, or have yet to pick a subject, there are several steps you can take to assure the salability of your manuscript. A marketable subject is vital for both commercial publication and self-publishing.

Subject matter greatly influences your book's track record. Choosing a marketable topic is the first step toward the best-seller dream to which all authors cling (secretly or admittedly). But how do you know what's marketable?

Catching the tide of current or anticipated trends is certainly one good way to find a salable topic. By staying alert you can recognize a hidden need for information before others. Tune in to hot topics. But be careful not to be trapped by a fad. The trick lies in determining the difference between a fad, which can be here today and gone tomorrow, and a genuine trend. Ignore the transient fads.

How can you tell a genuine ongoing trend from a mere novelty? The best you can do is a shrewd guess. Ask yourself if it's a single, freaky happening unrelated to anything else, or an eruption into wide popularity of something of long-standing interest. Ask yourself if a lot of people are likely to still be interested in it in a year or two.

Now spirituality and religion are hot—in the workplace as well as the home. Of course the subject of money continues to peak peoples' interest: earning it, investing it, making it, saving it.

Americans continue to be caught up in diet and exercise. There are hundreds of books on these topics. It would make no sense to come out with another run-of-the-mill (pardon the pun) tome on jogging. If you are clever, however, you may find a new way to tide the wave of interest others have generated. That's what Kenneth Cooper did with *The New Aerobics*. Exercise has been popular through the ages.

Speaking of aging, books for people fifty and older are in great demand as the baby boomers mature. They seek titles on managing personal finances, volunteerism, aging gracefully, health and fitness, part-time self-employment, downsizing your budget, gardening, and more.

When searching for a marketable subject, one trick is to look at what type of book is selling well, then take a different approach. Figure out how to be better than the pack.

For a self-publisher it's important to

- **Select a specific, clearly defined market.** By purposely ignoring big, general groups and targeting a select audience, you can find and penetrate your market.

- **Evaluate the possibilities carefully.** People are willing to buy and own several cookbooks or gardening guides, because these subjects are broad and of general interest. Remember that your book's success isn't just dependent on how good a book it is of its type; it'll depend on how many people need and want it.

- **Look for tiny crevices that have been passed over by the "big guys."** You're a lot less likely to be outscaled by the competition if you define a small niche and address yourself to that audience.

Write What You Know

There are things you can write about effectively and profitably even if you've never written anything in your life. No matter who you are, where you live, or how old you are, you know more about "something" than most other folks, and therefore you possess special knowledge that other people will pay for. All you have to do is write what you know!

Okay, so you can write what you know, but you're probably asking, "What *else* do I have to write about?" First, grab a pad of paper and a pencil.

- **Start listing your hobbies and interests.** Write down the jobs you've had, and especially note any job functions or procedures that you particularly enjoyed or were good at.

- **Now think about your successes.** Have you won any honors or contests? Received special recognition for something? That could contain the germ of a book, because if you are successful, you're better than most people, and thus you're an "expert" with information to sell.

- **Do your homework.** Find out what books are already available on the subject and what they are titled. An impossible task? Not really.

The Internet and your local library are ready to supply the answers. Look under all possible versions of your topic.

It's All in the Name

Now that you've isolated your subject, how will you tempt potential readers to partake of this offering?

Christen it with a zesty title. A dynamic title—one that turns a sleeper into a keeper—will motivate people to sip the sparkling prose of your pages. There are no absolute rules or proven formulas for this. As soon as we say, "The best titles are brief: ideally two or three words, certainly no more than six," we're reminded of *Chicken Soup for the _____ Soul*, which has to be one of the all-time best series titles. A close second is John Gray's *Men Are From Mars, Women Are From Venus*. Brief.

At least we'd all agree your title should be descriptive. Right? Then what about *Don't Make Me Stop This Car!* (Al Roker) or *Who Moved My Cheese?* (Spencer Johnson). The first, in case you didn't know, is about raising good kids; the second addresses change at work.

Well, then, humor. Should they be humorous? We could have *Beauty Secrets*, by Janet Reno, *Mike Tyson's Guide to Dating Etiquette*, *The Stripper's Guide to Woodworking*, *Things I Love Most About Bill*, by Hillary Clinton. Or what about *Spotted Owl Recipes*, by the Sierra Club?

Seriously, it usually works best to have a clear title over a catchy one. And ideally it should start with the two or three most relevant words, so when booksellers look it up on a database, they can immediately catch your drift. This will also help your book turn up more frequently in computer keyword searches.

When playing with titling, look at the power of numbers: 5 Ways to . . . , 7 Weeks to . . . , 21 Secrets for . . . , 101 Easy . . . , 307 Moneymaking Tips. It can go on and on. Studies show uneven numbers work best, by the way.

Start jotting down some ideas. Don't be judgmental. Write down every idea that comes to mind. Let your thoughts hopscotch across all possibilities. Use a thesaurus to find synonyms for likely candidates.

Check any fuzzy definitions. Cast out those with no possible application. String the remainder together in various combinations. You may end up with ten or twenty possibilities. All the better.

Next, do some preliminary market research. Big corporations spend hundreds of thousands of dollars to test people's reactions. You can sample public opinion for free. Carry your list of suggested titles everywhere you go. Ask co-workers, relatives, and friends which they like best, and least, and why. Capitalize on every opportunity to discuss your potential titles.

Other practical and helpful ways to stimulate ideas:

• Check magazine article titles on your subject to see what thought ticklers they provide.

• Look within the book itself for catchy phrases that might make a captivating title.

• Listen to songs and read poems to find a phrase that's just what you want.

• Toss around clichés and common sayings to see if a slight change of wording would yield an appealing title.

Just as there are guidelines for good titles, there are also some negatives to avoid:

• Stay away from trite titles like *All That Glitters Is Not Gold, Mother's Little Helper,* or *To Be or Not to Be.*

• Profane or controversial titles usually spell disaster—you'd have made at least some potential readers dislike your book on sight.

• Don't choose a title that gives misleading signals. As favored titles begin to emerge, play with them. See if by tossing two together you might mix in an appropriate subtitle for nonfiction.

While playing around with your titles, always create a subtitle. You do this for two very good reasons: One, important listing sources enter both the title and the subtitle, so you get more mileage out of your listing. It's like getting a brief sales message free. It also gives you more opportunity to describe the book. If you were looking to get a book on mail order, which would you buy: *Eureka!* or *Eureka! How to Build a Fortune in Mail Order?*

It's Up to You

The publishing business is a constant flow of exciting events. You will never forget that supreme moment when you hold the first copy of your very own book, just off the press.

When the book starts making the rounds, things happen. There's a domino effect. One day you get your first fan letter (most likely read with blurry vision). Then a prestigious person gets wind of the book and requests an examination copy. Magazines or newspaper syndicates inquire about subsidiary rights. Library orders start flowing in, and, lo and behold, the biggies—those publishers that previously rejected your work—just may decide to reverse their decision. Self-publishing can be the springboard to lucrative contracts with traditional publishers who were afraid to gamble before. Once the marketability of your book has been proven, they will be eager to take it off your hands.

Tom and Marilyn Ross are the authors of several books, including *The Complete Guide to Self-Publishing* (Writer's Digest Books) and *Jump Start Your Book Sales* (Communication Creativity).

 ## Embraced by the Light:
A Self-Published Best-Seller
BY KATIE STRUCKEL BROGAN

In November 1973, when Betty J. Eadie was thirty-one years old, she had a near-death experience during a routine surgical procedure. In 1992, her experience took the shape of a self-published nonfiction book—*Embraced by the Light.* Since that time, the book has sold more than six million copies, garnered national media attention, and created a presence on *The New York Times* best-seller list, where it held a place for more than two years—all because Eadie chose to turn down major publishing houses, follow her heart, and self-publish the book.

"My experience is strictly from the spirit," she says. "I had contact from other publishing houses, but I knew I would know that person, not only by the tone of her voice, but my spirit would connect with her."

Eventually, Eadie found the publisher that had the drive and the passion she was looking for—Gold Leaf Press. The company was formed by six people who, after reading *Embraced by the Light*, put their financial resources together to publish the book.

"They had great feelings that this was of interest to them. So, the success of the book actually benefited them in a tremendous way because of their faith in the project."

And, according to Eadie, that's what self-publishing boils down to: having faith in your message. Eadie believes that it was her faith, and the fact that the book went against publishing trends, that propelled it to the top of the charts. "It stood on its own and it became a phenomenal best-selling book because it shouldn't—according to all the other publishing houses—have worked by their formulas."

After It Was Published

When the book was published in 1992, Eadie began marketing the book out of her bag—literally. She took copies with her when she set up speaking events about the book. "I sold it book by book, often just paying for the tour or, depending on how much money I made, what I ate for dinner."

One of the most effective marketing strategies that Eadie used was setting up speaking events. She says that one of the best places to start is a learning annex, because people go to this place to learn about different subjects.

"You might start off with a group of twenty-five or so, but as word gets out, as your book gets out, more people come to listen to you."

She says that on one hand, marketing is the easiest part of self-publishing, but on the other hand, it's the hardest, because the media is not always readily available to unknown, self-published authors. However, in Eadie's case, she kept persisting and "going up against those locked doors."

For Eadie, being persistent and having faith in her message was one of the things that helped her get through the rough times. She says with self-published books, as with anything in life, authors need to have faith in themselves and their books, and they need to "go out, stir up the bees' nest and keep on stirring it."

The other thing that helped Eadie market her book was going the extra mile to make people aware of who she was and what she had to say. Her marketing advice for self-publishers: "Don't give up—because there are times when you want to. You just have to keep going and give the best of yourself.

"It requires work, but when you love what you are doing, you give that extra work. It's going the extra mile."

The Ins and Outs

For Eadie, one of the major advantages of self-publishing was that she got to publish what she wanted, and she was able to convey her own message to readers. She says that "most major publishing companies have the editorial rights. . . . If you are a new writer, they leave very little to you"—including the content of your book. Eadie says that self-publishing offers authors the ability to get a message out that may go against trends and not fit into the traditional publishing house idea.

Just as Eadie recognizes that there are advantages to self-publishing, she also recognizes that there are disadvantages. One of the biggest disadvantages, she says, is distribution.

"Most bookstores will only deal with large distribution companies like Ingram," she says. Many bookstores don't want to work with smaller companies because the booksellers tend to order books in large volumes, and if those books don't sell in what the stores consider a reasonable amount of time, the stores have to box the books up and ship them back to the publisher. It's much easier for the bookstores to send returns to one central distributor rather than a number of small publishers.

Eadie herself uses a large distributor to avoid any hassles with bookstores because she's learned that larger distributors have the advantage of being able to use books as a leverage tool. The distributor can go to a bookstore and say, "You're sending me back so many of these books, can I send you, in exchange, these books?"

Eadie did try doing the distribution on her own, but it just didn't work for her. "It is the worst thing to have to do because your energies then go into distribution and not into publishing," she says. "I think a small publisher has to decide where it's going to spend the most energy."

Changing Paths

Eadie made the important decision to focus her energies on publishing—she formed Onjinjinkta, her own publishing company, in 1992. "There were a lot of people who had messages similar to my own that were of the spiritual nature."

But Eadie soon found out that getting these kinds of spiritual books published by traditional publishing houses was difficult. On one occasion, shortly before Eadie formed her company, her son, who was acting as Eadie's agent, sent out one particular book to twenty different publishing houses, only to find out that the publishing houses felt that spiritual books were on the decline.

"My son called and told me that the book had been rejected, and I couldn't understand why—it was a great book," she says. "So, I decided to publish the book myself. Then, I started my own publishing company to publish my next book, and that's what I've been doing."

Prior to starting her own company, Eadie had been approached by several publishing houses to take her own imprint, but she declined. "They get a percentage of everything but are not willing to do all the work.

"Why do it through them just so that you can say you have an imprint? That's ego. It's not worth the money to me to spend that much to feed your ego to say you're with Random, Simon & Schuster, etc."

Eadie's assertion isn't unfounded. Her second book, *The Awakening Heart: My Continuing Journey to Love*, was published by Pocket Books, a division of Simon & Schuster. "From that experience I learned that they [major publishing houses] don't have the same drive as I do. Yes, they invest money, but they are eager to go on to the next project; whereas my work is my life, that's what I do."

She admits that the major publishers do put effort into the books they publish, but as soon as they're finished, they are off and running to the next book.

"I feel that each author is the creator of his work and responsible for it. If he wants to see it to its completion . . . then he needs to be the driving energy behind it"—and that's what Eadie tells her authors. "I'm very up front with my authors. I will only accept an author who has that push and drive behind [his or her] work"—the same drive that Eadie has for her own books.

The New York Times List

In 1993, *Embraced by the Light* hit *The New York Times* best-seller list, where it stayed for more than two years in hardback and paperback, including eighteen months in the prestigious number one spot. When it happened, though, Eadie didn't know why it was such a big deal.

"I didn't understand . . . what *The New York Times* best-seller list was all about. . . . I didn't feel any great joy because I didn't understand it."

Given that Eadie has been directly involved in the business of self-publishing for more than nine years, it's only natural that she's learned what works and what doesn't. "You know when you're doing the right thing, you feel it. And that's what a lot of people are doing now when they're self-publishing—they *feel* to self-publish."

But beyond feeling to self-publish, Eadie thinks that it's necessary for self-publishers to identify their reason for self-publishing, understand what self-publishing is, and realize that it's a lot of hard work.

"They need to learn about publishing so that they will use all the tools available to self-publish," she says. "They need to understand that publishing a book is one thing; distributing and marketing it are two separate energies that must be understood before someone wants to take on the task."

Katie Struckel Brogan is the editor of *Writer's Market* and former associate editor of *Writer's Digest*.

Conclusion

We've heard so many voices throughout this book—sometimes conflicting, often concurring—about publishing today. Some say e-books are the future; others are skeptical. Some scoff at the slush pile; others put a lot of faith in unsolicited submissions. But a few themes were brought up again and again by the editors and agents we talked with. If there are any universal "truths" to be gleaned from this book, perhaps these are a few of them:

- The competition to be published is fierce, but the opportunities for publication are more varied than ever before.
- The publishing industry is still looking for new, talented writers.
- Good writing really does matter.

I think that last statement is the most encouraging of all. Many writers say they feel powerless, disconnected, and "out of the loop" when it comes to dealing with getting their books published. And there's some truth to that—as a writer, you really can't control the forces that buffet the publishing world: the mergers, the changing editors, and the shifting publishing trends.

But the quality of your own writing—that *is* within your control. Your own work is something that you can influence and improve: Practice, strive to progress, hone your craft, get feedback from others around you, and always seek to make your writing even better.

Knowledge is power. I hope the insights and information within this book give you the power to better understand the publishing process and navigate the world of agents and editors. The rest is up to you. I've learned so much throughout the writing of this book; I hope you can say the same after reading it.

Index